working
SPANISH

for
TEACHERS AND EDUCATION PROFESSIONALS

working SPANISH

for TEACHERS AND EDUCATION PROFESSIONALS

Gail Stein

Wiley Publishing, Inc.

For general information on our other products and services or to obtain technical support please contact our Customer Care Department within the U.S. at (800) 762-2974, outside the U.S. at (317) 572-3993 or fax (317) 572-4002.

Wiley also publishes its books in a variety of electronic formats. Some content that appears in print may not be available in electronic books. For more information about Wiley products, please visit our web site at www.wiley.com.

Library of Congress Cataloging-in-Publication Data:
Stein, Gail.
     Working Spanish for teachers and education professionals / Gail Stein.
         p.   cm.
     ISBN-13 978-0-470-09523-2 (pbk.)
     ISBN-10 0-470-09523-7
  1. Spanish language—Conversation and phrase books (for school employees)
     I. Title.
PC4120.S34S84 2007
468.3'42102437—dc22

                                                2006103072

Printed in the United States of America

10 9 8 7 6 5 4 3 2 1

Book design by Melissa Auciello-Brogan
Book production by Wiley Publishing, Inc. Composition Services
Wiley Bicentennial Logo: Richard J. Pacifico

*This book is dedicated to the memory
of my father, Jack Bernstein, who
will always be with me.*

*This book is also dedicated to my
husband, Douglas, for his love and patience;
to my wonderful children, Eric, Michael,
and Katherine, for their encouragement and
support; and to my mother, Sara Bernstein,
for always being there for me.*

Acknowledgments

Many thanks to Roxane Cerda, my acquisitions editor, who was so helpful in getting this book off the ground; to Elizabeth Kuball, my project and copy editor, whose excellent editing skills and suggestions made this book a reality; to Wigberto Rivera, whose technical expertise and input were invaluable; and to Christina Stambaugh, Kristie Rees, and all the other people at Wiley Publishing, Inc., for their patience and help.

Contents

Chapter **1** Pronunciation Guide 1

    Stress and Accents 1
    Vowels 2
    Diphthongs 2
    Consonants 3

Chapter **2** Numbers 5

    Cardinal Numbers 5
    Ordinal Numbers 9

Chapter **3** Time 13

    Telling Time 13

Chapter **4** Days, Months, Dates, Seasons, Holidays,
             and the Weather 21

    Days 21
    Months 24
    Dates 25
    The Seasons 29
    Holidays 29
    The Weather 31

Chapter **5** Classroom Commands and Rules 35

    In the Classroom 35
    On the Playground 47

Chapter **6** Essential Phrases 51

    Greetings 51
    Common Courtesy 55
    Communication 55
    Question Words 58
    Starters and Joiners 61
    In a Few Words 63

Good Wishes 68
Words of Encouragement 68
Words of Praise 69

Chapter **7** Day Care and Pre-K   71

Hours and Costs 71
Baby Accessories 74
Food Habits 74
Sleep Habits 76
Bathroom Habits 77
Clothing 79
Developmental Skills 80
Toys and Activities 81
Moods and Behavior 83
Illnesses and Accidents 85

Chapter **8** Registration   89

Personal Information 89
Physical Descriptions 94
Personality Traits 95
Type of School 97
Family Members 97
Parental Contact 100

Chapter **9** In, Around, and After School   103

People 103
Classroom Fixtures 107
Locations 109
Giving Directions 112
Extracurricular Activities 115

Chapter **10** Medical   121

Parts of the Body 121
Accidents 123
Illnesses and Medical Conditions 127
Signs and Symptoms 132
Abuse 134

Nutritional Requirements 136
Emergencies 140

Chapter 11 Content Areas 143

School Subjects 143
In English Class 147
About Bilingual Education and ESL 149
In History and Geography Class. 149
In Math Class. 151
In Science Class 154
In Computer Science. 157
In Art Class 158
In Music Class 158
In Physical Education Class 159
Academic Skills 159
School Supplies 161

Chapter 12 Expectations and Consequences 165

Dress Codes. 165
Class Participation 169
Lateness. 171
Excessive Absence 172
Cutting Class 175
Homework. 176
Behavior and Interaction with Peers. 178
Attitude. 180
Work Habits. 181
Discipline. 183
Grades and Promotion 187
Conferences 189
On the Phone 191

Chapter 13 The Special-Needs Student 195

Special Needs 195
School Offerings. 199
Special Education 200
Parents' Rights 209
A Child's Progress. 210

Chapter **14** Planning for the Future   217

    Promotion and Graduation Requirements. 217
    Applying for a Job 219
    Applying to a College. 222

1

Pronunciation Guide

Spanish sounds are relatively easy to master because they resemble the sounds of English, and because Spanish letters and letter combinations are generally pronounced phonetically (unlike English letters and letter combinations, which may be pronounced in a variety of ways—"b<u>a</u>r" versus "b<u>a</u>t"; "c<u>ough</u>" versus "th<u>ough</u>"). When speaking Spanish, if you stress the wrong syllable or mispronounce a word, don't worry—you'll still be understood and your efforts will be appreciated.

Stress and Accents

The rules for stress in Spanish are:

1. If the word ends in a vowel (a, e, i, o, u), n, or s, stress the next to the last syllable:

amigo (friend)	*ah-**mee**-goh*
examen (test, exam)	*ehk-**sah**-mehn*
muchachos (boys)	*moo-**chah**-chohs*

2. If the word ends in a consonant other than n or s, stress the last syllable:

papel (paper)	*pah-**pehl***
profesor (teacher)	*proh-feh-**sohr***

3. Any exceptions to the above rules have accent marks to help you place the stress correctly:

composición (composition)	*kohm-poh-see-see-**yohn***
lápiz (pencil)	***lah**-pees*

The three accent marks in Spanish are:

* ´ This accent goes above a vowel to indicate that the syllable is stressed:

  álgebra (algebra)   *ahl-heh-brah*
  inglés (English)   *een-glehs*

* ˜ The tilde goes above an *n* to produce the ny sound in the word "union":

  año (year)   *ah-nyoh*
  mañana (tomorrow)   *mah-nyah-nah*

* ¨ The umlaut is used on the letter *u* in diphthongs (combinations of vowels) to show that each vowel is pronounced separately:

  vergüenza (shame)   *behr-goo-ehn-sah*

Vowels

The sound of each Spanish vowel consistently remains the same and is pronounced the way it is written. If you have to spell a word, the pronunciation of the vowels is in parentheses.

Vowels

Vowel	Sound	Example	Pronunciation
a	ah	**falta** (mistake)	*fahl-tah*
e	eh	**excelente** (excellent)	*ehk-seh-lehn-teh*
i	ee	**libro** (book)	*lee-broh*
o	oh	**ocho** (eight)	*oh-choh*
u	oo	**uno** (one)	*oo-noh*

Diphthongs

A diphthong is generally (but not always) a combination of one weak vowel (i or u) and one strong vowel (a, e, or o) that appear in the same syllable.

Diphthongs

Diphthong	Sound	Example	Pronunciation
ai	ah-ee	**aire** (air)	*ah-ee-reh*
au	ah-oo	**autor** (author)	*ah-oo-tohr*
ay	ah-ee	**hay** (there is/are)	*ah-ee*
ei	eh-ee	**seis** (six)	*seh-ees*
eu	eh-oo	**Europa** (Europe)	*eh-oo-roh-pah*
ia	ee-ah	**seria** (serious)	*seh-ree-ah*
ie	ee-eh	**siesta** (nap)	*see-ehs-tah*
io	ee-oh	**estudio** (study)	*ehs-too-dee-oh*
iu	ee-oo	**ciudad** (city)	*see-oo-dahd*
oi	oh-ee	**oigo** (I hear)	*oh-ee-goh*
ua	oo-ah	**cuatro** (four)	*koo-ah-troh*
ue	oo-eh	**bueno** (good)	*boo-eh-noh*
ui	oo-ee	**cuidado** (care)	*koo-ee-dah-doh*
uo	oo-oh	**cuota** (quota)	*koo-oh-tah*

Consonants

Most Spanish consonants are pronounced in the same way as they are pronounced in English. If you have to spell a word, the pronunciation of the consonants is in parentheses.

Consonants

Consonant	Sound	Example	Pronunciation
b (beh)	b	**bien** (well)	*bee-ehn*
c (seh)+ e or i	s	**cinco** (five)	*seen-koh*
c (seh)+ a, o, u	k	**banco** (bench)	*bahn-koh*
ch (cheh)	ch	**leche** (milk)	*leh-cheh*
d (deh)	d	**dama** (lady)	*dah-mah*
f (eh-feh)	f	**fiesta** (party)	*fee-ehs-tah*
g (heh)+ e or i	h	**general** (general)	*heh-neh-rahl*

continued

Consonant	Sound	Example	Pronunciation
g (heh)+ a, o, u	g	**goma** (eraser)	*gob-mah*
h (ah-cheh)	silent	**hora** (hour)	*oh-rah*
j (hoh-tah)	h	**junio** (June)	*hoo-nee-oh*
k (kah)	k	**kilo** (kilo)	*kee-loh*
l (eh-leh)	l	**sala** (room)	*sah-lah*
ll (eh-yeh)	y	**silla** (chair)	*see-yah*
m (eh-meh)	m	**madre** (mother)	*mah-dreh*
n (eh-neh)	n	**nombre** (name)	*nohm-breh*
p (peh)	p	**padre** (father)	*pah-dreh*
q (koo)	k	**quince** (fifteen)	*keen-seh*
r (eh-reh) (rolled)	r	**tarea** (homework)	*tah-reh-ah*
rr (eh-rreh) (rolled a lot)*	rr	**regla** (ruler)	*rreh-glah*
rr (rolled a lot)*	rr	**carro** (car)	*kah-rroh*
s (eh-seh)	s	**frase** (sentence)	*frah-seh*
t (teh)	t	**tiza** (chalk)	*tee-sah*
v (beh)	soft b	**veinte** (twenty)	*beh-een-teh*
w (doble beh)	w	**western** (western)	*wehs-tehrn*
x (eh-kees)	ks	**exacto** (exact)	*ehk-sahk-toh*
y (ee gree-eh-gah)	y	**yo** (I)	*yoh*
z (seh-tah)	s	**zoo** (zoo)	*soh*

*The r is rolled two or three times when it appears at the beginning of a word or when it is doubled within a word.

2

Numbers

> **Note:**
> 1. Letters or words in brackets are used when using the familiar you **[tú]** form.
> 2. When speaking to more than one adult, **Ud.** (you, singular) becomes **Uds.** (you, plural) and an n is added to the conjugated verb form.
> 3. The formal you form is expressed in the same way as the third-person singular **él** (he) and **ella** (she) forms.

Cardinal Numbers

Cardinal numbers are used for counting.

Number	Spanish	Pronunciation
0	cero	*seh-roh*
1	uno	*oo-noh*
2	dos	*dohs*
3	tres	*trehs*
4	cuatro	*koo-ah-troh*
5	cinco	*seen-koh*
6	seis	*seh-ees*
7	siete	*see-eh-teh*
8	ocho	*oh-choh*
9	nueve	*noo-eh-beh*
10	diez	*dee-ehs*
11	once	*ohn-seh*
12	doce	*doh-seh*

Number	Spanish	Pronunciation
13	trece	*treh-seh*
14	catorce	*kah-tohr-seh*
15	quince	*keen-seh*
16	dieciséis (diez y seis)	*dee-ehs-ee-seh-ees*
17	diecisiete (diez y siete)	*dee-ehs-ee-see-eh-teh*
18	dieciocho (diez y ocho)	*dee-ehs-ee-oh-choh*
19	diecinueve (diez y nueve)	*dee-ehs-ee-noo-eh-beh*
20	veinte	*beh-een-teh*
21	veintiuno (veinte y uno)	*beh-een-tee-oo-noh*
22	veintidós (veinte y dos)	*beh-een-tee-dohs*
23	veintitrés (veinte y tres)	*beh-een-tee-trehs*
24	veinticuatro (veinte y cuatro)	*beh-een-tee-koo-ah-troh*
25	veinticinco (veinte y cinco)	*beh-een-tee-seen-koh*
26	veintiséis (veinte y seis)	*beh-een-tee-seh-ees*
27	veintisiete (veinte y siete)	*beh-een-tee-see-eh-teh*
28	veintiocho (veinte y ocho)	*beh-een-tee-oh-choh*
29	veintinueve (veinte y nueve)	*beh-een-tee-noo-eh-beh*
30	treinta	*treh-een-tah*

From 30 on, compound numbers are always written separately:

Number	Spanish	Pronunciation
31	treinta y uno	*treh-een-tah ee oo-noh*
40	cuarenta	*koo-ah-rehn-tah*
45	cuarenta y cinco	*koo-ah-rehn-tah ee seen-koh*
50	cincuenta	*seen-koo-ehn-tah*
60	sesenta	*seh-sehn-tah*
70	setenta	*seh-tehn-tah*
80	ochenta	*oh-chehn-tah*
90	noventa	*noh-behn-tah*
100	ciento (cien)	*see-ehn-toh (see-ehn)*
101	ciento uno	*see-ehn-toh oo-noh*
200	doscientos	*dohs-see-ehn-tohs*
500	quinientos	*kee-nee-ehn-tohs*
1000	mil	*meel*
2000	dos mil	*dohs meel*
100.000	cien mil	*see-ehn meel*
1.000.000	un millón	*oon meel-yohn*

•

Number	Spanish	Pronunciation
2.000.000	**dos millones**	*dohs meel-yoh-nehs*
1.000.000.000	**mil millones**	*meel meel-yoh-nehs*
2.000.000.000	**dos mil millones**	*dos meel meel-yoh-nehs*

When you want to use Spanish cardinal numbers, remember to do the following:

* Use **uno** only when counting. **Uno** becomes **un** before a masculine noun and **una** before a feminine noun:

uno, dos, tres ...	one, two, three ...
un hombre y una mujer	a man and a woman
treinta y un libros	thirty-one books
veintiuna páginas	twenty-one pages

* Use the conjunction **y** (and) only for numbers between 16 and 99. Note, however, that compound numbers between 21 and 29 are frequently written as one word (see above):

sesenta y dos	62
but	
ciento sesenta y dos	162

* Show agreement with a feminine noun in compounds of **ciento** (for example, **doscientos, trescientos**):

<u>**doscientos**</u> **pesos**	two hundred pesos
<u>**trescientas**</u> **pesetas**	three hundred pesetas

* Use **cien** before nouns and before the numbers **mil** and **millones**. Before all other numbers, use **ciento**:

<u>**cien**</u> **alumnos**	one hundred students
<u>**cien**</u> **mil personas**	one hundred thousand people
<u>**cien**</u> **millones de habitantes**	one hundred million inhabitants
<u>**ciento**</u> **dos páginas**	one hundred and two pages

* Use **un** before **millón** but not before **cien(to)** or **mil**. When a noun follows **millón**, put **de** between **millón** and the noun:

<u>**cien**</u> **libros**	one hundred books
<u>**ciento**</u> **noventa páginas**	one hundred ninety pages
<u>**mil**</u> **personas**	one thousand people
<u>**un**</u> **millón de dólares**	a million dollars

* Use the following words to express common arithmetic functions:

y	plus (+)
menos	minus (–)
por	times (×)
dividido por	divided by (÷)
son	equals (=)

When reading Spanish numbers, keep in mind that the Spanish-speaking world writes numbers differently from the way Americans do. The number 1 has a little hook on top, which makes it look like a 7. So, to distinguish a 1 from a 7, a line is put through the 7, to look like this: 7̵

In numerals and decimals, Spanish uses commas where English uses periods, and vice versa:

English	Spanish
8,000	8.000
.75	0,75
$16.25	$16,25

The Spanish-speaking world reverses the numerical order to express dates:

Date	English	Spanish
August 7, 2006	8/7/06	7/8/06

Using Cardinal Numbers

We are on page 156.
Estamos en la página ciento cincuenta y seis.
ehs-tah-mohs ehn lah pah-hee-nah see-ehn-toh seen-koo-ehn-tah ee seh-ees

The book costs $32.
El libro cuesta treinta y dos dólares.
ehl lee-broh koo-ehs-tah treh-een-tah ee dohs doh-lah-rehs

You (He/She) received 95 on the test.
Recibió noventa y cinco en el examen.
rreh-see-bee-oh noh-behn-tah ee seen-koh ehn ehl ehk-sah-mehn

You are (He/She is) missing six homeworks.
Le faltan seis tareas.
leh fahl-tahn seh-ees tah-reh-ahs

You were (He/She was) absent 24 times.
Estuvo ausente veinticuatro veces.
ehs-too-boh ah-oo-sehn-teh beh-een-tee-koo-ah-troh beh-sehs

You were (He/She was) late ten times, often by 30 minutes or more.
Llegó tarde diez veces, frecuentemente con treinta minutos de retraso o más.
yeh-goh tahr-deh dee-ehs beh-sehs; freh-koo-ehn-teh-mehn-teh kohn treh-een-tah mee-noo-tohs deh rreh-trah-soh oh mahs

You have (He/She has) to spend at least an hour a day studying.
Tiene que pasar por lo menos una hora al día estudiando.
tee-eh-neh keh pah-sar pohr loh meh-nos oo-nah oh-rah ahl dee-ah ehs-too-dee-ahn-doh

You need (He/She needs) three notebooks for the class.
Necesita tres cuadernos para la clase.
neh-seh-see-tah trehs koo-ah-dehr-nohs pah-rah lah klah-seh

My telephone number at school is 555-6789.
Mi número de teléfono en la escuela es cinco, cinco, cinco, seis, siete, ocho, nueve.
mee noo-meh-roh deh teh-leh-foh-noh ehn lah ehs-koo-eh-lah ehs seen-koh, seen-koh, seen-koh, seh-ees, see-eh-teh, oh-choh, noo-eh-beh

Our class is going to take a trip on May 3rd.
Nuestra clase irá de excursión el tres de mayo.
noo-ehs-trah klah-seh ee-rah deh ehks-koor-see-yohn ehl trehs deh mah-yoh

We will leave at three o'clock.
Saldremos a las tres.
sahl-dreh-mohs ah lahs trehs

Ordinal Numbers

Ordinal numbers allow you to express numbers in a series.

Ordinal	Spanish	Pronunciation
1st	**primero**	*pree-meh-roh*
2nd	**segundo**	*seh-goon-doh*
3rd	**tercero**	*tehr-seh-roh*
4th	**cuarto**	*koo-ahr-toh*
5th	**quinto**	*keen-toh*
6th	**sexto**	*sehks-toh*

Ordinal	Spanish	Pronunciation
7th	**séptimo**	*sehp-tee-moh*
8th	**octavo**	*ohk-tah-boh*
9th	**noveno**	*noh-beh-noh*
10th	**décimo**	*deh-see-moh*

When you want to use Spanish ordinal numbers, remember to do the following:

* Use Spanish ordinal numbers only through the tenth. After that, use cardinal numbers:

el séptimo grado	the seventh grade
el siglo veintiuno	the 21st century

* Change the final o of the masculine form to a for agreement with a feminine noun:

el sexto día	the sixth day
la quinta semana	the fifth week

* Drop the final o before a masculine singular noun when using **primero** and **tercero:**

el primer año	the first year
el tercer piso	the third floor

  but

el siglo tercero	the third century

* Use **primero** in dates to express the first of a month:

el primero de enero	January 1st

* Use cardinal numbers before ordinal numbers:

los tres primeros capítulos	the first three chapters

When writing, keep in mind that Spanish ordinal numbers are abbreviated as follows:

Ordinal Number	Spanish	Abbreviation
1st	**primero** (masculine)	1°
	primera (feminine)	1^a
	primer (masculine before singular noun)	1er
2nd	**segundo** (masculine)	2°
	segunda (feminine)	2^a

Ordinal Number	Spanish	Abbreviation
3rd	**tercero** (masculine)	3º
	tercera (feminine)	3ª
	tercer (masculine before singular noun)	3er
4th	**cuarto** (masculine)	4º
	cuarta (feminine)	4ª
5th	**quinto** (masculine)	5º
	quinta (feminine)	5ª
6th	**sexto** (masculine)	6º
	sexta (feminine)	6ª
7th	**séptimo** (masculine)	7º
	séptima (feminine)	7ª
8th	**octavo** (masculine)	8º
	octava (feminine)	8ª
9th	**noveno** (masculine)	9º
	novena (feminine)	9ª
10th	**décimo** (masculine)	10º
	décima (feminine)	10ª

Using Ordinal Numbers

There is a test on March 1st.
Hay un examen el primero de marzo.
ah-ee oon ehk-sah-mehn ehl pree-meh-roh deh mahr-soh

That office is on the first floor.
Esa oficina está en el primer piso.
eh-sah oh-fee-see-nah ehs-tah ehn ehl pree-mehr pee-soh

That classroom is on the third floor.
Ese salón de clase está en el tercer piso.
eh-seh sah-lohn deh klah-seh ehs-tah ehn ehl tehr-sehr pee-soh

You have (He/She has) passed the sixth grade.
Ha aprobado el sexto grado.
ah ah-proh-bah-doh ehl sehks-toh grah-doh

You (He/[She]) came in fifth in the competition.
Terminó quinto (quinta) en la competición.
tehr-mee-noh keen-toh (keen-tah) ehn lah kohm-peh-tee-see-ohn

You (He/She) won second prize.
Ganó el segundo premio.
gah-noh ehl seh-goon-doh preh-mee-oh

You were (He/[She] was) first in the class.
Fue primero (primera) en la clase.
foo-eh pree-meh-roh (pree-meh-rah) ehn lah klah-seh

That wasn't the first time you were (he/she was) late.
No era la primera vez que llegó con retraso.
noh eh-rah lah pree-meh-rah behs keh yeh-goh kohn rreh-trah-soh

3

Time

Note:
1. Letters or words in brackets are used when using the familiar you **[tú]** form.
2. When speaking to more than one adult, **Ud.** (you, singular) becomes **Uds.** (you, plural) and an n is added to the conjugated verb form.
3. The formal you form is expressed in the same way as the third-person singular **él** (he) and **ella** (she) forms.

Telling Time

What time is it?
¿Qué hora es?
keh oh-rah ehs

It is one o'clock.
Es la una.
ehs lah oo-nah

It is two (three) o'clock.
Son las dos (tres).
sohn lahs dohs (trehs)

At what time . . . ?
A qué hora . . . ?
ah keh oh-rah

To answer, use **a** + **la** (singular) or **a** + **las** (plural) + a cardinal number:

at one o'clock
a la una
ah lah oo-nah

at eight o'clock
a las ocho
ah lahs oh-choh

The following table gives the times in Spanish before and after the hour:

Time	Spanish	Pronunciation
1:00	**la una**	*lah oo-nah*
2:05	**las dos y cinco**	*lahs dohs ee seen-koh*
3:10	**las tres y diez**	*lahs trehs ee dee-ehs*
4:15	**las cuatro y cuarto/ las cuatro y quince**	*lahs koo-ah-troh ee koo-ahr-toh/lahs koo-ah-troh ee keen-seh*
5:20	**las cinco y veinte**	*lahs seen-koh ee beh-een-teh*
6:25	**las seis y veinticinco**	*lahs seh-ees ee beh-een-tee-seen-koh*
7:30	**las siete y media**	*lahs see-eh-teh ee meh-dee-ah*
7:35	**las ocho menos veinticinco**	*lahs oh-choh meh-nohs beh-een-tee-seen-koh*
8:40	**las nueve menos veinte**	*lahs noo-eh-beh meh-nohs beh-een-teh*
9:45	**las diez menos cuarto**	*lahs dee-ehs meh-nohs koo-ahr-toh*
10:50	**las once menos diez**	*lahs ohn-seh meh-nohs dee-ehs*
11:55	**las doce menos cinco**	*lahs doh-seh meh-nohs seen-koh*
noon	**el mediodía**	*ehl meh-dee-oh-dee-ah*
midnight	**la medianoche**	*lah meh-dee-ah-noh-cheh*

When time is of the essence, remember the following:

* To express time after the hour (before half past) use **y** and the number of minutes:
    At 9:10.
    A las nueve y diez.
    ah lahs noo-eh-beh ee dee-ehs

* To express time before the next hour (after half past) use the number of the next hour + **menos** + the number of minutes:

    At 12:45

    A la una menos quince

    ah lah oo-nah meh-nohs keen-seh

* You may hear the verb **faltar** (to be needed) + minutes + **para** + the next hour to express the time before the hour:

    It's 1:59.

    Falta un minuto para las dos.

    fahl-tah oon mee-noo-toh pah-rah lahs dohs

    It's 3:50.

    Faltan diez minutos para las cuatro.

    fahl-tahn dee-ehs mee-noo-tohs pah-rah lahs koo-ah-troh

* Time may also be expressed by giving the hour and the number of minutes following it:

    It is 8:20.

    Son las ocho y veinte.

    sohn lahs oh-choh ee beh-een-teh

    At 8:45

    A las ocho y cuarenta y cinco

    ah lahs oh-choh ee koo-ah-rehn-tah ee seen-koh

Time-Related Vocabulary

English	Spanish	Pronunciation
a half hour	**media hora**	*meh-dee-yah oh-rah*
a minute	**un minuto**	*oon mee-noo-toh*
a quarter of an hour	**un cuarto de hora**	*oon koo-ahr-toh deh oh-rah*
a second	**un segundo**	*oon seh-goon-doh*
after three o'clock	**después de las tres**	*dehs-poo-ehs deh lahs trehs*
ago	**hace** [time] **que**	*ah-seh* [time] *keh*

continued

English	Spanish	Pronunciation
an hour	**una hora**	*oo-nah oh-rah*
at about two o'clock	**a eso de las dos**	*ah eh-soh deh lahs dohs*
at exactly nine o'clock	**a las nueve en punto**	*ah lahs noo-eh-beh ehn poon-toh*
before eight o'clock	**antes de las ocho**	*ahn-tehs deh lahs oh-choh*
early	**temprano**	*tehm-prah-noh*
eve	**la víspera**	*lah bees-peh-rah*
frequently	**frecuentemente**	*freh-koo-ehn-teh-mehn-teh*
from time to time	**a veces; de vez en cuando**	*ah beh-sehs; deh behs ehn koo-ahn-doh*
immediately	**inmediatamente (en seguida)**	*een-meh-dee-ah-tah-mehn-teh (ehn seh-gee-dah)*
in a while	**dentro de un rato**	*dehn-troh deh oon-rrah-toh*
in an hour	**en una hora**	*ehn oo-nah oh-rah*
in the afternoon	**por la tarde**	*pohr lah tahr-deh*
in the evening	**por la noche**	*pohr lah noh-cheh*
in the morning	**por la mañana**	*pohr lah mah-nyah-nah*
in the very early morning	**por la madrugada**	*pohr lah mah-droo-gah-dah*
late (in arriving)	**de retraso**	*deh rreh-trah-soh*
late (in arriving)	**tarde**	*tahr-deh*
later	**más tarde**	*mahs tahr-deh*
often	**a menudo**	*ah meh-noo-doh*
on time	**a tiempo**	*ah tee-ehm-poh*
per hour	**por hora**	*pohr oh-rah*
sharp	**en punto**	*en poon-toh*

English	Spanish	Pronunciation
since ten o'clock	**desde las diez**	*dehs-deh lahs dee-ehs*
since what time?	**¿desde qué hora?**	*dehs-deh keh oh-rah*
two hours ago	**hace dos horas**	*ah-seh dohs oh-rahs*
until one o'clock	**hasta la una**	*ahs-tah lah oo-nah*

Using Time and Time Expressions

The normal school day begins at 8:20 and ends at 3:45.
El horario normal de la escuela empieza a las ocho y veinte y termina a las cuatro menos cuarto.
ehl oh-rah-ree-oh nohr-mahl deh lah ehs-koo-eh-lah ehm-pee-eh-sah ah las oh-choh ee beh-een-teh ee tehr-mee-nah ah lahs koo-ah-troh meh-nohs koo-ahr-toh

Students may not arrive before 8 a.m. Your child should not arrive before 8 a.m.
Los estudiantes no deben llegar antes de las ocho. Su hijo (hija) no debe llegar antes de las ocho de la mañana.
lohs ehs-too-dee-ahn-tehs noh deh-behn yeh-gahr ahn-tehs deh lahs oh-choh soo ee-hoh (ee-hah) noh deh-beh yeh-gahr ahn-tehs deh lahs oh-choh deh lah mah-nyah-nah

There will be an early dismissal on Monday. Students will be dismissed at 2 p.m. sharp.
El lunes, las clases terminarán antes del horario habitual. Los estudiantes saldrán a las dos en punto.
ehl loo-nehs lahs klah-sehs tehr-mee-nah-rahn ahn-tehs dehl oh-rah-ree-yoh ah-bee-too-ahl lohs ehs-too-dee-ahn-tehs sahl-drahn ah lahs dohs ehn poon-toh

Our class is going on a trip from 8:30 a.m. until 2:15 p.m.
Nuestra clase va de excursión desde las ocho y media de la mañana hasta las dos y cuarto de la tarde.
noo-ehs-trah klah-seh bah deh ehks-koor-see-ohn dehs-deh lahs oh-choh ee meh-dee-ah deh lah mah-nyah-nah ahs-tah lahs dohs ee koo-ahr-toh deh lah tahr-deh

Your child is not succeeding because he (she) is frequently late to school.
Su hijo (hija) no sale bien porque llega tarde frecuentemente a la escuela.
soo ee-hoh (ee-hah) noh sah-leh bee-ehn pohr-keh yeh-gah tahr-deh freh-koo-ehn-teh-mehn-teh ah lah ehs-koo-eh-lah

He/She often arrives a half hour or more late.
Llega a menudo con media hora o más de retraso.
yeh-gah ah meh-noo-doh kohn meh-dee-ah oh-rah oh mahs deh rreh-trah-soh

How long does it take to get to school?
¿Cuánto tiempo le toma para llegar a la escuela?
koo-ahn-toh tee-ehm-poh leh toh-mah pah-rah yeh-gahr ah lah ehs-koo-eh-lah

At what time does he/she go to bed at night?
¿A qué hora se acuesta por la noche?
ah keh oh-rah seh ah-koo-ehs-tah pohr lah noh-cheh

How much time does he/she spend doing homework?
¿Cuánto tiempo pasa haciendo la tarea?
koo-ahn-toh tee-ehm-poh pah-sah ah-see-ehn-doh lah tah-reh-ah

He/She should spend at least an hour doing homework.
Debería pasar por lo menos una hora haciendo la tarea.
deh-beh-ree-ah pah-sahr pohr loh meh-nohs oo-nah oh-rah ah see-ehn-doh lah tah-reh-yah

Your child left school an hour ago.
Su hijo (hija) salió de la escuela hace una hora.
soo ee-hoh (ee-hah) sah-lee-oh deh lah ehs-koo-eh-lah ah-seh oo-nah oh-rah

Open School Night takes place from 6:30 p.m. until 9 p.m.
La reunión de padres y maestros tiene lugar desde las seis y media hasta las nueve de la noche.
lah rreh-oo-nyohn deh pah-drehs ee mah-ehs-trohs tee-eh-neh loo-gahr dehs-deh lahs seh-ees ee meh-dee-yah ahs-tah lahs noo-eh-beh deh lah noh-cheh.

We have an appointment at 7:35.
Tenemos una cita a las ocho menos veinticinco.
teh-neh-mohs oo-nah see-tah ah lahs oh-choh meh-nohs beh-een-tee-seen-koh

I will tell you after class.
Le diré después de la clase.
leh dee-reh dehs-poo-ehs deh lah klah-seh

I would like to speak to you about your child's work (attitude).
At what time can I call you at home?
**Me gustaría hablarle acerca del trabajo (de la actitud) de su
hijo (hija). ¿A qué hora puedo telefonearle a casa?**
*meh goos-tah-ree-ah ah-blahr-leh ah-sehr-kah dehl trah-bah-hoh (deh lah ahk-
tee-tood) deh soo ee-hoh (ee-hah) ah keh oh-rah poo-eh-doh teh-leh-foh-neh-
ahr-leh ah kah-sah*

Chapter

4

Days, Months, Dates, Seasons, Holidays, and the Weather

Days

What day is it today?
¿Qué día es hoy?
keh dee-ah ehs oh-ee

Today is Monday.
Hoy es lunes.
oh-ee ehs loo-nehs

What is today's date?
¿Cuál es la fecha de hoy?
koo-ahl ehs lah feh-chah deh oh-ee

Today is April 10th.
Hoy es el diez de abril.
oh-ee ehs ehl dee-ehs deh ah-breel

The days of the week in Spanish are not capitalized.

English	Spanish	Pronunciation
Monday	**lunes**	*loo-nehs*
Tuesday	**martes**	*mahr-tehs*
Wednesday	**miércoles**	*mee-ehr-koh-lehs*
Thursday	**jueves**	*hoo-eh-behs*
Friday	**viernes**	*bee-ehr-nehs*
Saturday	**sábado**	*sah-bah-doh*
Sunday	**domingo**	*doh-meen-goh*

To express "on a particular day," use the masculine, singular definite article **el** + singular day of the week:

There is an assembly program in the school auditorium on Monday.
Hay una asamblea en el salón de actos de la escuela el lunes.
ah-ee oo-nah ah-sahm-bleh-ah ehn ehl sah-lohn deh ahk-tohs deh lah ehs-koo-eh-lah ehl loo-nehs

To express "on" when speaking about the day in a general sense, use the masculine, plural definite article **los** + plural day of the week:

There is an assembly program in the school auditorium on Mondays.
Hay una asamblea en el salón de actos de la escuela los lunes.
ah-ee oo-nah ah-sam-bleh-ah ehn ehl sah-lohn deh ahk-tohs deh lah ehs-koo-eh-lah lohs loo-nehs

Using Days of the Week

The normal school schedule is Monday through Friday from 8 a.m. until 3 p.m.
El horario normal de la escuela es de lunes a viernes, desde las ocho hasta las tres.
ehl oh-rah-ree-oh nohr-mahl deh lah ehs-koo-eh-lah ehs deh loo-nehs ah bee-ehr-nehs dehs-deh lahs oh-choh ahs-tah lahs trehs

There are no classes on Saturday or Sunday.
No hay clases el sábado o el domingo.
noh ah-ee klah-sehs ehl sah-bah-doh oh ehl doh-meen-goh

School is closed on Monday.
La escuela está cerrada el lunes.
lah ehs-koo-eh-lah ehs-tah seh-rrah-dah ehl loo-nehs

• A normal schedule will resume on Tuesday.
La escuela reanudará su horario habitual el martes.
lah ehs-koo-eh-lah rreh-ah-noo-dah-rah soo oh-rah-ree-oh ah-bee-too-ahl ehl
mahr-tehs

The cafeteria will be open on Thursday.
La cafetería estará abierta el jueves.
lah kah-feh-teh-ree-ah eh-stah-rah ah-bee-ehr-tah ehl hoo-eh-behs

Your child was absent on Friday.
Su hijo (hija) faltó el viernes.
soo ee-hoh (ee-hah) fahl-toh ehl bee-ehr-nehs

There is a test on Wednesday.
Hay un examen el miércoles.
ah-ee oon ehk-sah-mehn ehl mee-ehr-koh-lehs

There is no homework on Fridays.
No hay tarea los viernes.
noh ah-ee tah-reh-ah lohs bee-ehr-nehs

The assignment is due on Friday.
Hay que entregar la tarea el viernes.
ah-ee keh ehn-treh-gahr lah tah-reh-ah ehl bee-ehr-nehs

Your child misbehaved in school. He (She) has detention on
Thursday from 3 p.m. until 4 p.m.
Su hijo (hija) se ha portado mal en la escuela. Por eso debe
cumplir una penitencia el jueves desde las tres hasta las cuatro
de la tarde.
soo ee-hoh (ee-hah) seh hah pohr-tah-doh mahl ehn lah ehs-koo-eh-lah pohr
eh-soh deh-beh koom-pleer oon peh-nee-tehn-see-ah el hoo-eh-behs des-deh
lahs trehs ahs-tah lahs koo-ah-troh deh lah tahr-deh

I will speak to you (call you) again on Tuesday.
Le hablaré (telefonearé) otra vez el martes.
leh ah-blah-reh (teh-leh-foh-neh-ah-reh) oh-trah behs ehl mahr-tehs

We have an appointment for Thursday.
Tenemos una cita para el jueves.
teh-neh-mohs oo-nah see-tah pah-rah ehl hoo-eh-behs

Your child must bring his gym uniform on Mondays, Wednesdays, and Fridays.
Su hijo (hija) debe traer su uniforme de gimnasio los lunes, miércoles, y viernes.
soo ee-hoh (ee-hah) deh-beh trah-ehr soo oo-nee-fohr-meh deh heem-nah-see-oh lohs loo-nehs mee-ehr-koh-lehs ee bee-ehr-nehs

Months

English	Spanish	Pronunciation
January	**enero**	*eh-neh-roh*
February	**febrero**	*feh-breh-roh*
March	**marzo**	*mahr-soh*
April	**abril**	*ah-breel*
May	**mayo**	*mah-yoh*
June	**junio**	*hoo-nee-oh*
July	**julio**	*hoo-lee-oh*
August	**agosto**	*ah-gohs-toh*
September	**septiembre**	*sehp-tee-ehm-breh*
October	**octubre**	*ohk-too-breh*
November	**noviembre**	*noh-bee-ehm-breh*
December	**diciembre**	*dee-see-ehm-breh*

To express "in" a particular month, use **en**:

There are no classes in July and August.
No hay clases en julio y en agosto.
noh ah-ee klah-sehs ehn hoo-lee-oh ee ehn ah-gohs-toh

Classes begin in September.
Las clases empiezan en septiembre.
lahs klah-sehs ehm-pee-eh-sahn ehn sehp-tee-ehm-breh

Classes end in June.
Las clases terminan en junio.
lahs klah-sehs tehr-mee-nahn ehn hoo-nee-oh

We celebrate Christmas in December.
Celebramos la Navidad en diciembre.
seh-leh-brah-mohs lah nah-bee-dahd ehn dee-see-ehm-breh

Dates

What is today's date?
¿Cuál es la fecha de hoy? (¿A cuántos estamos?)
koo-ahl ehs lah feh-chah deh oh-ee (ah koo-ahn-tohs ehs-tah-mohs)

To answer, use the following formula:

> **Es (Estamos a)** day + **(el)** + cardinal number (use **primero**
> only for the first day of each month) + **de** + month + **de** + year

or
> **Hoy es lunes el primero de enero de dos mil siete.**

It's (Monday) the first of January (2007).
Es (Estamos a) (lunes) el primero de enero (de dos mil siete).
ehs (ehs-tah-mohs ah) (loo-nehs) ehl pree-meh-roh deh eh-neh-roh (deh dohs meel see-eh-teh)

Was he (she) born (Tuesday) the fourteenth of May (1977)?
¿Nació (martes) el catorce de mayo (de mil novecientos setenta y siete)?
nah-see-oh (mahr-tehs) ehl kah-tohr-seh deh mah-yoh (deh meel noh-beh-see-ehn-tohs seh-tehn-tah ee see-eh-teh)

When expressing a date in Spanish, remember that although
English dates are generally expressed in hundreds, Spanish years
are expressed in thousands and hundreds:

1983 (nineteen [hundred] eighty three)
mil novecientos ochenta y tres
meel noh-beh-see-ehn-tohs oh-chehn-tah ee trehs

If you have to read or write a date in Spanish, remember that the
numerals are written with the day before the month:

> April 12, 2007   **el 12 de abril de 2007** or 12/4/07

Words and Expressions Pertaining to Dates

English	Spanish	Pronunciation
a day	**un día**	*oon dee-ah*
a week	**una semana**	*oo-nah seh-mah-nah*
a month	**un mes**	*oon mehs*
a year	**un año**	*oon ah-nyoh*
a week from today	**de hoy en una semana**	*deh oh-ee ehn oo-nah seh-mah-nah*
ago	**hace**	*ah-seh*
always	**siempre**	*see-ehm-preh*
day after tomorrow	**pasado mañana**	*pah-sah-doh mah-nyah-nah*
day before yesterday	**anteayer**	*ahn-teh-ah-yehr*
during	**durante**	*doo-rahn-teh*
from	**desde**	*dehs-deh*
in	**en**	*ehn*
last (in a series)	**último(a)**	*ool-tee-moh(mah)*
last (most recent)	**pasado(a)**	*pah-sah-doh(dah)*
never	**nunca**	*noon-kah*
next	**próximo(a)**	*prohk-see-moh(mah)*
sometimes	**a veces**	*ah beh-sehs*
today	**hoy**	*oh-ee*
tomorrow	**mañana**	*mah-nyah-nah*
tomorrow afternoon	**mañana por la tarde**	*mah-nyah-nah pohr lah tahr-deh*
tomorrow morning	**mañana por la mañana**	*mah-nyah-nah pohr lah mah-nyah-nah*
tomorrow night	**mañana por la noche**	*mah-nyah-nah pohr lah noh-cheh*

continued

English	Spanish	Pronunciation
two weeks from tomorrow	**de mañana en dos semanas**	*deh mah-nyah-nah ehn dohs seh-mah-nahs*
until	**hasta**	*ahs-tah*
yesterday	**ayer**	*ah-yehr*

Using Dates, Words, and Expressions Pertaining to Dates

We have a meeting (an appointment) for Thursday, May 10th at 4 p.m.
Tenemos una reunión (una cita) para el jueves, el diez de mayo, a las cuatro.
teh-neh-mohs oo-nah rreh-oo-nyohn (oo-nah see-tah) pah-rah ehl hoo-eh-behs ehl dee-ehs deh mah-yoh ah lahs koo-ah-troh

There are no classes on Tuesday, June 15.
No hay clases el martes, quince de junio.
noh ah-ee klah-sehs ehl mahr-tehs keen-seh deh hoo-nee-on

We are on vacation from Monday, December 23rd through Thursday, January 2nd.
Estamos de vacaciones desde el lunes, veintitrés de diciembre hasta el jueves, dos de enero.
ehs-tah-mohs deh bah-kah-see-oh-nehs dehs-deh ehl loo-nehs beh-een-tee-trehs deh dee-see-ehm-breh ahs-tah ehl hoo-eh-behs dohs deh eh-neh-roh

Your child was absent yesterday (on Wednesday, January 12th).
Su hijo (hija) faltó ayer (el miércoles, doce de enero).
soo ee-hoh (ee-hah) fahl-toh ah-yehr (ehl mee-ehr-koh-lehs doh-seh deh eh-neh-roh)

I have scheduled an appointment for a conference concering the progress of your son (daughter) for Monday, April 22nd.
He programado una reunión con Ud. acerca del progreso de su hijo (hija) para el lunes, veintidós de abril.
eh proh-grah-mah-doh oo-nah rreh-oo-nyohn kohn oo-stehd ah-sehr-kah dehl proh-greh-soh deh soo ee-hoh (ee-hah) pah-rah ehl loo-nehs beh-een-tee-dohs deh ah-breel

I would like to remind you of our meeting for Wednesday, February 9th.
Me gustaría recordarle nuestra reunión para el miércoles, el nueve de febrero.
meh goos-tah-ree-ah rreh-kohr-dahr-leh noo-ehs-trah rreh-oo-nyohn pah-rah ehl mee-ehr-koh-lehs ehl noo-eh-beh deh feh-breh-roh

I am available to meet with you on Monday, April 12th.
Estoy disponible para reunirme con Ud. el lunes, el doce de abril.
ehs-toh-ee dees-poh-nee-bleh pah-rah rreh-oo-neer-meh kohn oo-stehd ehl loo-nehs ehl doh-seh deh ah-breel

We invite you to come to school on Monday, October 1st for a special program.
Lo (La) invitamos a venir a la escuela el lunes, el primero de octubre para un programa especial.
loh (lah) een-bee-tah-mohs ah beh-neer ah lah ehs-koo-eh-lah ehl loo-nehs pree-meh-roh deh ohk-too-breh pah-rah oon proh-grah-mah ehs-peh-see-ahl

Our class is taking a trip (having a party) on Monday, November 21st.
Nuestra clase irá de excursión (tendrá una fiesta) el lunes, veintiuno de noviembre.
noo-ehs-trah klah-seh ee-rah deh ehks-koor-see-ohn (tehn-drah oo-nah fee-ehs-tah) ehl loo-nehs beh-een-tee-oo-noh deh noh-bee-ehm-breh

School pictures will be taken on Tuesday, March 3rd.
Las fotos escolares se tomarán el martes, tres de marzo.
lahs foh-tohs ehs-koh-lah-rehs seh toh-mah-rahn ehl mahr-tehs trehs deh mahr-soh

Your child always (sometimes, never) does his (her) homework.
Su hijo (hija) siempre (a veces, nunca) hace su tarea.
soo ee-hoh (ee-hah) see-ehm-preh (ah beh-sehs, noon-kah) ah-seh soo tah-reh-ah

I will call (tell) you tomorrow morning (afternoon, night).
Le telefonearé (diré) mañana por la mañana (por la tarde, por la noche).
leh teh-leh-foh-neh-ah-reh (dee-reh) mah-nyah-nah pohr lah mah-nyah-nah (pohr lah tahr-deh, pohr lah noh-cheh)

The last day of school is Friday, June 30th.
El último día de clases es viernes, el treinta de junio.
ehl ool-tee-moh dee-ah deh klah-sehs ehs bee-ehr-nehs ehl treh-een-tah deh hoo-nee-oh

The Seasons

English	Spanish	Pronunciation
winter	**el invierno**	*ehl een-bee-ehr-noh*
spring	**la primavera**	*lah pree-mah-beh-rah*
summer	**el verano**	*ehl beh-rah-noh*
autumn, fall	**el otoño**	*ehl oh-toh-nyoh*

There is no school in the summer.
No hay clases en el verano.
noh ah-ee klah-sehs ehn ehl beh-rah-noh

Holidays

New Year's Day
el Día de Año Nuevo
ehl dee-ah deh ah-nyoh noo-eh-boh

Martin Luther King Day
el Natalicio de Martin Luther King
ehl nah-tah-lee-see-oh deh Martin Luther King

Presidents' Week
la Semana de los Presidentes
lah seh-mah-nah deh lohs preh-see-dehn-tehs

Valentine's Day
el Día de San Valentín
ehl dee-ah deh sahn bah-lehn-teen

Easter
(la) Pascua
(lah)pahs-koo-ah

Mother's Day
el Día de las Madres
ehl dee-ah deh lahs mah-drehs

Memorial Day
el Día de los Caídos
ehl dee-ah deh lohs kah-ee-dohs

Father's Day
el Día de los Padres
ehl dee-ah deh lohs pah-drehs

Independence Day
el Día de la Independencia
ehl dee-ah deh lah een-deh-pehn-dehn-see-ah

Labor Day
el Día del Trabajo
ehl dee-ah dehl trah-bah-hoh

Columbus Day
el Día de la Raza
ehl dee-ah dehl lah rrah-sah

Halloween
la Víspera de Todos los Santos
lah bees-peh-rah deh toh-dohs lohs sahn-tohs

Election Day
el Día de las Elecciones
ehl dee-ah deh lahs eh-lehk-see-oh-nehs

Veterans' Day
el Día del Armisticio
ehl dee-ah dehl ahr-mees-tee-see-oh

Thanksgiving
el Día de Acción de Gracias
ehl dee-ah deh ahk-see-ohn deh grah-see-ahs

Christmas Eve
la Nochebuena
lah noh-cheh-boo-eh-nah

Christmas
la Navidad
lah nah-bee-dahd

New Year's Eve
la Víspera de Año Nuevo
lah bee-speh-rah deh ah-nyoh noo-eh-boh

There is a parade to celebrate Thanksgiving.
Hay un desfile para celebrar el Día de Acción de Gracias.
ah-ee oon dehs-fee-leh pah-rah seh-leh-brahr ehl dee-ah deh ahk-see-ohn deh grah-see-ahs

There is no school on Christmas.
No hay clases en Navidad.
noh ah-ee klah-sehs en nah-bee-dahd

Students have to come to school on Election Day.
Los alumnos tienen que venir a la escuela el Día de las Elecciones.
lohs ah-loom-nohs tee-eh-nehn keh beh-neer ah lah ehs-koo-eh-lah ehl dee-ah deh lahs eh-lehk-see-oh-nehs

We celebrate Mother's Day the second Sunday in May.
Celebramos el Día de las Madres el segundo domingo de mayo.
seh-leh-brah-mohs ehl dee-ah deh lahs mah-drehs ehl seh-goon-doh doh-meen-goh deh mah-yoh

The Weather

It's bad weather.
Hace mal tiempo.
ah-seh mahl tee-ehm-poh

It's cloudy.
Está nublado.
ehs-tah noo-blah-doh

It's cold.
Hace frío.
ah-seh free-oh

It's cool.
Hace fresco.
ah-seh frehs-koh

It's foggy.
Hay niebla (neblina).
ah-ee nee-eh-blah(neh-blee-nah)

It's hot.
Hace calor.
ah-seh kah-lohr

It's humid.
Está húmedo.
ehs-tah oo-meh-doh

There's lightning.
Hay relámpagos.
ah-ee rreh-lahm-pah-gohs

It's nice weather.
Hace buen tiempo.
ah-seh boo-ehn tee-ehm-poh

It's overcast.
Está nublado.
ehs-tah noo-blah-doh

It's pouring.
Llueve torrencialmente.
yoo-eh-beh toh-rrehn-see-ahl-mehn-teh

It's pouring.
Hay un aguacero.
ah-ee oon ah-goo-ah-seh-roh

It's raining.
Llueve.
yoo-eh-beh

It's raining.
Está lloviendo.
ehs-tah yoh-bee-ehn-doh

It's showery.
Está lluvioso.
ehs-tah yoo-bee-oh-soh

It's drizzling.
Está lloviznando.
ehs-tah yoh-bees-nahn-doh

It's snowing.
Nieva.
nee-eh-bah

It's snowing.
Está nevando.
ehs-tah neh-bahn-doh

It's sunny.
Hace sol.
ah-seh sohl

It's sunny.
Está soleado.
ehs-tah soh-leh-ah-doh

It's thundering.
Truena.
troo-eh-nah

It's thundering.
Está tronando.
ehs-tah troh-nahn-doh

It's windy.
Hace viento.
ah-seh bee-ehn-toh

There's a hurricane.
Hay un huracán.
ah-ee oon oo-rah-kahn

There's a tornado.
Hay un tornado.
ah-ee oon tohr-nah-doh

There are showers.
Hay lloviznas.
ah-ee yoh-bees-nahs

There are gale winds.
Hay un vendaval.
ah-ee oon behn-dah-bahl

There's hail.
Hay granizo.
ah-ee grah-nee-soh

There's a storm.
Hay una tormenta (tempestad).
ah-ee oo-nah tohr-mehn-tah (tehm-pehs-tahd)

Discussing the Weather

School is closed because of the bad weather.
La escuela está cerrada a causa del mal tiempo.
lah ehs-koo-eh-lah ehs-tah seh-rrah-dah ah kah-oo-sah dehl mahl tee-ehm-poh

School is open despite the snow.
La escuela está abierta a pesar de la nieve.
lah ehs-koo-eh-lah ehs-tah ah-bee-ehr-tah ah peh-sahr deh lah nee-eh-beh

The buses are running a half-hour late because of the rain.
Los autobuses corren media hora de retraso a causa de la lluvia.
lohs ah-oo-toh-boo-sehs koh-rrehn meh-deee-ah oh-rah deh rreh-trah-soh ah kah-oo-sah deh lah yoo-bee-ah

The buses aren't running today because of the storm.
Los autobuses no corren hoy a causa de la tormenta.
lohs ah-oh-toh-boo-sehs noh koh-rrehn oh-ee ah kah-oo-sah deh lah tohr-mehn-tah

5

Classroom Commands and Rules

> **Note:**
> 1. Letters or words in brackets are used when using the familiar you **[tú]** form.
> 2. When speaking to more than one adult, **Ud.** (you, singular) becomes **Uds.** (you, plural) and an n is added to the conjugated verb form.
> 3. The formal you form is expressed in the same way as the third-person singular **él** (he) and **ella** (she) forms.

In the Classroom

Again.
Otra vez.
oh-trah behs

All together.
Todos juntos.
toh-dohs hoon-tohs

Answer the questions.
Conteste(n) [Contesta, No contestes] las preguntas.
kohn-tehs-teh(n) [kohn-tehs-tah, noh kohn-tehs-tehs] lahs preh-goon-tahs

Arrange the chairs (in a circle).
Arregle(n) [Arregla, No arregles] las sillas (en un círculo).
ah-rreh-gleh(n) [ah-rreh-glah, noh ah-rreh-glehs] lahs see-yahs (ehn oon seer-koo-loh)

Arrive at eight o'clock (on time, late) every day.
Llegue(n) [Llega, No llegues] a las ocho (a tiempo, tarde) cada día.
yeh-geh(n) [yeh-gah, no yeh-gehs] ah lahs oh-choh (ah-tee-ehm-poh, tahr-deh) kah-dah dee-ah

Ask for the pass.
Pida(n) [Pide, No pidas] permiso.
pee-dah(n) [pee-deh, noh pee-dahs] ehl pehr-mee-soh

Ask Juan if he wants to help you.
Pregúntele [Pregúntale, No le preguntes] a Juan si quiere ayudarle [te].
preh-goon-teh-leh [preh-goon-tah-leh, noh leh preh-goon-tehs] ah hoo-ahn see kee-eh-reh ah-yoo-dahr-leh [teh]

Attention.
Atención.
ah-tehn-see-ohn

Be careful.
Tenga(n) [Ten, No tengas] cuidado.
tehn-gah(n) [tehn, noh tehn-gahs] koo-ee-dah-doh

Be proud.
Sea(n) [Sé, No seas] orgulloso(s).
seh-ah(n) [seh, noh seh-ahs] ohr-goo-yoh-soh(s)

Be quiet.
Cálle(n)se [Cállate, No te calles].
kah-yeh(n)-seh (kah-yah-teh, noh teh kah-yehs)

Be responsible.
Sea(n) [Sé, No seas] responsable(s).
seh-ah(n) [seh, no seh-ahs] rrehs-pohn-sah-bleh(s)

Behave yourself.
Pórte(n)se [Pórtate] bien.
pohr-teh(n)-seh [pohr-tah-teh] bee-ehn

Bring me the book.
Tráigame [Tráeme] el libro.
trah-ee-gah-meh [trah-eh-meh] el libro.

Bring your book every day.
Traiga(n) [Trae, No traigas] sus [tus] libros cada día.
trah-ee-gah(n) [trah-eh, noh trah-ee-gahs] soos [toos] lee-brohs kah-dah dee-ah

Careful.
Cuidado.
koo-ee-dah-doh

Carry your ID card.
Lleve(n) [Lleva] la tarjeta de identificación.
yeh-beh(n) [yeh-bah] lah tahr-heh-tah deh ee-dehn-tee-fee-kah-see-ohn]

Check your answers.
Revise(n) [Revisa] sus [tus] respuestas.
rreh-bee-seh(n) [rreh-bee-sah] soos [toos] rrehs-poo-ehs-tahs

Choose the answer.
Escoja(n) [Escoje, No escojas] la respuesta.
ehs-koh-hah(n) [ehs-koh-heh, noh ehs-koh-hahs] lah rrehs-poo-ehs-tah

Clean the desks.
Limpie(n) [Limpia, No limpies] los pupitres.
leem-pee-eh(n) [leem-pee-ah, noh leem-pee-ehs] lohs poo-pee-trehs

Close your books.
Cierre(n) [Cierra, No cierres] los libros.
see-eh-rreh(n) [see-eh-rrah, noh see-eh-rrehs] lohs lee-brohs

Come here.
Venga(n) [Ven, No vengas] aquí.
behn-gah(n) [behn, noh behn-gahs] ah-kee

Come to school on time.
Venga(n) [Ven] a la escuela a tiempo.
behn-gah(n) [behn] ah lah ehs-koo-eh-lah ah tee-ehm-poh

Continue working.
Continúe(n) [Continúa, No continúes] trabajando. Siga(n) [Sigue, No sigas] trabajando.
kohn-tee-noo-eh(n) [kohn-tee-noo-ah, noh kohn-teen-oo-ehs] trah-bah-hahn-doh see-gah(n) [see-geh, noh see-gahs] trah-bah-hahn-doh

Correct your answers.
Corrija(n) [Corrige, No corrijas] sus [tus] respuestas.
koh-rree-hah(n) [koh-rree-heh, noh koh-rree-hahs] soos [toos] rrehs-poo-ehs-tahs

Count the money.
Cuente(n) [Cuenta, No cuentes] el dinero.
koo-ehn-teh(n) [koo-ehn-tah, noh koo-ehn-tehs] ehl dee-neh-roh

Cut the paper.
Corte(n) [Corta, No cortes] el papel.
kohr-teh(n) [kohr-tah, noh kohr-tehs] ehl pah-pehl.

Describe what happened.
Describa(n) [Describe, No describas] lo que pasó.
dehs-kree-bah(n) [dehs-kree-beh, noh dehs-kree-bahs] loh keh pah-soh

Do it like this.
Hága(n)lo (Hazlo, No lo hagas) así.
ah-gah(n)-loh (ahs-loh, noh loh ah-gahs) ah-see

Do it this way.
Hága(n)lo [Hazlo, No lo hagas] de esta manera.
ah-gah(n)-loh [ahs-loh, noh loh ah-gahs] deh ehs-tah mah-neh-rah

Do the exercises now.
Haga(n) [Haz, No hagas] los ejercicios ahora.
ah-gah(n) [ahs, noh ah-gahs] lohs eh-hehr-see-see-ohs ah-oh-rah

(Don't) Do your homework (in class).
(No) Haga(n) [Haz, No hagas] su [tu] tarea (en clase).
(noh) ah-gah(n) [ahs, noh ah-gahs] soo [too] tah-reh-ah (ehn klah-seh)

Don't be afraid.
No tenga [tengas] miedo.
noh tehn-gah[s] mee-eh-doh

Don't arrive late.
No llegue(n) [No llegues] tarde.
noh yeh-geh(n) [noh yeh-gehs] tahr-deh

Don't be silly (nervous).
No sea(n) [No seas] tonto (a) (s) (nervioso (a)(s)).
noh seh-ah(n) [noh seh-ahs] tohn-toh (tah)(s)(nehr-bee-oh-soh(sah)(s))

Don't bother other students.
No moleste(n) [No molestes] a los demás estudiantes (a los otros estudiantes).
noh moh-lehs-teh(n) [noh moh-lehs-tehs] ah lohs deh-mahs ehs-too-dee-ahn-tehs (ah lohs oh-trohs ehs-too-dee-ahn-tehs)

Don't chew gum.
No mastique(n) [mastiques] chicle.
noh mahs-tee-keh(n) [mahs-tee-kehs] chee-kleh

Don't complain.
No se queje(n) [No te quejes].
noh seh keh-heh(n) [noh teh keh-hehs]

Don't cry.
No llore [llores].
noh yoh-reh [yoh-rehs]

Don't cut class.
No falte(n) [faltes] a su [tu] clase.
noh fahl-teh(n) [fahl-tehs] ah soo [too] klah-seh

Don't forget to bring your English book tomorrow.
No olvide(n) [olvides] traer su [tu] libro de inglés mañana.
noh ohl-bee-deh(n) [ohl-bee-dehs] trah-ehr soo [too] lee-broh deh een-glehs mah-nyah-nah

Don't lose your book.
No pierda(n) [No pierdas] su [tu] libro.
noh pee-ehr-dah(n) [noh pee-ehr-dahs] soo [too] lee-broh

Don't smoke.
No fume(n) [fumes].
noh foo-meh(n) [foo-mehs]

Don't take too long.
No se demore [te demores] mucho.
noh seh deh-moh-reh [teh deh-moh-rehs] moo-choh

Don't touch.
No toque(n) [toques].
noh toh-keh(n) [toh-kehs]

Don't turn around.
No se den [No te des] vuelta.
noh seh dehn [noh teh dehs] boo-ehl-tah

Don't use drugs.
No use(n) [No uses] drogas.
noh oo-seh(n) [noh oo-sehs] droh-gahs

Don't whistle.
No silbe(n) [silbes].
noh seel-beh(n) [seel-behs]

Draw a triangle.
Dibuje(n) [Dibuja, No dibujes] un triángulo.
dee-boo-heh(n) [dee-boo-hah, noh dee-boo-hehs] oon tree-ahn-goo-loh

Enter the classroom.
Entre(n) [Entra, No entres] en el salón de clase.
ehn-treh(n) [ehn-trah, noh ehn-trehs] ehn ehl sah-lohn deh klah-seh

Erase the chalkboard.
Borre(n) [Borra, No borres] la pizarra.
boh-rreh(n) [boh-rrah, noh boh-rrehs] lah pee-sah-rrah

Fill out the form.
Llene(n) [Llena, No llenes] el formulario.
yeh-neh(n) [yeh-nah, noh yeh-nehs] ehl fohr-moo-lah-ree-oh

Fill the glass with water.
Llene(n) [Llena, No llenes] el vaso de agua.
yeh-neh(n) [yeh-nah, no yeh-nehs] ehl bah-soh deh ah-goo-ah

Fold the paper in half.
Doble(n) [Dobla, No dobles] el papel en dos.
doh-bleh(n) [doh-blah, noh doh-blehs] ehl pah-pehl ehn dohs

Follow the explanations carefully.
Siga(n) [Sigue, No sigas] con atención las explicaciones.
see-gah(n) [see-geh, noh see-gahs] kohn ah-tehn-see-ohn lahs ehk-splee-kah-see-oh-nehs

Follow the model.
Siga(n) [Sigue, No sigas] el modelo.
see-gah(n) [see-geh, noh see-gahs] ehl moh-deh-loh

Give me your paper.
Deme [Dame] su [tu] papel.
deh-meh [dah-meh] soo [too] pah-pehl

Go to the dean's office.
Vaya(n) [Ve, No vayas] a la oficina del decano.
bah-yah(n) [beh, noh bah-yahs] ah lah oh-fee-see-nah dehl deh-kah-noh

Get into your groups.
Formen sus grupos.
fohr-mehn soos groo-pohs

Hand in your test (homework).
Entregue(n) [Entrega, No entregues] su [tu] examen (tarea).
ehn-treh-geh(n) [ehn-treh-gah, noh ehn-treh-gehs] soo [too] ehk-sah-mehn (tah-reh-ah)

Hang your coat in the closet (wardrobe).
Cuelgue(n) [Cuelga, No cuelgues] su [tu] abrigo en el armario.
koo-ehl-geh(n) [koo-ehl-gah, noh koo-ehl-gehs] soo [too] ah-bree-goh ehn ehl ahr-mah-ree-oh

In a loud voice
En voz alta
ehn bohs ahl-tah

In English
En inglés
ehn een-glehs

In Spanish
En español
ehn ehs-pah-nyohl

Keep going.
Siga(n) [Sigue, No sigas].
see-gah(n) [see-geh, noh see-gahs]

Know how to spell the words.
Sepa(n) deletrear las palabras.
seh-pah(n) deh-leh-treh-ahr lahs pah-lah-brahs

Learn the rules.
Aprenda(n) [Aprende, No aprendas] las reglas.
ah-prehn-dah(n) [ah-prehn-deh, noh ah-prehn-dahs] lahs rreh-glahs

Leave the classroom.
Salga(n) [Sal, No salgas] del sálon.
sahl-gah(n) [sahl, noh sahl-gahs] dehl sah-lohn

Listen.
Escuche(n) [Escucha, No escuches].
ehs-koo-cheh(n) [ehs-koo-chah, noh ehs-koo-chehs]

Look at the chalkboard.
Mire(n) [Mira, No mires] la pizarra.
mee-reh(n) [mee-rah, noh mee-rehs] lah pee-sah-rrah

Look for the correct answer.
Busque(n) [Busca, No busques] la respuesta correcta.
boos-keh(n) [boos-kah, noh boos-kehs] lah rrehs-poo-ehs-tah koh-rrehk-tah

Louder (slower), please.
Más alto (despacio), por favor.
mahs ahl-toh (dehs-pah-see-oh) pohr fah-bohr

Memorize the words.
Aprenda(n) [Aprende, No aprendas] de memoria las palabras.
ah-prehn-dah(n) [ah-prehn-deh, noh ah-prehn-dahs] deh meh-moh-ree-ah lahs pah-lah-brahs

Move the basket.
Mueva(n) [Mueve, No muevas] la canasta.
moo-eh-bah(n) [moo-eh-beh, noh moo-eh-bahs] lah kah-nahs-tah

Obey the rules.
Obedezca(n) [Obedece] las reglas.
oh-beh-dehs-kah(n) [oh-beh-deh-seh] lahs rreh-glahs

One at a time.
Uno a la vez.
oo-noh ah lah behs

Open the door (window).
Abra(n) [Abre, No abras] la puerta (ventana).
ah-brah(n) [ah-breh, noh ah-brahs] lah poo-ehr-tah (behn-tah-nah)

Paint a house.
Pinte(n) [Pinta, No pintes] una casa.
peen-teh(n) [peen-tah, noh peen-tehs] oo-nah kah-sah

Pass out the books.
Reparta(n) [Reparte, No repartas] los libros.
rreh-pahr-tah(n) [rreh-pahr-teh, noh rreh-pahr-tahs] lohs lee-brohs

Pay attention (Listen).
Preste(n) [Presta, No prestes] atención.
prehs-teh(n) [prehs-tah, noh prehs-tehs] ah-tehn-see-ohn

Pick up the papers.
Recoja(n) [Recoge, No recojas] los papeles.
rreh-koh-hah(n) [rreh-koh-heh, noh rreh-koh-hahs] lohs pah-peh-lehs

Point to the person.
Señale(n) [Señala, No señales] a la persona.
seh-nyah-leh(n) [seh-nyah-lah, noh seh-nyah-lehs] ah lah pehr-soh-nah

Practice the vocabulary words.
Practique(n) [Practica, No practiques] las palabras del vocabulario.
prahk-tee-keh(n) [prahk-tee-kah, noh prahk-tee-kehs] lahs pah-lah-brahs dehl boh-kah-boo-lah-ree-oh

Prepare your homework well.
Prepare(n) [Prepara, No preparen] bien su [tu] tarea.
preh-pah-reh(n) [preh-pah-rah, noh preh-pah-rehn] bee-ehn soo [too] tah-reh-ah

Pronounce these words.
Pronuncie(n) [Pronuncia, No pronuncies] estas palabras.
proh-noon-see-eh(n) [proh-noon-see-ah, no proh-noon-see-ehs] ehs-tahs pah-lah-brahs

Raise your hand.
Levante(n) [Levanta, No levantes] la mano.
leh-bahn-teh(n) [leh-bahn-tah, noh leh-bahn-tehs] lah mah-noh

Read aloud (silently).
Lea(n) [Lee, No leas] en voz alta (en silencio).
leh-ah(n) [leh-eh, noh leh-ahs] ehn bohs ahl-tah (ehn see-lehn-see-oh)

Remember that there is a test tomorrow.
Recuerde(n) [Recuerda, No recuerdes] que hay un examen mañana.
rreh-koo-ehr-deh(n) [rreh-koo-ehr-dah, noh rreh-koo-ehr-dehs] keh ah-ee oon ehk-sah-men mah-nyah-nah

Repeat the words after me.
Repita(n) [Repite, No repitas] las palabras después de mí.
rreh-pee-tah(n) [rreh-pee-teh, noh rreh-pee-tahs] lahs pah-lah-brahs dehs-poo-ehs deh mee

Respect the property of others.
Respete(n) [Respeta] la propiedad de los demás.
rrehs-peh-teh(n) [rrehs-peh-tah] lah proh-pee-eh-dahd deh lohs deh-mahs

Return this paper with your parent's signature.
Devuelva(n) [Devuelve, No devuelvas] este papel con la firma de sus [tus] padres.
deh-boo-ehl-bah(n) [deh-boo-ehl-beh, noh deh-boo-ehl-bahs] ehs-teh pah-pehl kohn lah feer-mah deh soos [toos] pah-drehs

Review your work.
Revise(n) [Revisa, No revises] su [tu] trabajo.
rreh-bee-seh(n) [rreh-bee-sah, noh rreh-bee-sehs] soo [too] trah-bah-hoh

Say what happened.
Diga(n) [Di, No digas] lo que pasó.
dee-gah(n) [dee, noh dee-gahs] loh keh pah-soh

Show me your answer.
Muéstre(n)me [Muéstrame, No me muestres] su [tu] respuesta.
moo-ehs-treh(n)-meh [moo-ehs-trah-meh, noh meh moo-ehs-trehs] soo [too] rrehs-poo-ehs-tah

Show your work to your friend.
Muestre(n) [Muestra, No muestres] su [tu] trabajo a su [tu] amigo.
moo-ehs-treh(n) [moo-ehs-trah, noh moo-ehs-trehs] soo [too] trah-bah-hoh ah soo [too] ah-mee-goh

Silence.
Silencio.
see-lehn-see-oh

Sing.
Cante(n) [Canta, No cantes].
kahn-teh(n) [kahn-tah, noh kahn-tehs]

Sit.
Siénte(n)se [Siéntate, No te sientes].
see-ehn-teh(n)-seh [see-ehn-tah-teh, noh teh see-ehn-tehs]

Speak only English in class.
Hable(n) [Habla, No hables] solamente inglés en clase.
ah-bleh(n) [ah-blah, noh ah-blehs] soh-lah-mehn-teh een-glehs ehn klah-seh

Spell these words.
Deletree(n) [Deletrea, No deletrees] estas palabras.
deh-leh-treh-eh(n) [deh-leh-treh-ah, noh deh-leh-treh-ehs] ehs-tahs pah-lah-brahs

Stack the books.
Amontone(n) [Amontona, No amontones] los libros.
ah-mohn-toh-neh(n) [ah-mohn-toh-nah, noh ah-mohn-toh-nehs] lohs lee-brohs

Stand up.
Levánte(n)se [Levántate, No te levantes].
leh-bahn-teh(n)-seh [leh-bahn-tah-teh, noh teh leh-bahn-tehs]

Start the work now.
Empiece(n) [Empieza, No empieces] el trabajo ahora.
ehm-pee-eh-seh(n) [ehm-pee-eh-sah, noh ehm-pee-eh-sehs] ehl trah-bah-hoh ah-oh-rah

Stop talking.
Pare(n) [Para, No pares] de hablar.
pah-reh(n) [pah-rah, noh pah-rehs] deh ah-blahr

Study for the test.
Estudie(n) [Estudia, No estudies] para el examen.
ehs-too-dee-eh(n) [ehs-too-dee-ah, noh ehs-too-dee-ehs] pah-rah ehl ehk-sah-mehn

Take out your homework.
Saque(n) [Saca, No saques) su [tu] tarea.
sah-keh(n) [sah-kah, noh sah-kehs] soo [too] tah-reh-ah

Take this paper.
Tome(n) [Toma, No tomes] este papel.
toh-meh(n) [toh-mah, noh toh-mehs] ehs-teh pah-pehl

Tell me the truth.
Díga(n)me [Dime] la verdad.
dee-gah(n)-meh [dee-meh] lah behr-dahd

Turn around.
De(n)se [Date, No te des] la vuelta.
deh(n)-seh [dah-teh, noh teh dehs] lah boo-ehl-tah

Turn to page. . . .
Pase(n) [Pasa, No pases] a la página. . . .
pah-seh(n) [pah-sah, noh pah-sehs] ah lah pah-hee-nah

Use a pencil.
Emplee(n) [Emplea, No emplees] un lápiz.
ehm-pleh-eh(n) [ehm-pleh-ah, noh ehm-pleh-ehs] oon lah-pees

Use a pencil.
Use(n) [Usa, No uses] un lápiz.
oo-seh(n) [oo-sah, noh oo-sehs] oon lah-pees

Wait for the bell to ring.
Espere(n) [Espera, No esperes] hasta que suene el timbre.
ehs-peh-reh(n) [ehs-peh-rah, noh ehs-peh-rehs] ahs-tah keh soo-eh-neh ehl teem-breh

Wash your hands.
Láve(n)se [Lávate] las manos.
lah-beh(n)-seh [lah-bah-teh] lahs mah-nohs

Wear appropriate clothing.
Pónga(n)se [Ponte] ropa apropiada.
poh-gah(n)-seh [pohn-teh] rroh-pah ah-proh-pee-ah-dah

Work with a partner.
Trabaje(n) [Trabaja, No trabajes] con un compañero.
trah-bah-heh(n) [trah-bah-hah, noh trah-bah-hehs] kohn oon kohm-pah-nyeh-roh

Write in blue or black ink.
Escriba(n) [Escribe, No escribas] con tinta azul o negra.
ehs-kree-bah(n) [ehs-kree-beh, noh ehs-kree-bahs] kohn teen-tah ah-sool oh neh-grah

Your attention, please.
Atención, por favor.
ah-tehn-see-ohn pohr fah-bohr

On the Playground

To the Student

Come here.
Venga(n) [ven] acá.
behn-gah(n) [behn] ah-kah

Bring the _____ to me.
Tráiga(n)me [Tráeme] _____.
trah-ee-gah[n]-meh [trah-eh-meh]

ball	**la pelota**	*lah peh-loh-tah*
equipment	**el equipo**	*ehl eh-kee-poh*
jump rope	**la cuerda para brincar**	*lah koo-ehr-dah pah-rah breen-kahr*
racket	**la raqueta**	*lah rrah-keh-tah*

Don't _____.
No _____.
noh

argue	**discutas**	*dees-koo-tahs*
bite	**muerdas**	*moo-ehr-dahs*
bother the others	**molestes a los demás**	*moh-lehs-tehs ah lohs deh-mahs*
climb	**subas**	*soo-bahs*
complain	**te quejes**	*teh keh-hehs*
cry	**llores**	*yoh-rehs*
curse	**digas palabrotas**	*dee-gahs pah-lah-broh-tahs*
fall	**te caigas**	*teh kah-ee-gahs*
fight	**pelees**	*peh-leh-ehs*
grab	**agarres**	*ah-gah-rrehs*
hide	**te escondas**	*teh ehs-kohn-dahs*
jump	**saltes**	*sahl-tehs*
kick	**patees**	*pah-teh-ehs*
play roughly	**juegues brutamente**	*hoo-eh-gehs broo-tah-mehn-teh*
pull	**jales**	*hah-lehs*
push	**empujes**	*ehm-poo-hehs*
run	**corras**	*koh-rrahs*

spit	**escupas**	*ehs-koo-pahs*
talk to	**hables con**	*ah-blehs kohn dehs-*
strangers	**desconocidos**	*koh-noh-see-dohs*
throw things	**tires cosas**	*tee-rehs koh-sahs*
touch	**toques**	*toh-kehs*
trip anybody	**hagas caer a nadie**	*ah-gahs kah-ehr ah nah-dee-eh*
yell	**grites**	*gree-tehs*

Line up.
Hagan una fila.
ah-gahn oo-nah fee-lah

Stay in line.
Quédense en fila.
keh-dehn-seh ehn fee-lah

Come here.
Vengan [Ven] aquí.
behn-gahn [behn] ah-kee

Keep to the left (right).
Quéde(n)se a la izquierda (derecha).
keh-deh(n)-seh ah lah ees-kee-ehr-dah (deh-reh-chah)

Remain quiet.
Quéde(n)se callado(a)(s).
keh-deh(n)-seh kah-yah-doh(dah)(s)

Put that away.
Favor de guardar esa cosa.
fah-bohr deh goo-ahr-dahr eh-sah koh-sah

Go to class.
Vaya(n) [Ve, No vayas] a la clase.
bah-yah(n) [beh, noh bah-yahs] ah lah klah-seh

Wait your turn.
Espere(n) [Espera] su [tu] turno.
ehs-peh-reh(n) [ehs-peh-rah] soo [too] toor-noh

To the Parent

Your child loves playground activities.
A su hijo (hija) le encantan las actividades en el patio de recreo.
ah soo ee-hoh (ee-hah) leh ehn-kahn-tahn lahs ahk-tee-bee-dah-dehs ehn ehl pah-tee-oh deh rreh-kreh-oh

He/She plays well with others.
Juega bien con los demás.
hoo-eh-gah bee-ehn kohn lohs deh-mahs

He/She should participate more in organized games.
Debería participar más en partidos organizados.
deh-beh-ree-ah pahr-tee-see-pahr mahs ehn pahr-tee-dohs ohr-gah-nee-sah-dohs

Your child doesn't cooperate with others on the playground.
Su hijo (hija) no coopera con los demás en el patio de recreo.
soo ee-hoh (ee-hah) noh koh-oh-peh-rah kohn lohs deh-mahs ehn ehl pah-tee-oh deh rreh-kreh-oh

Recently, there have been several incidents regarding his (her) playground behavior.
Recientemente, han ocurrido varios incidentes relacionados con su conducta en el patio.
rreh-see-ehn-teh-mehn-teh ahn oh-koo-rree-doh bah-ree-ohs een-see-dehn-tehs rreh-lah-see-oh-nah-dohs kohn soo kohn-dook-tah ehn ehl pah-tee-oh

He/She is bossy on the playground.
Es muy dominante en el patio de recreo.
ehs moo-ee doh-mee-nahn-teh ehn ehl pah-tee-oh deh rreh-kreh-oh

Would you please speak to him (her) about this?
¿Podría Ud. hablarle de esto?
poh-dree-ah oo-stehd ah-blahr-leh deh ehs-toh

He/She must play more carefully.
Tiene que jugar con más cuidado.
tee-eh-neh keh hoo-gahr kohn mahs koo-ee-dah-doh

When he/she doesn't listen, it becomes necessary to remove him (her) from playground activities.

Cuando no escucha, es necesario sacarlo(la) de las actividades del patio de recreo.

koo-ahn-doh noh ehs-koo-chah ehs neh-seh-sah-ree-oh sah-kahr-loh(lah) deh lahs ahk-tee-bee-dah-dehs dehl pah-tee-oh deh rreh-kreh-oh

When can we speak about this problem?

¿Cuándo podemos hablar de este problema?

koo-ahn-doh poh-deh-mohs ah-blahr deh ehs-teh proh-bleh-mah

6

Essential Phrases

> **Note:**
> 1. Letters or words in brackets are used when using the familiar you **[tú]** form.
> 2. When speaking to more than one adult, **Ud.** (you, singular) becomes **Uds.** (you, plural) and an n is added to the conjugated verb form.
> 3. The formal you form is expressed in the same way as the third-person singular **él** (he) and **ella** (she) forms.

Greetings

To Parents

Good morning.
Buenos días.
boo-eh-nohs dee-ahs

Good afternoon.
Buenas tardes.
boo-eh-nahs tahr-dehs

Good evening/Good night.
Buenas noches.
boo-eh-nahs noh-chehs

Welcome.
Bienvenido(a)(s).
bee-ehn-beh-nee-doh(dah)(s)

It's nice to meet you.
Mucho gusto en conocerlo(a)(s).
moo-choh goos-toh ehn koh-noh-sehr-loh(lah)(s)

How nice to see you!
¡Qué gusto verlo(a)(s)!
keh goos-toh behr-loh(lah)(s)

The pleasure is mine.
El gusto es mío.
ehl goos-toh ehs mee-oh

How are you?
¿Cómo está Ud.?
koh-moh ehs-tah oos-tehd

Please come in.
Entre(n), por favor.
ehn-treh(n) pohr fah-bohr

Please sit down.
Siénte(n)se, por favor.
see-ehn-teh(n)-seh, pohr fah-bohr

What is your name?
¿Cómo se llama(n) Ud(s).?
koh-moh seh yah-mah(n) oos-tehd(ehs)

What is your child's name?
¿Cómo se llama su hijo (hija)?
koh-moh seh yah-mah soo ee-hoh (ee-hah)

I'm Mr. (Miss, Mrs.) _____.
Soy el (la) señor (señorita, señora) _____.
soh-ee ehl (lah) seh-nyohr (seh-nyoh-ree-tah, sehn-yoh-rah)

I am your child's teacher.
Soy el profesor (la profesora) de su hijo (hija).
soh-ee ehl proh-feh-sohr (lah proh-feh-soh-rah) deh soo ee-hoh (ee-hah)

I would like to introduce you to your child's counselor.
Quisiera presentarle al consejero (a la consejera) de su hijo (hija).
kee-see-eh-rah preh-sehn-tahr-leh ahl kohn-seh-heh-roh (ah lah kohn-seh-heh-rah) deh soo ee-hoh (ee-hah)

It is nice to see you.
Me alegro mucho de verlo(a)(s) a Ud(s).
meh ah-leh-groh moo-choh deh behr-loh(lah)(s) ah oos-tehd (oos-teh-dehs)

It was nice to see you.
Me he alegrado mucho de verlo(a)(s) a Ud(s).
meh eh ah-leh-grah-doh moo-choh de behr-loh(lah)(s) ah oos-tehd (oos-teh-dehs)

Goodbye.
Adiós.
ah-dee-ohs

Have a nice day.
Que tenga(n) un buen día.
keh tehn-gah(n) oon boo-ehn dee-ah

Have a nice day!
¡Que le(s) vaya bien!
keh leh(s) bah-yah bee-ehn

Same to you.
Igualmente.
ee-goo-ahl-mehn-teh

Thank you for coming.
Muchas gracias por haber venido.
moo-chahs grah-see-ahs pohr ah-behr beh-nee-doh

You're welcome.
De nada. (No hay de qué.)
deh nah-dah (noh ah-ee deh keh)

To a Young or Familiar Student

Hi!
¡Hola!
oh-lah

What is your name?
¿Cómo te llamas?
koh-moh teh yah-mahs

How are you?
¿Cómo estás?
koh-moh ehs-tahs

What's happening?
¿Qué pasa?
keh pah-sah

How are things going?
¿Qué tal?
keh tahl

What's new?
¿Que hay de nuevo?
keh ah-ee deh noo-eh-boh

Please come in.
Pasa, por favor.
pah-sah pohr fah-bohr

Please sit down.
Siéntate, por favor.
see-ehn-tah-teh pohr fah-bohr

How nice to see you!
¡Qué gusto verte!
keh goos-toh behr-teh

See you later.
Hasta luego.
ahs-tah loo-eh-goh

See you tomorrow.
Hasta mañana.
ahs-tah mah-nyah-nah

Have a nice day.
Qué pases un buen día.
keh pah-sehs oon boo-ehn dee-ah

Same to you.
Igualmente.
ee-goo-ahl-mehn-teh

Common Courtesy

Please.
Por favor.
pohr fah-bohr

Thank you (very much).
(Muchas) Gracias.
(moo-chahs) grah-see-ahs

Thanks a million.
Un millón de gracias.
oon mee-yohn deh grah-see-ahs

You're welcome.
De nada. (No hay de qué.)
deh nah-dah (noh ah-ee deh keh)

Bless you!
¡Salud!
sah-lood

Excuse me. (*Note:* Use if you have bumped into or disturbed someone.)
Perdón. (Perdóneme.) [Perdóname.]
pehr-dohn (pehr-doh-neh-meh) [pehr-doh-nah-meh]

Excuse me. (*Note:* Use if you are leaving a group, passing through a crowd, or trying to get someone's attention.)
Con permiso.
kohn pehr-mee-soh

I'm (very) sorry.
Lo siento (mucho).
loh see-ehn-toh (moo-choh)

Communication

Do you speak Englilsh?
¿Habla(n) [Hablas] inglés?
ah-blah(n) [ah-blahs] een-glehs

I speak a little Spanish.
Hablo español un poco.
ah-bloh ehs-pah-nyohl oon poh-koh

I'm learning Spanish.
Estoy aprendiendo español.
ehs-toh-ee ah-prehm-dee-ehn-doh ehs-pah-nyohl

I don't speak Spanish (well).
No hablo (bien) español.
noh ah-bloh (bee-ehn) ehs-pah-nyohl

Does anyone here speak English?
¿Alguien habla inglés aquí?
ahl-gee-ehn ah-blah een-glehs ah-kee

Do you need an interpreter?
¿Necesita(n) [necesitas] un intérprete?
neh-seh-see-tah(n) [neh-seh-see-tahs] oon een-tehr-preh-teh

I don't understand.
No comprendo. (No entiendo.)
noh kohm-prehn-doh (noh ehn-tee-ehn-doh)

I couldn't understand you.
No lo (la)(s) [te] entendí.
noh loh (lah)(s) (teh) ehn-tehn-dee

What?
¿Cómo?
koh-moh

What did you say?
¿Qué dijo (dijeron) [dijiste]?
keh dee-hoh (dee-heh-rohn) [dee-hees-teh] ·

I can't hear a thing.
No oigo nada.
noh oh-ee-goh nah-dah

Again. (One more time.)
Otra vez.
oh-trah behs

Please repeat (word for word).
Repita(n) [Repite] (palabra por palabra), por favor.
rreh-pee-tah(n) [rreh-pee-teh] (pah-lah-brah pohr pah-lah-brah) pohr fah-bohr

Speak more slowly.
Hable(n) [Habla] más despacio.
ah-bleh(n) [ah-blah] mahs dehs-pah-see-oh

Did you say _____ or _____?
¿Dijo (Dijeron) [Dijiste] _____ o _____?
dee-hoh (dee-heh-rohn) [dee-hees-teh _____ oh _____

What does this (that) mean?
¿Qué quiere decir esto (eso)?
keh kee-eh-reh deh-seer ehs-toh (eh-soh)

What does this (that) mean?
¿Qué significa esto (eso)?
keh seeg-nee-fee-kah ehs-toh (eh-soh)

How do you say _____ in Spanish?
¿Cómo se dice _____ en español?
koh-moh seh dee-seh _____ ehn ehs-pah-nyohl

How do you spell that (that word)?
¿Cómo se deletrea eso (esa palabra)?
koh-moh seh deh-leh-treh-ah eh-soh (eh-sah pah-lah-brah)

What do you call this (that) in Spanish?
¿Cómo se llama esto (eso) en español?
koh-moh seh yah-mah ehs-toh (eh-soh) ehn ehs-pah-nyohl

Do you understand (me)?
¿(Me) Comprende(n) [Comprendes]?
meh kohm-prehn-deh(n) [kohm-rehn-dehs]

Do you understand (me)?
¿(Me) Entiende(n) [Entiendes]?
(meh) ehn-tee-ehn-deh(n) [ehn-tee-ehn-dehs]

Thank you for your patience.
Gracias por su [tu] paciencia.
grah-see-ahs pohr soo [too] pah-see-ehn-see-ah

I'm grateful to you.
Se [Te] lo agradezco.
seh [teh] loh ah-grah-dehs-koh

Question Words

How much (many) (+ noun)?
¿Cuánto? (¿Cuántos?, ¿Cuánta?, ¿Cuántas?)
koo-ahn-toh (koo-ahn-tohs, koo-ahn-tah, koo-ahn-tahs)

How many people are in your family?
¿Cuántas personas hay en su [tu] familia?
koo-ahn-tahs pehr-soh-nahs ah-ee ehn soo [too] fah-mee-lee-ah

How much (+ verb)?
¿Cuánto?
koo-ahn-toh

How much is it worth?
¿Cuánto vale?
koo-ahn-toh bah-leh

How?
¿Cómo?
koh-moh

How do you spell your name?
¿Cómo se deletrea su [tu] nombre?
koh-moh seh deh-leh-treh-ah soo [too] nohm-breh

When?
¿Cuándo?
koo-ahn-doh

When can you come?
¿Cuándo puede(n) [puedes] venir?
koo-ahn-doh poo-eh-deh(n) [poo-eh-dehs] beh-neer

When are you available to come to school?
Cuándo está(n) [estás] disponible(s) para venir a la escuela?
koo-ahn-doh ehs-tah(n)[ehs-tahs] dees-poh-nee-bleh(s) pah-rah beh-neer ah lah ehs-koo-eh-lah

Until when?
¿Hasta cuándo?
ahs-tah koo-ahn-doh

Until when do you work?
¿Hasta cuándo trabaja(n) [trabajas]?
ahs-tah koo-ahn-doh trah-bah-hah(n) [trah-bah-hahs]

For when?
¿Para cuándo?
pah-rah koo-ahn-doh

For when do you need this information?
¿Para cuándo necesita(n) [necesitas] esta información?
pah-rah koo-ahn-doh neh-seh-see-tah(n) [neh-seh-see-tahs] ehs-tah een-fohr-mah-see-ohn

Where?
¿Dónde?
dohn-deh

Where do you live?
¿Dónde vive(n) Ud(s). [vives]?
dohn-deh bee-beh(n) oos-tehd (oos-teh-dehs) [bee-behs]

To where?
¿Adónde?
ah-dohn-deh

Where would you like to go?
¿Adónde querría(n) [querrías] ir?
ah-dohn-deh keh-rree-ah(n) [keh-ree-ahs] eer

From where?
¿De dónde?
deh dohn-deh

Where are you from?
¿De dónde es (son) Ud(s). [eres]?
deh dohn-deh ehs (sohn) oo-stehd (ehs) [eh-rehs]

What?
¿Qué?
keh

What do you think of this idea?
¿Qué piensa(n) [piensas] de esta idea?
keh pee-ehn-sah(n) [pee-ehn-sahs] deh ehs-tah ee-deh-ah

With what?
¿Con qué?
kohn keh

What are you writing with?
¿Con qué está(n) (estás) escribiendo?
kohn keh ehs-tah(n) [ehs-tahs] ehs-kree-bee-ehn-doh

Why?
¿Por qué?
pohr keh

Why doesn't (don't) he/she (you) arrive on time?
¿Por qué no llega(n) [llegas] a tiempo?
pohr keh noh yeh-gah(n) [yeh-gahs] ah tee-ehm-poh

Why?/For what purpose?
¿Para qué?
pah-rah keh

Why are you using a pencil?
¿Para qué usa(n) [usas] un lápiz?
pah-rah keh oo-sah(n) [oo-sahs] oon lah-pees

Who(m)?
¿Quién(es)?
kee-ehn(ehs)

Who is your child's teacher?
¿Quién es el profesor (la profesora) [el maestro, la maestra] de su hijo (hija)?
kee-ehn ehs ehl proh-feh-sohr (lah proh-feh-soh-rah) [ehl mah-ehs-troh, lah mah-ehs-trah] deh soo ee-hoh (ee-hah)

Who are your child's friends?
¿Quiénes son los amigos de su hijo (hija)?
kee-ehn-ehs sohn lohs ah-mee-gohs deh soo ee-hoh (ee-hah)

To whom?
¿A quién(es)?
ah kee-ehn(ehs)

To whom have you already spoken?
¿A quién(es) ya ha hablado?
ah kee-ehn(ehs) yah ah ah-blah-doh

About whom?
¿De quién(es)?
deh kee-ehn(ehs)

About whom are you speaking?
¿De quién(es) habla(n) [hablas]?
deh kee-ehn(ehs) ah-blah(n) [ah-blahs]

With whom?
¿Con quién(es)?
kohn kee-ehn(ehs)

With whom would you like to speak?
¿Con quién(es) quisiera(n) [quisieras] hablar?
kohn kee-ehn(ehs) kee-see-eh-rah(n) [kee-see-eh-rahs] ah-blahr

Which?/Which one (ones)?
¿Cuál(es)?
koo-ahl(ehs)

Which one(s) of his (her, your) friends said that?
¿Cuál(es) de sus [tus] amigos ha(n) dicho eso?
koo-ahl(ehs) deh soos [toos] ah-mee-gohs ah(n) dee-choh eh-soh

Is (Are) there?
¿Hay?
ah-ee

Is there a problem?
¿Hay un problema?
ah-ee oon proh-bleh-mah

Starters and Joiners

Above all
Sobre todo
soh-breh toh-doh

According to
Según
seh-goon

At first
Al principio
ahl preen-see-pee-oh

At least
Por lo menos
pohr loh meh-nohs

Besides
Además
ah-deh-mahs

By the way
A propósito
ah proh-poh-see-toh

Finally
Finalmente
fee-nahl-mehn-teh

For example
Por ejemplo
pohr eh-hehm-ploh

Fortunately
Afortunadamente
ah-fohr-too-nah-dah-mehn-teh

However
Sin embargo
seen ehm-bahr-goh

In general
En general
ehn heh-neh-rahl

In other words
O sea
oh seh-ah

In spite of
A pesar de
ah peh-sahr deh

Little by little
Poco a poco
poh-koh ah poh-koh

Then
Entonces
ehn-tohn-sehs

Therefore
Por lo tanto
pohr loh tahn-toh

Unfortunately
Desgraciadamente
dehs-grah-see-ah-dah-mehn-teh

Without a doubt
Sin duda
seen doo-dah

In a Few Words

Are you sure?
¿Está(n) [Estás] seguro(a)(s)?
ehs-tah(n) [ehs-tahs] seh-goo-roh(rah)(s)

Don't worry.
No se [te] preocupe(n) [preocupes]
noh seh [teh] preh-oh-koo-peh(n) [preh-oh-koo-pehs]

Good luck!
¡Buena suerte!
boo-eh-nah soo-ehr-teh

How beautiful!
¡Qué hermoso!
keh ehr-moh-soh

How great!
¡Qué bueno!
keh boo-eh-noh

I agree.
De acuerdo.
deh ah-koo-ehr-doh

I don't know.
No sé.
noh seh

I doubt that!
¡Lo dudo!
loh doo-doh

I hope so.
Ojalá.
oh-hah-lah

I see.
Ya veo.
yah beh-oh

I think not.
Creo que no.
kreh-oh keh noh

I think so.
Creo que sí.
kreh-oh keh see

I'm so glad.
Me alegro.
meh ah-leh-groh

I'm very happy to hear it!
¡Me alegro de oírlo!
meh ah-leh-groh deh oh-eer-loh

Is that okay?
¿Está bien?
ehs-tah bee-ehn

It doesn't matter./Never mind.
No importa.
noh eem-pohr-tah

It goes without saying.
Dicho está.
dee-choh ehs-tah

It's a bad idea.
Es una mala idea.
ehs oo-nah mah-lah ee-deh-ah

It's a good idea.
Es una buena idea.
ehs oo-nah boo-eh-nah ee-deh-ah

It's important.
Es importante.
ehs eem-pohr-tahn-teh

It's interesting.
Es interesante.
ehs een-teh-reh-sahn-teh

It's necessary.
Es necesario.
ehs neh-seh-sah-ree-oh

It's obvious.
Es obvio.
ehs ohb-bee-oh

It's possible.
Es posible.
ehs poh-see-bleh

Many times.
Muchas veces.
moo-chahs beh-sehs

Maybe (perhaps).
Quizás.
kee-sahs

Me neither.
Yo tampoco.
yoh tahm-poh-koh

Me, too.
Yo también.
yoh tahm-bee-ehn

More or less.
Más o menos.
mahs oh meh-nohs

No.
No.
noh

No problem!
¡No hay problema!
noh ah-ee proh-bleh-mah

No wonder!
¡Con razón!
kohn rah-sohn

Not now.
Ahora no.
ah-oh-rrah noh

Not yet.
Todavía no.
toh-dah-bee-ah noh

Of course!
¡Por supuesto!
pohr soo-poo-ehs-toh

Of course!
¡Cómo no!
koh-moh noh

On the contrary.
Al contrario.
ahl kohn-trah-ree-oh

Really?
¿Es verdad?
ehs behr-dahd

Really?
¿De veras?
deh beh-rahs

Sure!
¡Claro!
klah-roh

That depends.
Depende.
deh-pehn-deh

That's good.
Está bien.
ehs-tah bee-ehn

That's okay!
¡Está bien!
ehs-tah bee-ehn

There's no hurry.
No corre prisa.
noh koh-rreh pree-sah

What a good idea!
¡Qué buena idea!
keh boo-eh-nah ee-deh-ah

What a shame/pity!
¡Qué lástima!
keh lahs-tee-mah

What's the matter?
¿Qué le(s) [te] pasa?
keh leh(s) [teh] pah-sah

Who knows?
¿Quién sabe?
kee-ehn sah-beh

Why not!
¡Cómo no!
koh-moh noh

With pleasure.
Con mucho gusto.
kohn moo-choh goos-toh

Without a doubt.
Sin duda.
seen doo-dah

Yes.
Sí.
see

Good Wishes

Congratulations!
¡Felicitaciones!
feh-lee-see-tah-see-oh-nehs

Good luck!
¡Buena suerte!
boo-eh-nah soo-ehr-teh

Happy birthday!
¡Feliz cumpleaños!
feh-lees koom-pleh-ah-nyohs

Happy Easter!
¡Felices Pascuas!
feh-lee-sehs pahs-koo-ahs

Happy (Prosperous) New Year!
¡Feliz (Próspero) Año Nuevo!
feh-lees (prohs-peh-roh) ah-nyoh noo-eh-boh

Merry Christmas!
¡Feliz Navidad!
feh-lees nah-bee-dahd

Words of Encouragement

A little more effort!
¡Un poquito más de esfuerzo!
oon poh-kee-toh mahs deh ehs-foo-ehr-soh

Don't hesitate!
¡No vacile!
noh bah-see-leh

It's coming along!
¡Está progresando!
ehs-tah proh-greh-sahn-doh

Keep going!
¡Continúe(n)! [¡Continúa!]
kohn-tee-noo-eh(n) [kohn-tee-noo-ah]

Keep going!
¡Siga(n)! [¡Sigue!]
see-gah(n) [see-geh]

That's fine!
¡Está bien!
ehs-tah bee-ehn

You have to try!
¡Tiene(n) [Tienes] que tratar!
tee-eh-neh(n) [tee-eh-nehs] keh trah-tahr

You're getting there!
¡Está(n) [Estás] a punto de lograrlo!
ehs-tah(n) [ehs-tahs] ah poon-toh deh loh-grahr-loh

Words of Praise

What a great job!
¿Qué trabajo fenomenal!
keh trah-bah-hoh feh-noh-meh-nahl

Very good!
¡Muy bien!
moo-ee bee-ehn

Well done!
¡Bien hecho!
bee-ehn eh-choh

You did it!
¡Lo hizo (hicieron) [hiciste]!
loh ee-soh (ee-see-eh-rohn) [ee-sees-teh]

You learn quickly!
¡Aprende(n) [Aprendes] rápido!
ah-prehn-deh(n) [ah-prehn-dehs] rrah-pee-doh

How _____!
¡Qué _____!
keh

excellent	**excelente**	*ehk-seh-lehn-teh*
exceptional	**excepcional**	*ehk-sehp-see-oh-nahl*
extraordinary	**extraordinario**	*ehks-trah-ohr-dee-nah-ree-oh*
fantastic	**fantástico**	*fahn-tahs-tee-koh*
important	**importante**	*eem-pohr-tahn-teh*
incredible	**increíble**	*een-kreh-ee-bleh*
interesting	**interesante**	*een-teh-reh-sahn-teh*
magnificent	**magnífico**	*mahg-nee-fee-koh*
marvelous	**maravilloso**	*mah-rah-bee-yoh-soh*
outstanding	**destacado**	*dehs-tah-kah-doh*
sensational	**sensacional**	*sehn-sah-see-oh-nahl*
super	**estupendo**	*ehs-too-pehn-doh*
superb	**fenomenal**	*feh-noh-meh-nahl*

I like his (her, your [your]) _____.
Me gusta su [tu] _____.
meh goos-tah (soo) [too]

ambition	**ambición**	*ahm-bee-see-ohn*
attitude	**actitud**	*ahk-tee-tood*
commitment	**compromiso**	*kohm-proh-mee-soh*
competence	**competencia**	*kohm-peh-tehn-see-ah*
confidence	**confianza**	*kohn-fee-ahn-sah*
enthusiasm	**entusiasmo**	*ehn-too-see-ahs-moh*
honesty	**honradez**	*ohn-rah-dehs*
independence	**independencia**	*een-deh-pehn-dehn-see-ah*
initiative	**iniciativa**	*een-ee-see-ah-tee-bah*
integrity	**integridad**	*een-teh-gree-dahd*
patience	**paciencia**	*pah-see-ehn-see-ah*
punctuality	**puntualidad**	*poon-too-ah-lee-dahd*
sense of humor	**sentido del humor**	*sehn-tee-doh dehl oo-mohr*
spirit	**espíritu**	*ehs-pee-ree-too*

7

Day Care and Pre-K

Note:
1. Letters or words in brackets are used when using the familiar you **[tú]** form.
2. When speaking to more than one adult, **Ud.** (you, singular) becomes **Uds.** (you, plural) and an n is added to the conjugated verb form.
3. The formal you form is expressed in the same way as the third-person singular **él** (he) and **ella** (she) forms.

Hours and Costs

The center opens at 6 a.m. and closes at 6 p.m.
La guardería infantil abre a las seis de la mañana y cierra a las seis de la tarde.
lah goo-ahr-deh-ree-ah een-fahn-teel ah-breh ah lahs seh-ees deh lah mah-nyah-nah ee see-eh-rrah ah lahs seh-ees deh lah tahr-deh

You must pick up your child no later than 6:10 p.m.
Ud. debe recoger a su hijo (hija) no más tarde de las seis y diez de la tarde.
oo-stehd deh-beh rreh-koh-hehr ah soo ee-hoh (ee-hah) noh mahs tahr-deh deh lahs seh-ehs ee dee-ehs deh lah tahr-deh

How many days a week will you need child care?
¿Cuántos días por semana necesitará Ud. el cuidado de niños?
koo-ahn-tohs dee-ahs pohr seh-mah-nah neh-seh-see-tah-rah oo-stehd ehl koo-ee-dah-doh deh nee-nyohs

How many hours a day will you need child care?
¿Cuántas horas al día necesitará Ud. el cuidado de niños?
koo-ahn-tahs oh-rahs ahl dee-ah neh-seh-see-tah-rah oos-tehd ehl koo-ee-dah-doh deh nee-nyohs

At what time will you be dropping off your child?
¿A qué hora dejará Ud. a su hijo (hija)?
ah keh oh-rah deh-hah-rah oo-stehd ah soo ee-hoh (ee-hah)

At what time will you be picking up your child?
¿A qué hora recogerá Ud. a su hijo (hija)?
ah keh oh-rah rreh-koh-heh-rah oo-stehd ah soo ee-hoh (ee-hah)

We are (not) open on Saturdays and Sundays.
(No) Está abierto los sábados y los domingos.
(noh) ehs-tah ah-bee-ehr-toh lohs sah-bah-dohs ee lohs doh-meen-gohs

You must sign a contract.
Ud. debe firmar un contrato.
oos-tehd deh-beh feer-mahr oon kohn-trah-toh

You must give two weeks' advance notice to cancel your contract.
Ud. debe darnos dos semanas de aviso previo para anular su contrato.
oo-stehd deh-beh dahr-nohs dohs seh-mah-nahs deh ah-bee-soh preh-bee-oh pah-rah ah-noo-lahr soo kohn-trah-toh

Your contract can be cancelled at any time (for a valid reason).
Ud. puede cancelar su contrato en cualquier momento (por una razón legítima).
oo-stehd poo-eh-deh kahn-seh-lahr soo kohn-trah-toh ehn koo-ahl-kee-ehr moh-mehn-toh (pohr oo-nah rrah-sohn leh-hee-tee-mah)

The weekly rate is $_____.
La tarifa semanal es _____ dólares.
lah tah-ree-fah seh-mah-nahl ehs _____ doh-lah-rehs

The daily rate is $_____.
La tarifa diaria es _____ dólares.
lah tah-ree-fah dee-ah-ree-ah ehs _____ doh-lah-rehs

You may drop off your child no more than ten minutes early.

Ud. puede dejar a su hijo (hija) no más de diez minutos antes del horario.

oo-stehd poo-eh-deh deh-hahr ah soo ee-hoh (ee-hah) noh mahs deh dee-ehs mee-noo-tohs ahn-tehs del oh-rah-ree-oh

There is no charge if you arrive after 5:50 a.m.

No hay tarifa si Ud. llega después de las seis menos diez de la mañana.

no ah-ee tah-ree-fah see oo-stehd yeh-gah dehs-poo-ehs deh lahs seh-ees meh-nohs dee-ehs deh lah mah-nyah-nah

If you are going to be late, please call us.

Si estuviera retrasado(a), llámenos, por favor.

see ehs-too-bee-eh-rah rreh-trah-sah-doh(dah) yah-meh-nohs pohr fah-bohr

There is no charge if you arrive before 6:10 p.m.

No hay tarifa si Ud. llega antes de las seis y diez de la tarde.

no ah-ee tah-ree-fah see oo-stehd yeh-gah ahn-tehs deh lahs seh-ees ee dee-ehs deh lah tahr-deh

There is a grace period of ten minutes.

Hay un período de gracia de diez minutos.

ah-ee oon peh-ree-oh-doh deh grah-see-ah deh dee-ehs mee-noo-tohs

If you arrive after 6:10 p.m., you will be charged $_____ per minute (hour or portion thereof).

Si Ud. llegara después de las seis y diez de la tarde, habrá una tarifa de _____ dólares por minuto (por hora o por un porcentaje del mismo).

see oo-stehd yeh-gah-rah dehs-poo-ehs deh lahs seh-ees ee dee-ehs deh lah tahr-deh ah-brah oo-nah tah-ree-fah deh _____ doh-lah-rehs pohr mee-noo-toh (pohr oh-rah oh pohr oon pohr-sehn-tah-heh dehl mees-moh)

If your child isn't picked up by 6:15 p.m., the police (Child Protective Services) will be called.

Si Ud. llegara después de las seis y cuarto, llamaremos a la policía (a los Servicios Protectivos de Menores).

see oo-stehd yeh-gah-rah dehs-poo-ehs deh lahs seh-ees ee koo-ahr-toh yah-mah-reh-mohs ah lah poh-lee-see-ah (ah lohs sehr-bee-see-ohs proh-tehk-tee-bohs deh meh-noh-rehs)

Baby Accessories

Your child needs (more) _____.
Su hijo (hija) necesita (más) _____.
soo ee-hoh (ee-hah) neh-seh-see-tah (mahs) _____

a blanket	**una manta**	*oo-nah mahn-tah*
a change of	**un cambio**	*oon kahm-bee-oh*
clothing	**de ropa**	*deh rroh-pah*
a pacifier	**un chupete**	*oon choo-peh-teh*
a pillow	**una almohada**	*oo-nah ahl-moh-ah-dah*
a snack	**una merienda**	*oo-nah meh-ree-ehn-dah*
a towel	**una toalla**	*oo-nah toh-ah-yah*
baby food	**comida para**	*koh-mee-dah pah-rah*
	bebés	*beh-behs*
baby wipes	**toallitas**	*toh-ah-yee-tahs*
	desechables	*deh-seh-chah-blehs*
bottles	**biberones**	*bee-beh-roh-nehs*
diapers	**pañales**	*pah-nyah-lehs*
formula	**leche**	*leh-cheh*
	maternizada	*mah-tehr-nee-sah-dah*
juice	**jugo**	*hoo-goh*
milk	**leche**	*leh-cheh*

Please bring _____ the next time you come.
Por favor, traiga _____ la próxima vez que venga.
pohr fah-bohr trah-ee-gah _____ lah prohk-see-mah behs keh behn-gah

Please take your child's _____ home and wash it (them).
Por favor, llévese el (la/los/las) _____ de su hijo (hija) y lávelo (lávela/lávelos/lávelas).
pohr fah-bohr yeh-beh-seh ehl (lah/lohs/lahs) _____ de soo ee-hoh (ee-hah) ee lah-beh-loh (lah-beh-lah/lah-beh-lohs/lah-beh-lahs)

Food Habits

You must (do not have to) provide food and drinks for your child.
Ud. (no) debe traer comida y bebidas para su hijo (hija).
oo-stehd (noh) deh-beh trah-ehr koh-mee-dah ee beh-bee-dahs pah-rah soo ee-hoh (ee-hah)

How often does your child take a bottle?
¿Con qué frecuencia toma el biberón su hijo (hija)?
kohn keh freh-koo-ehn-see-ah toh-mah ehl bee-beh-rohn soo ee-hoh (ee-hah)

How much does he/she usually drink?
¿Cuánta leche bebe generalmente?
koo-ahn-tah leh-cheh beh-beh heh-neh-rahl-mehn-teh

Your child usually drinks four 6-ounce bottles of milk (formula).
Su hijo (hija) bebe generalmente cuatro biberones de seis onzas de leche (de leche maternizada).
soo ee-hoh (ee-hah) beh-beh hen-neh-rahl-mehn-teh koo-ah-troh bee-beh-roh-nehs deh seh-ees ohn-sahs deh leh-cheh (deh leh-cheh mah-tehr-nee-sah-dah)

Do you give him/her cold or warm milk?
¿Le da Ud. leche fría o caliente?
leh dah oo-stehd leh-cheh free-ah oh kah-lee-ehn-teh

Please label the foods and drinks you send for your child.
Por favor, rotule la comida y todas las bebidas que envíe para su hijo (hija).
pohr fah-bohr rroh-too-leh lah koh-mee-dah ee toh-dahs lahs beh-bee-dahs keh ehn-bee-eh pah-rah soo ee-hoh (ee-hah)

We are equipped to handle breast milk.
Estamos preparados para manejar leche materna.
ehs-tah-mohs preh-pah-rah-dohs pah-rah mah-neh-hahr leh-cheh mah-tehr-nah

Please label your child's bottle with his (her) name, the date and time the milk was expressed, and the number of ounces in the bottle.
Por favor, rotule el biberón de su hijo (hija) con su nombre, la fecha y la hora cuando la leche fue extraída, y la cantidad de onzas que contiene.
pohr fah-bohr rroh-too-leh ehl bee-beh-rohn deh soo ee-hoh (ee-hah) kohn soo nohm-breh lah feh-chah ee lah oh-rah koo-ahn-doh lah leh-cheh foo-eh ehks-trah-ee-dah ee lah kahn-tee-tahd deh ohn-sahs keh kohn-tee-eh-neh

Please write your child's full name, the date, and the meal on the label.
Por favor, escriba el nombre y apellidos de su hijo (hija), la fecha, y la comida en la etiqueta.
pohr fah-bohr ehs-kree-bah ehl nohm-breh ee ah-peh-yee-dohs deh soo ee-hoh (ee-hah) lah feh-chah ee lah koh-mee-dah ehn lah eh-tee-keh-tah

Name	Date	Meal
Nombre y apellidos	Fecha	Comida
Juan Rivera	Jueves, el once de mayo	Almuerzo

What food does your child like (dislike)?
¿Qué alimentos le gustan (disgustan) a su hijo (hija)?
keh ah-lee-mehn-tohs leh goos-tahn (dees-goos-tahn) ah soo ee-hoh (ee-hah)

Today your child drank _____ glasses of _____.
Hoy su hijo (hija) bebió _____ vasos de _____.
oh-ee soo ee-hoh (ee-hah) beh-bee-oh _____ bah-sohs deh _____

Your child wasn't hungry and didn't eat anything today.
Hoy su hijo (hija) no tuvo hambre y no comió nada.
oh-ee soo ee-hoh (ee-hah) noh too-boh ahm-breh ee noh koh-mee-oh nah-dah

Today your child ate half of his (her) breakfast (lunch, dinner).
Hoy su hijo (hija) comió la mitad de su desayuno (almuerzo, cena).
oh-ee soo ee-hoh (ee-hah) koh-mee-oh lah mee-tahd deh soo deh-sah-yoo-noh (ahl-moo-ehr-soh seh-nah)

Today your child ate his (her) entire breakfast (lunch).
Hoy su hijo (hija) comió todo su desayuno (almuerzo).
oh-ee soo ee-hoh (ee-hah) koh-mee-oh toh-doh soo deh-sah-yoo-noh (ahl-moo-ehr-soh)

Today your child ate his (her) entire dinner.
Hoy su hijo (hija) comió toda su cena.
oh-ee soo ee-hoh (ee-hah) koh-mee-oh toh-dah soo seh-nah

Sleep Habits

Does your child generally take a nap?
¿Su hijo (hija) echa una siesta generalmente?
soo ee-hoh (ee-hah) eh-chah oo-nah see-ehs-tah heh-neh-rahl-mehn-teh

Your child did not take a nap today.
Su hijo (hija) no echó una siesta hoy.
soo ee-hoh (ee-hah) noh eh-choh oon-nah see-ehs-tah oh-ee

Your child took one (two) nap(s) today.
Su hijo (hija) echó una (dos) siesta(s) hoy.
soo ee-hoh (ee-hah) eh-choh oo-nah (dohs) see-ehs-tah(s) oh-ee

He/She slept for two hours.
Durmió dos horas.
door-mee-oh dohs oh-rahs

He/She woke up and then fell back to sleep.
Se despertó y luego se durmió de nuevo.
seh dehs-pehr-toh ee loo-eh-goh seh door-mee-oh deh noo-eh-boh

He/She woke up crying.
Se despertó llorando.
seh dehs-pehr-toh yoh-rahn-doh

He/She had a nightmare.
Tuvo una pesadilla.
too-boh oo-nah peh-sah-dee-yah

Bathroom Habits

Your child wet (dirtied) his diaper _____ times today.
Su hijo (hija) orinó (evacuó) en su pañal _____ veces hoy.
soo ee-hoh (ee-hah) oh-ree-noh (eh-bah-koo-oh) ehn soo pah-nyahl _____ beh-sehs oh-ee

He/She has diaper rash.
Está sarpullido(a).
ehs-tah sahr-poo-yee-doh(dah)

He/She had diarrhea (_____ times).
Tuvo diarrea (_____ veces).
too-boh dee-ah-rreh-ah (_____ beh-sehs)

He/She was constipated.
Estuvo estreñido(a).
ehs-too-boh ehs-treh-nyee-doh(dah)

He/She had _____ bowel movements today.
Evacuó _____ veces hoy.
eh-bah-koo-oh _____ beh-sehs oh-ee

He/She did not have a bowel movement today.
No evacuó hoy.
noh eh-bah-koo-oh oh-ee

Your child must be toilet trained to attend this center (school).
Su hijo (hija) tiene que estar acostumbrado(a) a ir solo(a) al baño para ir a esta guardería (escuela).
soo ee-hoh (ee-hah) tee-eh-neh keh ehs-tahr ah-kohs-toom-brah-doh(dah) ah eer soh-loh(lah) ahl bah-nyoh pah-rah ah-sees-teer ah ehs-tah goo-ahr-deh-ree-ah (ehs-koo-eh-lah)

Is your child toilet trained?
¿Está su hijo (hija) acostumbrado(a) a ir solo(a) al baño?
ehs-tah soo ee-hoh (ee-hah) ah-kohs-toom-brah-doh(dah) ah eer soh-loh(lah) ahl bah-nyoh

Is he (she) ready to be toilet trained?
¿Está listo(a) a acostumbrarse a ir solo(a) al baño?
ehs-tah lees-toh(tah) ah ah-kohs-toom-brahr-seh ah eer soh-loh(lah) ahl bah-nyoh

Does he/she wear underpants or pull-ups?
¿Lleva pañales con elástico?
yeh-bah pah-nyah-lehs kohn eh-lahs-tee-koh

Does he/she need help using the toilet?
¿Necesita ayuda cuando va al baño?
neh-seh-see-tah ah-yoo-dah koo-ahn-doh bah ahl bah-nyoh

We will (not) toilet-train your child.
(No) Entrenaremos a su hijo (hija) a ir al baño solo(a).
(noh) ehn-treh-nah-reh-mohs ah soo ee-hoh (ee-hah) ah eer ahl bah-nyoh soh-loh(lah)

At what age was your child toilet trained?
¿A qué edad entrenó a su hijo (hija) a ir solo(a) al baño?
ah keh eh-dahd ehn-treh-noh ah soo ee-hoh (ee-hah) ah eer soh-loh(lah) ahl bah-nyoh

Please bring your child's potty to the daycare center (school).
Por favor, traiga el orinal del niño (de la niña) a la guardería (la escuela).
pohr fah-bohr trah-ee-gah ehl oh-ree-nahl dehl nee-nyoh (deh lah nee-nyah) ah lah goo-ahr-deh-ree-ah (lah ehs-koo-eh-lah)

How many diapers does your child generally need per day?
¿Generalmente, cuántos pañales al día necesita su hijo (hija)?
*heh-neh-rahl-mehn-teh koo-ahn-tohs pah-nyah-lehs ahl dee-ah neh-seh-see-tah
soo ee-hoh (ee-hah)*

Please bring extra diapers.
Traiga pañales adicionales, por favor.
trah-ee-gah pah-nyah-lehs ah-dee-see-oh-nah-lehs pohr fah-bohr

Clothing

Your child is going to need the next size clothing soon.
**Su hijo (hija) va a necesitar una talla de ropa más grande
pronto.**
*soo ee-hoh (ee-hah) bah ah neh-seh-see-tahr oo-nah tah-yah deh rroh-pah
mahs grahn-deh prohn-toh*

Please send a change of clothing for your child.
Por favor, envíe un cambio de ropa para su hijo (hija).
*pohr fah-bohr ehn-bee-eh oon kahm-bee-oh deh rroh-pah par-rah soo ee-hoh
(ee-hah)*

Today your child dirtied (lost, tore) _____.
Hoy su hijo (hija) ensució (perdió, desgarró) _____.
oh-ee soo ee-hoh (ee-hah) ehn-soo-see-oh (pehr-dee-oh, dehs-gah-rroh)

his/her coat	**su abrigo**	*soo ah-bree-goh*
her dress	**su vestido**	*soo behs-tee-doh*
his/her gloves	**sus guantes**	*soos goo-ahn-tehs*
his/her hat	**su sombrero**	*soo sohm-breh-roh*
his/her pajamas	**sus pijamas**	*soos pee-hah-mahs*
his/her pants	**sus pantalones**	*soos pahn-tah-loh-nehs*
his/her scarf	**su bufanda**	*soo boo-fahn-dah*
his/her shirt	**su camisa**	*soo kah-mee-sah*
her skirt	**su falda**	*soo fahl-dah*
his/her socks	**sus calcetines**	*soos kahl-seh-tee-nehs*
his/her underwear	**su ropa interior**	*soo rroh-pah een-teh-ree-ohr*

Your child forgot to wear his (her) _____.
Su hijo (hija) olvidó llevar su(s) _____.
soo ee-hoh (ee-hah) ohl-bee-doh yeh-bahr soo(s) _____

Yesterday your child left his (her) _____ in the center (school).
Ayer su hijo (hija) dejó su(s) _____ en la guardería (la escuela).
ah-yehr soo ee-hoh (ee-hah) deh-hoh soo(s) _____ ehn lah goo-ahr-deh-ree-ah (lah ehs-koo-eh-lah)

Developmental Skills

Today your child _____ for the first time.
Hoy, por primera vez, su hijo (hija) _____.
oh-ee pohr pree-meh-rah behs soo ee-hoh (ee-hah) _____

crawled	**gateó**	*gah-teh-oh*
drank from a glass	**bebió de un vaso**	*beh-bee-oh deh oon bah-soh*
fed himself (herself)	**comió solo(a)**	*koh-mee-oh soh-loh(lah)*
ran	**corrió**	*koh-rree-oh*
rolled over	**se dio la vuelta**	*seh dee-oh lah boo-ehl-tah*
said a word	**dijo una palabra**	*dee-hoh oo-nah pah-lah-brah*
sat	**se sentó solo(a)**	*seh sehn-toh soh-loh(lah)*
stood	**se paró solo(a)**	*seh pah-roh soh-loh(lah)*
took a step	**tomó un pequeño paso**	*toh-moh oon peh-keh-nyoh pah-soh*
used a spoon (fork)	**usó una cuchara (un tenedor)**	*oo-soh oo-nah koo-chah-rah (oon teh-neh-dohr)*
used his (her) potty	**usó su orinal**	*oo-soh soo oh-ree-nahl*
walked	**andó solo(a)**	*ahn-doh soh-loh(lah)*

Your child still needs a pacifier.
Su hijo (hija) todavía necesita un chupete.
soo ee-hoh (ee-hah) toh-dah-bee-ah neh-seh-see-tah oon choo-peh-teh

It is time for your child to give up his (her) bottle.
Es tiempo que su hijo (hija) deje de beber de un biberón.
ehs tee-ehm-poh keh soo ee-hoh (ee-hah) deh-heh deh beh-behr deh oon bee-beh-rohn

Your child continues to suck his (her) thumb.
Su hijo (hija) sigue chupándose el dedo.
soo ee-hoh (ee-hah) see-geh choo-pahn-doh-seh ehl deh-doh

Your child can ride a tricycle.
Su hijo (hija) puede montar en triciclo.
soo ee-hoh (ee-hah) poo-eh-deh mohn-tahr ehn tree-see-kloh

Your child is developmentally delayed.
El desarrollo de su hijo (hija) está retrasado.
ehl deh-sah-rroh-yoh deh soo ee-hoh (ee-hah) ehs-tah rreh-trah-sah-doh

He/She has trouble _____.
Le es difícil _____.
leh ehs dee-fee-seel

behaving well	**portarse bien**	*pohr-tahr-seh bee-ehn*
concentrating	**concentrarse**	*kohn-sehn-trahr-seh*
listening	**escuchar**	*ehs-koo-char*
manipulating things	**manipular las cosas**	*mah-nee-poo-lahr lahs koh-sahs*
reading	**leer**	*leh-ehr*
relating to others	**relacionarse con los demás**	*rreh-lah-see-oh-nahr-seh kohn lohs deh-mahs*
speaking	**hablar**	*ah-blahr*
writing	**escribir**	*ehs-kree-beer*

He/She is entitled to be evaluated for Early Intervention Services.
Tiene derecho de recibir evaluaciones para los servicios del Programa de Intervención Temprana.
tee-eh-neh deh-reh-choh deh rreh-see-beer eh-bah-loo-ah-see-oh-nehs pah-rah lohs sehr-bee-see-ohs dehl proh-grah-mah deh een-tehr-behn-see-ohn tehm-prah-nah

To obtain a recommendation for this program, call this number.
Para conseguir una recomendación para este programa, llame a este número.
pah-rah kohn-seh-geer oo-nah rreh-koh-mehn-dah-see-ohn pah-rah ehs-teh proh-grah-mah yah-meh ah ehs-teh noo-meh-roh

Toys and Activities

Your child likes to play with _____.
A su hijo (hija) le gusta jugar con _____.
ah soo ee-hoh (ee-hah) leh goos-tah hoo-gahr kohn _____

a wagon	**un vagón**	*oon bah-gohn*
balloons	**globos**	*gloh-bohs*
blocks	**bloques de madera**	*bloh-kehs deh mah-deh-rah*
dolls	**muñecas**	*moo-nyeh-kahs*
games	**juegos**	*hoo-eh-gohs*
marbles	**canicas**	*kah-nee-kahs*
modeling clay	**plasticina**	*plahs-tee-see-nah*
puppets	**títeres**	*tee-teh-rehs*
puzzles	**rompecabezas**	*rrohm-peh-kah-beh-sahs*
stuffed animals	**animales de peluche**	*ah-nee-mah-lehs deh peh-loo-cheh*
toy cars	**coches de juguete**	*koh-chehs deh hoo-geh-teh*
toy trains	**trenes de juguete**	*treh-nehs deh hoo-geh-teh*

Your child likes (especially enjoys) _____.
A su hijo (hija) le gusta (sobre todo) _____.
ah soo ee-hoh (ee-hah) leh goos-tah (soh-breh toh-doh) _____

to color	**colorear**	*koh-loh-reh-ahr*
to dance	**bailar**	*bah-ee-lahr*
to draw	**dibujar**	*dee-boo-hahr*
to fly a kite	**volar cometas**	*boh-lahr koh-meh-tahs*
to go to the park	**ir al parque**	*eer ahl pahr-keh*
to jump rope	**saltar la cuerda**	*sahl-tahr lah koo-ehr-dah*
to listen to music	**escuchar música**	*ehs-koo-chahr moo-see-kah*
to paint	**pintar**	*peen-tahr*
to play an instrument	**tocar un instrumento**	*toh-kahr oon een-stroo-mehn-toh*
to play cards	**jugar a los naipes**	*hoo-gahr ah lohs nah-ee-pehs*
to play checkers	**jugar a las damas**	*hoo-gahr ah lahs dah-mahs*
to play chess	**jugar al ajedrez**	*hoo-gahr ahl ah-heh-drehs*
to play dominoes	**jugar al dominó**	*hoo-gahr ahl doh-mee-noh*
to play sports	**practicar deportes**	*prahk-tee-kahr deh-pohr-tehs*

to read	**leer**	*leh-ehr*
to ride a tricycle	**montar en triciclo**	*mohn-tahr ehn tree-see-kloh*
to sing	**cantar**	*kahn-tahr*
to skate	**patinar**	*pah-tee-nahr*
to use the computer	**usar la computadora**	*oo-sahr lah kohm-poo-tah-doh-rah*
to watch cartoons	**mirar los dibujos animados**	*mee-rahr lohs dee-boo-hohs ah-nee-mah-dohs*
to watch television	**mirar la televisión**	*mee-rahr lah teh-leh-bee-see-ohn*

When we go to the playground, your child prefers _____.

Cuando vamos al campo de recreo, su hijo (hija) prefiere _____.

koo-ahn-doh bah-mohs ahl kahm-poh deh rreh-kreh-oh soo ee-hoh (ee-hah) preh-fee-eh-reh _____

the merry-go-round	**el carrusel**	*ehl kah-rroo-sehl*
the monkey bars	**la trepadora**	*lah treh-pah-doh-rah*
the sandbox	**el cajón de arena**	*ehl kah-hohn deh ah-reh-nah*
the seesaw	**el subibaja**	*ehl soo-bee-bah-hah*
the slide	**el tobogán**	*ehl toh-boh-gahn*
the swings	**los columpios**	*lohs koh-loom-pee-ohs*

Moods and Behavior

Today your child _____.

Hoy su hijo (hija) _____.

oh-ee soo ee-hoh (ee-hah) _____

was affectionate	**estaba cariñoso(a)**	*ehs-tah-bah kah-ree-nyoh-soh(sah)*
was aggressive	**estaba agresivo(a)**	*ehs-tah-bah ah-greh-see-boh(bah)*
was alert	**estaba despierto(a)**	*ehs-tah-bah dehs-pee-ehr-toh(tah)*
was bashful	**estaba tímido(a)**	*ehs-tah-bah tee-mee-doh(dah)*

was calm	**estaba tranquilo(a)**	*ehs-tah-bah trahn-kee-loh(lah)*
was content	**estaba contento(a)**	*ehs-tah-bah kohn-tehn-toh(tah)*
was disobedient	**estaba desobediente**	*ehs-tah-bah dehs-oh-beh-dee-ehn-teh*
was happy	**estaba feliz**	*ehs-tah-bah feh-lees*
was mischievous	**estaba travieso(a)**	*ehs-tah-bah trah-bee-eh-soh(sah)*
was obedient	**estaba obediente**	*ehs-tah-bah oh-beh-dee-ehn-teh*
was playful	**estaba alegre**	*ehs-tah-bah ah-leh-greh*
was quiet	**estaba callado(a)**	*ehs-tah-bah kah-yah-doh(dah)*
was restless	**estaba inquieto(a)**	*ehs-tah-bah een-kee-eh-toh(tah)*
was sad	**estaba triste**	*ehs-tah-bah trees-teh*
was selfish	**fue egoísta**	*foo-eh eh-goh-ees-tah*
was sensitive	**fue sensible**	*foo-eh sehn-see-bleh*
was sociable	**fue sociable**	*foo-eh soh-see-ah-bleh*
was talkative	**fue hablador(a)**	*foo-eh ah-blah-dohr (doh-rah)*
was tired	**tenía sueño**	*teh-nee-ah soo-eh-nyoh*
was unhappy	**fue infeliz**	*foo-eh een-feh-lees*
was unsociable	**fue insociable**	*foo-eh een-soh-see-ah-bleh*

Your child behaved well today.
Su hijo (hija) se portó bien hoy.
soo ee-hoh (ee-hah) seh pohr-toh bee-ehn oh-ee

In general, your child gets along with others.
En general, su hijo (hija) se lleva bien con los demás.
ehn heh-neh-rahl soo ee-hoh (ee-hah) seh yeh-bah bee-ehn kohn lohs deh-mahs

Your child has a pleasant disposition.
Su hijo (hija) tiene un temperamento agradable.
soo ee-hoh (ee-hah) tee-eh-neh oon tehm-peh-rah-mehn-toh ah-grah-dah-bleh

Your child did (not) listen.
Su hijo (hija) (no) escuchó.
soo ee-hoh (ee-hah) (noh) ehs-koo-choh

Your child hit (bit) another child.
Su hijo (hija) agredió (mordió) a otro(a) niño(a).
soo ee-hoh (ee-hah) ah-greh-dee-oh (mohr-dee-oh) ah oh-troh (oh-trah)
nee-nyoh (nee-nyah)

Illnesses and Accidents

Your child wasn't feeling well today.
Su hijo (hija) no se sentía bien hoy.
soo ee-hoh (ee-hah) noh seh sehn-tee-ah bee-ehn oh-ee

He/She is sick.
Está enfermo(a).
ehs-tah ehn-fehr-moh(mah)

He/She spilled milk on himself/herself.
Derramó leche en su ropa.
deh-rrah-moh leh-cheh ehn soo rroh-pah

He/She overate.
Comió en exceso.
koh-mee-oh ehn ehk-seh-soh

He/She has a fever.
Tiene fiebre.
tee-eh-neh fee-eh-breh

He/She was wheezing all day.
Respiró con dificultad todo el día.
rrehs-pee-roh kohn dee-fee-kool-tahd toh-doh ehl dee-ah

He/She was pulling on his/her ears all day.
Se tiró las orejas todo el día.
seh tee-roh lahs oh-reh-hahs toh-doh ehl dee-ah

He/She had a discharge from his/her (left/right) ear(s).
Le salió una descarga de su(s) oído(s) (su oído izquierdo/ derecho).
leh sah-lee-oh oo-nah dehs-kahr-gah deh soo(s) oh-ee-doh(s) (soo oo-ee-doh
ees-kee-ehr-doh/deh-reh-choh)

He/She was crying all day.
Estuvo llorando todo el día.
ehs-too-boh yoh-rahn-doh toh-doh ehl dee-ah

He/She has a runny nose.
Estuvo mocoso(a).
ehs-too-boh moh-koh-soh(sah)

He/She is coughing.
Estuvo tosiendo.
ehs-too-boh toh-see-ehn-doh

He/She is sneezing.
Estuvo estornudando.
ehs-too-boh ehs-tohr-noo-dahn-doh

He/She cut himself/herself.
Se cortó.
seh kohr-toh

He/She is bleeding.
Está sangrando.
ehs-tah sahn-grahn-doh

He/She bled (a little).
Sangró (un poquito).
sahn-groh (oon poh-kee-toh)

He/She has a bruise (scrape, abrasion).
Tiene un cardenal/moretón (rasguño).
tee-eh-neh oon kahr-deh-nahl/moh-reh-tohn) (rrahs-goo-nyoh)

He/She has an abrasion.
Tiene una abrasión.
tee-eh-neh oo-nah ah-brah-see-ohn

He/She lost a front (back) tooth.
Se le cayó un diente (una muela).
seh leh kah-yoh oon dee-ehn-teh (oo-nah moo-eh-lah)

He (She) was bitten.
Lo (la) mordieron.
loh (lah) mohr-dee-eh-rohn

He/She vomited.
Vomitó.
boh-mee-toh

He/She had diarrhea (_____ times).
Tuvo diarrea (_____ veces).
too-boh dee-ah-rreh-ah (_____ beh-sehs)

He/She wet (dirtied) himself/herself.
Se orinó (ensució).
seh oh-ree-noh (ehn-soo-see-ohn)

He/She is cutting a tooth.
Le está saliendo un diente de leche.
leh ehs-tah sah-lee-ehn-doh oon dee-ehn-teh deh leh-cheh

He/She has a discharge from his/her eye.
Los ojos le gotean.
lohs oh-hohs leh goh-teh-ahn

He/She had an accident.
Tuvo un accidente.
too-boh oon ahk-see-dehn-teh

He/She fell.
Se cayó.
seh kah-yoh

He/She is limping.
Está cojeando.
ehs-tah koh-heh-ahn-doh

It is possible that he/she has a sprained wrist (ankle).
Es posible que se haya doblado la muñeca (el tobillo).
*ehs poh-see-bleh keh seh ah-yah doh-blah-doh lah moo-nyeh-kah
(ehl toh-bee-yoh)*

Perhaps he/she has broken his/her arm (leg).
Quizás se haya roto el brazo (la pierna).
kee-sahs seh ah-yah rroh-toh ehl brah-soh (lah pee-ehr-nah)

He/She should see a doctor (dentist).
Debería ir al médico (dentista).
deh-beh-ree-ah eer ahl meh-dee-koh (dehn-tees-tah)

He/She needs medical attention.
Necesita atención médica.
neh-seh-see-tah ah-tehn-see-ohn meh-dee-kah

It is (not) an emergency.

(No) es una urgencia.

(noh) ehs oo-nah oor-hehn-see-ah

Your child may not come to this center (school) when he (she) is sick.

Su hijo (hija) no puede venir a esta guardería (escuela) cuando esté enfermo(a).

soo ee-hoh (ee-hah) noh poo-eh-deh beh-neer ah ehs-tah goo-ahr-deh-ree-ah koo-ahn-doh ehs-teh ehn-fehr-moh(mah)

Please keep your child home until he (she) is better.

Por favor, mantenga a su hijo (hija) en casa hasta que se sienta mejor.

pohr fah-bohr mahn-tehn-gah ah soo ee-hoh (ee-hah) ehn kah-sah ahs-tah keh seh see-ehn-tah meh-hohr

8

Registration

Note:
1. Letters or words in brackets are used when using the familiar you **[tú]** form.
2. When speaking to more than one adult, **Ud.** (you, singular) becomes **Uds.** (you, plural) and an n is added to the conjugated verb form.
3. The formal you form is expressed in the same way as the third-person singular **él** (he) and **ella** (she) forms.

Personal Information

What is your _____?
¿Cuál es su _____?
koo-ahl ehs soo

address	**dirección**	*dee-rehk-see-ohn*
apartment number	**número de apartamento**	*noo-meh-roh deh ah-pahr-tah-mehn-toh*
area code	**prefijo local**	*preh-fee-hoh loh-kahl*
cellphone number	**número de teléfono celular**	*noo-meh-roh deh teh-leh-foh-noh seh-loo-lahr*
e-mail address	**dirección de correo electrónico**	*dee-rehk-see-ohn deh koh-rreh-oh eh-lehk-troh-nee-koh*
first name	**primer nombre**	*pree-mehr nohm-breh*
full name	**nombre y apellido**	*nohm-breh ee ah-peh-yee-doh*
last name	**apellido**	*ah-peh-yee-doh*

maiden name	**nombre de soltera**	*nohm-breh deh sohl-teh-rah*
nationality	**nacionalidad**	*nah-see-oh-nah-lee-dahd*
native language	**lengua materna**	*lehn-goo-ah mah-tehr-nah*
occupation	**profesión**	*proh-feh-see-ohn*
race	**raza**	*rrah-sah*
relationship to ____	**parentesco con**	*pah-rehn-tehs-koh kohn*
telephone number	**número de teléfono**	*noo-meh-roh deh teh-leh-foh-noh*
zip code	**código postal**	*koh-dee-goh pohs-tahl*

What is your child's ____?
¿Cuál es ____ de su hijo (hija)?
koo-ahl ehs ____ deh soo ee-hoh (ee-hah)

age	**la edad**	*lah eh-dahd*
date of birth	**la fecha de nacimiento**	*lah feh-chah deh nah-see-mee-ehn-toh*
full name	**el nombre y apellido**	*ehl nohm-breh ee ah-peh-yee-doh*
nickname	**el apodo**	*ehl ah-poh-doh*
place of birth	**el lugar de nacimiento**	*ehl loo-gahr deh nah-see-mee-ehn-toh*
Social Security number	**el número de seguro social**	*ehl noo-meh-roh deh seh-goo-roh soh-see-ahl*

May I help you?
¿Puedo ayudarle?
poo-eh-doh ah-yoo-dahr-leh

You need to speak with ____.
Debe hablar con ____.
deh-beh ah-blahr kohn ____

He/She is in room ____.
Está en la sala ____.
ehs-tah ehn lah sah-lah ____

His (Her) office hours are ____.
Sus horas de oficina son ____.
soos oh-rahs deh oh-fee-see-nah sohn ____

Someone will help you in a few minutes.
Alguien lo (la) atenderá en algunos minutos.
ahl-gee-ehn loh (lah) ah-tehn-deh-rah ehn ahl-goo-nohs mee-noo-tohs

Please have a seat.
Siéntese, por favor.
see-ehn-teh-seh pohr fah-bohr

Your child's student ID number is _____.
El número de estudiante de su hijo (hija) es _____.
ehl noo-meh-roh deh ehs-too-dee-ahn-teh deh soo ee-hoh (ee-hah) ehs _____

Do you (Does your child) have a cellphone?
¿Tiene Ud. (su hijo/hija) un teléfono celular?
tee-eh-neh oo-stehd (soo ee-hoh/ee-hah) oon teh-leh-foh-noh seh-loo-lahr

What is your (his/her) number?
¿Cuál es su número?
koo-ahl ehs soo noo-meh-roh

Do you (Does your child) have an e-mail address?
¿Tiene Ud. (su hijo/hija) una dirección de correo electrónico?
tee-eh-neh oo-stehd (soo ee-hoh/ee-hah) oo-nah dee-rehk-see-ohn deh koh-rreh-oh eh-lehk-troh-nee-koh

What is it?
¿Cuál es?
koo-ahl ehs

What language(s) do you speak at home?
¿Qué idioma(s) hablan Uds. en casa?
keh ee-dee-oh-mahs ah-blahn oo-steh-dehs ehn kah-sah

What school(s) did your child attend?
¿A qué escuela(s) asistió su hijo (hija)?
ah keh ehs-koo-eh-lah(s) ah-sees-tee-oh soo ee-hoh (ee-hah)

Where is this (are these) school(s) located?
¿Dónde está(n) localizada(s) esta(s) escuela(s)?
dohn-deh ehs-tah(n) loh-kah-lee-sah-dah(s) ehs-tah(s) ehs-koo-eh-lah(s)

What school did he/she attend last?
¿Cuál fue la última escuela a la que asistió?
koo-ahl foo-eh lah ool-tee-mah ehs-koo-eh-lah ah lah keh ah-sees-tee-oh

What grade level did he/she complete?
¿Qué grado terminó?
keh grah-doh tehr-mee-noh

Do you have his (her) scholastic (medical) records from his (her)
previous school(s)?
¿Tiene Ud. sus expedientes académicos (médicos) anterior(es)?
*tee-eh-neh oo-stehd soos ehks-peh-dee-ehn-tehs ah-kah-deh-mee-kohs
(meh-dee-kohs) ahn-teh-ree-ohr(es)*

You have the right to obtain all of your child's school records.
**Ud. tiene derecho a obtener todos los expedientes académicos
de su hijo (hija).**
*oo-stehd tee-eh-neh deh-reh-choh ah ohb-teh-nehr toh-dohs lohs ehks-peh-dee-
ehn-tehs ah-kah-deh-mee-kohs deh soo ee-hoh (ee-hah)*

May I see his (her) report card to verify his (her) grades?
¿Puedo ver su boletín de notas para verificar sus notas?
*poo-eh-doh behr soo boh-leh-teen deh noh-tahs pah-rah beh-ree-fee-kahr soos
noh-tahs*

We have (not) received his (her) permanent record yet.
Todavía no hemos recibido su expediente permanente.
*toh-dah-bee-ah noh eh-mohs rreh-see-bee-doh soo ehks-peh-dee-ehn-teh pehr-
mah-nehn-teh*

Your child must take a placement (diagnostic, proficiency) test.
**Su hijo (hija) tiene que pasar un examen de nivel (diagnóstico,
de competencia).**
*soo ee-hoh (ee-hah) tee-eh-neh keh pah-sahr oon ehk-sah-mehn deh nee-behl
(dee-ahg-nohs-tee-koh, de kohm-peh-tehn-see-ah)*

He/She must come on this date at this time.
Tiene que venir en esta fecha a esta hora.
tee-eh-neh keh beh-neer ehn ehs-tah feh-chah ah ehs-tah oh-rah

You can call for the results (scores).
Puede llamar para recibir los resultados (las calificaciones).
*poo-eh-deh yah-mahr pah-rah rreh-see-beer lohs rreh-sool-tah-dohs (lahs kah-
lee-fee-kah-see-oh-nehs)*

We will give him (her) _____ credits (units) from his (her) previous school.
Le daremos _____ créditos (unidades) de su escuela anterior.
leh dah-reh-mohs _____ kreh-dee-tohs (oo-nee-dah-dehs) deh soo ehs-koo-eh-lah ahn-teh-ree-ohr

He/She has reached a (an) _____ level.
Ha logrado un nivel _____.
ah loh-grah-doh oon nee-behl _____

advanced	**avanzado**	*ah-bahn-sah-doh*
average	**promedio**	*proh-meh-dee-oh*
beginning	**inicial**	*ee-nee-see-ahl*
intermediate	**intermedio**	*een-tehr-meh-dee-oh*

Your child is _____.
Su hijo (hija) es _____.
soo ee-hoh (ee-hah) ehs _____

above average	**sobresaliente**	*soh-breh-sah-lee-ehn-teh*
average	**promedio**	*proh-meh-dee-o*
below average	**deficiente**	*deh-fee-see-ehn-teh*
gifted	**talentoso(a)**	*tah-lehn-toh-soh(sah)*

We have advanced (remedial) programs.
Tenemos programas avanzados (de refuerzo).
teh-neh-mohs proh-grah-mahs ah-bahn-sah-dohs (deh rreh-foo-ehr-soh)

Are his (her) medical (dental) records up to date?
¿Están actualizados sus archivos médicos (dentales)?
ehs-tahn ahk-too-ah-lee-sah-dohs soos ahr-chee-bohs meh-dee-kohs (dehn-tah-lehs)

Please give them to me and I will make copies of them.
Démelos por favor y yo los fotocopiaré.
deh-meh-lohs pohr fah-bohr ee yoh lohs foh-toh-koh-pee-ah-reh

Has he/she had all the necessary vaccinations?
¿Ha tenido todas las vacunaciones necesarias?
ah teh-nee-doh toh-dahs lahs bah-koo-nah-see-oh-nehs neh-seh-sah-ree-ahs

Which ones has he/she had?
¿Cuáles ha tenido?
koo-ah-lehs ah teh-nee-doh

What is your child's doctor's name?
¿Cómo se llama el médico de su hijo (hija)?
koh-moh seh yah-mah ehl meh-dee-koh deh soo ee-hoh (ee-hah)

Please fill out everything on these forms and sign them.
Por favor, complete estos formularios y fírmelos.
pohr fah-bohr kohm-pleh-teh ehs-tohs fohr-moo-lah-ree-ohs ee feer-meh-lohs

Here are the instructions.
Aquí están las instrucciones.
ah-kee ehs-tahn lahs een-strook-see-oh-nehs

Read all the information carefully.
Lea toda la información cuidadosamente.
leh-ah toh-dah lah een-fohr-mah-see-ohn koo-ee-dah-doh-sah-mehn-teh

Physical Descriptions

What does your child look like?
¿Cómo es su hijo (hija)?
koh-moh ehs soo ee-hoh (ee-hah)

Is he/she _____?
¿Es _____?
ehs _____

big	**grande**	*grahn-deh*
blond	**rubio(a)**	*rroo-bee-oh(ah)*
brunette	**moreno(a)**	*moh-reh-noh(nah)*
impaired in any way	**incapacitado(a) en alguna manera**	*een-kah-pah-see-tah-doh(dah) ehn ahl-goo-nah mah-neh-rah*
left-handed	**zurdo(a)**	*soor-doh(dah)*
red-headed	**pelirrojo(a)**	*peh-lee-rroh-hoh(hah)*
right-handed	**diestro(a)**	*dee-ehs-troh(trah)*
short	**bajo(a)**	*bah-hoh(hah)*
small	**pequeño(a)**	*peh-keh-nyoh(nyah)*
stout	**gordo(a)**	*gohr-doh(dah)*
tall	**alto(a)**	*ahl-toh(tah)*
thin	**delgado(a)**	*dehl-gah-doh(dah)*

Does he/she have _____?
¿Tiene _____?
tee-eh-neh _____

blue (brown, black, green, hazel) eyes	**ojos azules, (pardos, negros, verdes, color de avellana)**	*oh-hohs ah-soo-lehs (pahr-dohs, neh-grohs, behr-dehs, koh-lohr deh ah-beh-yah-nah)*
curly hair	**pelo rizado**	*peh-loh rree-sah-doh*
freckles	**pecas**	*peh-kahs*
straight hair	**pelo lacio**	*peh-loh lah-see-oh*
wavy hair	**pelo ondulado**	*peh-loh ohn-doo-lah-doh*

Personality Traits

Is your child _____?
¿Es su hijo (hija) _____?
ehs su ee-hoh (ee-hah) _____

Your child is _____.
Su hijo (hija) es _____.
soo ee-hoh (ee-hah) ehs _____

adventuresome	**aventurero(a)**	*ah-behn-too-reh-roh(rah)*
affectionate	**cariñoso(a)**	*kah-ree-nyoh-soh(sah)*
aggressive	**agresivo(a)**	*ah-greh-see-boh(bah)*
athletic	**atlético(a)**	*aht-leh-tee-koh(kah)*
attentive	**atento(a)**	*ah-tehn-toh(tah)*
bright	**brillante**	*bree-yahn-teh*
candid	**cándido(a)**	*kahn-dee-doh(dah)*
clumsy	**torpe**	*tohr-peh*
confident	**seguro(a)**	*seh-goo-roh(rah)*
cooperative	**dispuesto(a)**	*dees-poo-ehs-toh(tah)*
courteous	**cortés**	*kohr-tehs*
curious	**curioso(a)**	*koo-ree-oh-soh(sah)*
discourteous	**descortés**	*dehs-kohr-tehs*
ethical	**ético(a)**	*eh-tee-koh(kah)*
fair	**justo(a)**	*hoos-toh(tah)*
forgetful	**olvidadizo(a)**	*ohl-bee-dah-dee-soh(sah)*
friendly, kind	**amable**	*ah-mah-bleh*
funny	**cómico(a)**	*koh-mee-koh(kah)*
generous	**generoso(a)**	*heh-neh-roh-soh(sah)*
happy	**contento(a)**	*kohn-tehn-toh(tah)*

hard-working	**trabajador(a)**	*trah-bah-hah-dohr(doh-rah)*
helpful	**servicial**	*sehr-bee-see-ahl*
honest	**honesto(a)**	*oh-nehs-toh(tah)*
hyperactive	**hiperactivo(a)**	*ee-pehr-ahk-tee-boh(bah)*
immature	**inmaduro(a)**	*een-mah-doo-roh(rah)*
impatient	**impaciente**	*eem-pah-see-ehn-teh*
impulsive	**impulsivo(a)**	*eem-pool-see-boh(bah)*
insightful	**perspicaz**	*pehr-spee-kahs*
intelligent	**inteligente**	*een-teh-lee-hehn-teh*
intuitive	**intuitivo(a)**	*een-too-ee-tee-boh(bah)*
kind	**simpático(a)**	*seem-pah-tee-koh(kah)*
lazy	**perezoso(a)**	*peh-reh-soh-soh(sah)*
lively	**animado(a)**	*ah-nee-mah-doh(dah)*
mature	**maduro(a)**	*mah-doo-roh(rah)*
messy	**desorganizado(a)**	*dehs-ohr-gah-nee-sah-doh(dah)*
neat	**organizado(a)**	*ohr-gah-nee-sah-doh(dah)*
open-minded	**flexible**	*flehk-see-bleh*
optimistic	**optimista**	*ohp-tee-mees-tah*
outgoing	**sociable**	*soh-see-ah-bleh*
patient	**paciente**	*pah-see-ehn-teh*
pessimistic	**pesimista**	*peh-see-mees-tah*
pleasant	**agradable**	*ah-grah-dah-bleh*
proud	**orgulloso(a)**	*ohr-goo-yoh-soh(sah)*
responsible	**responsable**	*rrehs-pohn-sah-bleh*
rigid	**rígido(a)**	*rree-hee-doh(dah)*
sad	**triste**	*trees-teh*
selfish	**egoísta**	*eh-goh-ees-tah*
sensitive	**sensible**	*sehn-see-bleh*
serious	**serio(a)**	*seh-ree-oh(ah)*
shy	**tímido(a)**	*tee-mee-doh(dah)*
sincere	**sincero(a)**	*seen-seh-roh(rah)*
strong	**fuerte**	*foo-ehr-teh*
talkative	**hablador(a)**	*ah-blah-dohr(doh-rah)*
thoughtful	**considerado(a)**	*kohn-see-deh-rah-doh(dah)*
uncooperative	**poco cooperador(a)**	*poh-koh koh-oh-peh-rah-dohr(doh-rah)*
weak	**débil**	*deh-beel*
well-mannered	**bien educado(a)**	*bee-ehn eh-doo-kah-doh(dah)*
withdrawn	**reservado(a)**	*rreh-sehr-bah-doh(dah)*

Type of School

This is a/an _____ school.
Es una escuela _____.
ehs oo-nah ehs-koo-eh-lah _____

alternative	**alternativa**	*ahl-tehr-nah-tee-bah*
boys'	**para niños**	*pah-rah nee-nyohs*
coeducational	**mixta**	*meeks-tah*
elementary	**primaria**	*pree-mah-ree-ah*
girls'	**para niñas**	*pah-rah nee-nyahs*
high	**secundaria**	*seh-koon-dah-ree-ah*
magnet	**imán**	*ee-mahn*
middle	**intermedia**	*een-tehr-meh-dee-ah*
parochial	**parroquial**	*pah-rroh-kee-ahl*
pilot	**piloto**	*pee-loh-toh*
preschool	**preescolar**	*preh-ehs-koh-lahr*
private	**privada**	*pree-bah-dah*
public	**pública**	*poo-blee-kah*
religious	**religiosa**	*rreh-lee-hee-oh-sah*
satellite	**satélite**	*sah-teh-lee-teh*
trade	**de artes y oficios**	*deh ahr-tehs ee oh-fee-see-ohs*
vocational	**vocacional**	*boh-kah-see-oh-nahl*

Your child is in a/an _____ class.
Su hijo (hija) está en una clase _____.
soo ee-hoh (ee-hah) ehs-tah ehn oo-nah klah-seh _____

accelerated	**avanzada**	*ah-bahn-sah-dah*
regular	**normal**	*nohr-mahl*
special education	**de educación especial**	*deh eh-doo-kah-see-ohn ehs-peh-see-ahl*

Family Members

Are you his (her) _____?
¿Es Ud. su _____?
ehs oo-stehd soo _____

aunt	**tía**	*tee-ah*
brother	**hermano**	*ehr-mah-noh*
cousin	**primo(a)**	*pree-moh(mah)*
father	**padre**	*pah-dreh*

godfather	**padrino**	*pah-dree-noh*
godmother	**madrina**	*mah-dree-nah*
grandfather	**abuelo**	*ah-boo-eh-loh*
grandmother	**abuela**	*ah-boo-eh-lah*
legal guardian	**encargado(a)**	*ehn-kahr-gah-doh(dah)*
mother	**madre**	*mah-dreh*
sister	**hermana**	*ehr-mah-nah*
stepbrother	**hermanastro**	*ehr-mah-nahs-troh*
stepfather	**padrastro**	*pah-drahs-troh*
stepmother	**madrastra**	*mah-drahs-trah*
stepsister	**hermanastra**	*ehr-mah-nahs-trah*
uncle	**tío**	*tee-oh*

Is he/she your _____?
¿Es su _____?
ehs soo _____

daughter	**hija**	*ee-hah*
goddaughter	**ahijada**	*ah-ee-hah-dah*
godson	**ahijado**	*ah-ee-hah-doh*
nephew	**sobrino**	*soh-bree-noh*
niece	**sobrina**	*soh-bree-nah*
son	**hijo**	*ee-hoh*
stepdaughter	**hijastra**	*ee-hahs-trah*
stepson	**hijastro**	*ee-hahs-troh*

How many people are in your family?
¿Cuántas personas hay en su familia?
koo-ahn-tahs pehr-soh-nahs ah-ee ehn soo fah-meel-yah

Who are they?
¿Quiénes son?
kee-eh-nehs sohn

What other family members live with you?
¿Qué otros miembros de su familia viven con Uds.?
keh oh-trohs mee-ehm-brohs deh soo fah-meel-yah bee-behn kohn oo-steh-dehs

Who is your child's legal guardian?
¿Quién es el (la) encargado(a) de su hijo (hija)?
kee-ehn ehs ehl (lah) ehn-kahr-gah-doh(dah) deh soo ee-hoh (ee-hah)

Do you have a recent picture of your child for our records?
¿Tiene Ud. una fotografía reciente de su hijo (hija) para nuestros archivos?
tee-eh-neh oo-stehd oo-nah foh-toh-grah-fee-ah rreh-see-ehn-teh deh soo ee-hoh (ee-hah) pah-rah noo-ehs-trohs ahr-chee-bohs

With whom does your child come to school?
¿Con quién viene su hijo (hija) a la escuela?
kohn kee-ehn bee-eh-neh soo ee-hoh (ee-hah) ah lah ehs-koo-eh-lah

Who drops your child off at school?
¿Quién trae a su hijo (hija) a la escuela?
kee-ehn trah-eh ah soo ee-hoh (ee-hah) ah lah ehs-koo-eh-lah

Who picks up your child from school?
¿Quién recoge a su hijo (hija) después de las clases?
kee-ehn rreh-koh-heh ah soo ee-hoh (ee-hah) dehs-poo-ehs deh lahs klah-sehs

Is there someone else who has permission to pick up your child from school?
¿Quién más tiene permiso de recoger a su hijo (hija)?
kee-ehn mahs tee-eh-neh pehr-mee-soh deh rreh-koh-hehr ah soo ee-hoh (ee-hah)

¿What is his (her) name?
¿Cómo se llama?
koh-moh seh yah-mah

If you cannot pick up your child, who has permission to do so?
En su ausencia, ¿quién tiene permiso de recoger a su hijo (hija)?
ehn soo ah-oo-sehn-see-ah kee-ehn tee-eh-neh pehr-mee-soh deh rreh-koh-hehr ah soo ee-hoh (ee-hah)

If you cannot be here to pick up your child, please notify us in advance with a letter or phone call.
Si Ud. no pudiera venir a recoger a su hijo (hija), haga el favor de darnos notificación avanzada por escrito o por teléfono.
see oo-stehd noh poo-dee-eh-rah beh-neer ah rreh-koh-hehr ah soo ee-hoh (ee-hah) ah-gah ehl fah-bohr deh dahr-nohs noh-tee-fee-kah-see-ohn ah-bahn-sah-dah pohr ehs-kree-toh oh pohr teh-leh-foh-noh

The person who comes to pick up your child must show picture identification.

La persona que venga a recoger a su hijo (hija) tiene que mostrarnos identificación fotográfica.

lah pehr-soh-nah keh behn-gah ah rreh-koh-hehr ah soo ee-hoh (ee-hah) tee-eh-neh keh mohs-trahr-nohs ee-dehn-tee-fee-kah-see-ohn foh-toh-grah-fee-kah

Does anyone at home speak English?

¿Hay alguien en su casa que hable inglés?

ah-ee ahl-gee-ehn ehn soo kah-sah keh ah-bleh een-glehs

Do any of your child's siblings attend this school?

¿Asiste a esta escuela algún hermano o hermana de su hijo (hija)?

ah-sees-teh ah ehs-tah ehs-koo-eh-lah ahl-goon ehr-mah-noh oh ehr-mah-nah deh soo ee-hoh (ee-hah)

Parental Contact

What are your work hours?

¿Cuál es su horario de trabajo?

koo-ahl ehs soo oh-rah-ree-oh deh trah-bah-hoh

When are your days off from work?

¿Cuándo está Ud. libre?

koo-ahn-doh ehs-tah oo-stehd lee-breh

How can I contact you?

¿Cómo puedo ponerme en contacto con Ud.?

koh-moh poo-eh-doh poh-nehr-meh ehn kohn-tahk-toh kohn oo-stehd

When is the best time to reach you?

¿Qué hora es la más conveniente para comunicarme con Ud.?

keh oh-rah ehs lah mahs kohn-beh-nee-ehn-teh pah-rah koh-moo-nee-kahr-meh kohn oo-stehd

What is your work (home) number?

¿Cuál es el número de teléfono de su trabajo (casa)?

koo-ahl ehs ehl noo-meh-roh deh teh-leh-foh-noh deh soo trah-bah-hoh (kah-sah)

Do you have a cellphone (fax, beeper)?

¿Tiene Ud. un teléfono celular (fax, bíper)?

tee-eh-neh oo-stehd oon teh-leh-foh-noh seh-loo-lahr (fahks, bee-pehr)

What is the number?
¿Cuál es el número?
koo-ahl ehs ehl noo-meh-roh

What is your extension?
¿Cuál es su número interno?
koo-ahl ehs soo noo-meh-roh een-tehr-noh

Do you have an answering machine?
¿Tiene Ud. un contestador telefónico?
tee-eh-neh oo-stehd oon kohn-tehs-tah-dohr teh-leh-foh-nee-koh

May I leave you a voicemail message?
¿Puedo dejarle un mensaje en su buzón de voz?
poo-eh-doh deh-hahr-leh oon mehn-sah-heh ehn soo boo-sohn deh bohs

Whom can we call in case of an emergency?
¿A quién podemos telefonear en caso de urgencia?
ah kee-ehn poh-deh-mohs teh-leh-foh-neh-ahr ehn kah-soh deh oor-hehn-see-ah

In, Around, and After School

Note:
1. Letters or words in brackets are used when using the familiar you **[tú]** form.
2. When speaking to more than one adult, **Ud.** (you, singular) becomes **Uds.** (you, plural) and an n is added to the conjugated verb form.
3. The formal you form is expressed in the same way as the third-person singular **él** (he) and **ella** (she) forms.

People

English	Spanish	Pronunciation
administrator	el (la) administrador(a)	*ehl (lah) ahd-mee-nee-strah-dohr (doh-rah)*
advisor	el (la) consejero(a)	*ehl (lah) kohn-seh-heh-roh (rah)*
aide	el (la) ayudante	*ehl (lah) ah-yoo-dahn-teh*
assistant	el (la) asistente	*ehl (lah) ah-sees-tehn-teh*
assistant principal	el (la) subdirector(a)	*ehl (lah) soob-dee-rehk-tohr (toh-rah)*
assistant superintendent	el (la) subsuperintendente	*ehl (lah) soob-soo-pehr-een-tehn-dehn-teh*

English	Spanish	Pronunciation
bus driver	el (la) **conductor(a) de autobús**	*ehl (lah) kohn-dook-tohr (toh-rah) deh ah-oo-toh-boos*
coach	el (la) **entrenador(a)**	*ehl (lah) ehn-treh-nah-dohr (doh-rah)*
consultant	el (la) **consultor(a)**	*ehl (lah) kohn-sool-tohr (toh-rah)*
coordinator	el (la) **coordinador(a)**	*ehl (lah) koh-ohr-dee-nah-dohr (doh-rah)*
counselor	el (la) **consejero(a)**	*ehl (lah) kohn-seh-heh-roh (rah)*
crossing guard	el (la) **guardia escolar**	*ehl (lah) goo-ahr-dee-ah ehs-koh-lahr*
custodian	el (la) **guardián (guardiana)**	*ehl (lah) goo-ahr-dee-ahn (goo-ahr-dee-ah-nah)*
dean	el (la) **decano(a)**	*ehl (lah) deh-kah-noh(nah)*
doctor	el (la) **médico(a)**	*ehl (lah) meh-dee-koh(kah)*
interpreter	el (la) **intérprete**	*ehl (lah) een-tehr-preh-teh*
kitchen staff	el (la) **empleado(a) de la cocina**	*ehl (lah) ehm-pleh-ah-doh (dah) deh lah koh-see-nah*
librarian	el (la) **bibliotecario(a)**	*ehl (lah) bee-blee-oh-teh-kah-ree-oh(ah)*
nurse	el (la) **enfermero(a)**	*ehl (lah) ehn-fehr-meh-roh (rah)*
para-professional	el (la) **paraprofesional**	*ehl (lah) pah-rah-proh-feh-see-oh-nahl*
police officer	el (la) **policía**	*ehl (lah) poh-lee-see-ah*
principal	el (la) **director(a)**	*ehl (lah) dee-rehk-tohr (toh-rah)*
programmer	el (la) **programador(a)**	*ehl (lah) proh-grah-mah-dohr (doh-rah)*
psychiatrist	el (la) **psiquiatra**	*ehl (lah) see-kee-ah-trah*
psychologist	el (la) **psicólogo(a)**	*ehl (lah) see-koh-loh-goh (gah)*
PTA president	el (la) **presidente de la asociación de padres de alumnos**	*ehl (lah) preh-see-dehn-teh deh lah ah-soh-see-ah-see-ohn deh pah-drehs de ah-loom-nohs*
secretary	el (la) **secretario(a)**	*ehl (lah) seh-kreh-tah-ree-oh (ah)*

English	Spanish	Pronunciation
security staff	el personal de seguridad	*ehl pehr-soh-nahl deh seh-goo-ree-dahd*
social worker	el (la) trabajador(a) social	*ehl (lah) trah-bah-hah-dohr (trah-bah-hah-doh-rah) soh-see-ahl*
specialist	el (la) especialista	*ehl (lah) ehs-peh-see-ah-lees-tah*
speech therapist	el (la) logopeda	*ehl (lah) loh-goh-peh-dah*
student	el (la) alumno(a), estudiante	*ehl (lah) ah-loom-noh (nah), ehs-too-dee-ahn-teh*
superintendent	el (la) superintendente	*ehl (lah) soo-pehr-een-tehn-dehn-teh*
supervisor	el (la) supervisor(a)	*ehl (lah) soo-pehr-bee-sohr (soo-pehr-bee-soh-rah)*
teacher	el (la) maestro(a)	*ehl (lah) mah-ehs-troh (trah)*
teacher (secondary school)	el (la) profesor(a)	*ehl (lah) proh-feh-sohr (soh-rah)*
teaching assistant	el (la) ayudante de cátedra	*ehl (lah) ah-yoo-dahn-teh deh kah-teh-drah*
teaching staff	el profesorado	*ehl proh-feh-soh-rah-doh*
therapist	el (la) terapeuta	*ehl (lah) teh-rah-peh-oo-tah*

To the Parent

I don't speak Spanish very well. Do you need an interpreter?
No hablo muy bien español. ¿Necesita un intérprete?
noh ah-bloh moo-ee bee-ehn ehs-pah-nyohl neh-seh-see-tah oon een-tehr-preh-teh

I am your child's teacher.
Soy el (la) profesor(a) (maestro[a]) de su hijo (hija).
soh-ee ehl (lah) proh-feh-sohr(soh-rah) (mah-ehs-troh[trah]) deh soo ee-hoh (ee-hah)

You should speak to the supervisor of the department.
Debería hablar con el supervisor del departamento.
deh-beh-ree-ah ahb-lahr kohn ehl soo-pehr-bee-sohr dehl
deh-pahr-tah-mehn-toh

Who is your child's teacher?
¿Quién es el (la) profesor (profesora) / el (la) maestro (maestra) de su hijo (hija)?
kee-ehn ehs ehl (lah) proh-feh-sohr (proh-feh-soh-rah)/ehl (lah) mah-ehs-troh (mah-ehs-trah) deh soo ee-hoh (ee-hah)

Your child is with the school nurse.
Su hijo (hija) está con la enfermera de la escuela.
soo ee-hoh (ee-hah) ehs-tah kohn lah ehn-fehr-meh-rah deh lah ehs-koo-eh-lah

Would you like an appointment with your child's counselor?
¿Quisiera una cita con el (la) consejero (consejera) de su hijo (hija)?
kee-see-yeh-rah oo-nah see-tah kohn ehl (lah) kohn-seh-heh-roh (kohn-seh-heh-rah) deh soo ee-hoh (ee-hah)

Our school secretary will help you register your child.
Nuestra secretaria lo (la) ayudará a inscribir a su hijo (hija).
noo-ehs-trah seh-kreh-tah-ree-ah loh (lah) ah-yoo-dah-rah ah een-skree-beer ah soo ee-hoh (ee-hah)

Would you like to speak to the bus driver?
¿Quisiera hablar con el (la) conductor (conductora) de autobús?
kee-see-eh-rah ahb-lahr kohn ehl (lah) kohn-dook-tohr (kohn-dook-toh-rah) deh ah-oh-toh-boos

Do you have an appointment (meeting) with your child's teacher?
¿Tiene una cita (una reunión) con el (la) maestro (maestra)/ el (la) profesor (profesora) de su hijo (hija)?
tee-eh-neh oo-nah see-tah (oo-nah rreh-oo-nyohn) kohn ehl (lah) mah-ehs-troh (mah-ehs-trah)/ehl (lah) proh-feh-sohr (proh-feh-soh-rah) deh soo ee-hoh (ee-hah)

Our social worker will help you in a few minutes.
Nuestro(a) trabajador (trabajadora) social lo (la) atenderá en algunos minutos.
noo-ehs-troh (noo-ehs-trah) trah-bah-hah-dohr (trah-bah-hah-doh-rah) soh-see-ahl loh (lah) ah-tehn-deh-rah ehn ahl-goo-nohs mee-noo-tohs

The assistant principal is (not) available now.
El (La) subdirector (subdirectora) (no) está disponible ahora.
ehl (lah) soob-dee-rehk-tohr (soob-dee-rehk-toh-rah) (noh) ehs-tah dees-poh-nee-bleh ah-oh-rah

The reading specialist is absent (busy now).
El (La) especialista en lectura está ausente (ocupado[a] ahora).
ehl (lah) ehs-peh-see-ah-lees-tah ehn lehk-too-rah ehs-tah ah-oo-sehn-teh (oh-koo-pah-doh[dah] ah-oh-rah)

Would you like to speak with the principal?
¿Quisiera hablar con el (la) director (directora)?
kee-see-eh-rah ah-blahr kohn ehl (lah) dee-rehk-tohr (dee-rehk-toh-rah)

Your child's teacher can help you with that problem.
El (La) profesor (profesora) / El (La) maestro (maestra) de su hijo (hija) puede ayudarle a Ud. con ese problema.
ehl (lah) proh-feh-sohr (proh-feh-soh-rah) / ehl (lah) mah-ehs-troh (mah-ehs-trah) deh soo ee-hoh (ee-hah) poo-eh-deh ah-yoo-dahr-leh ah oo-stehd kohn eh-seh proh-bleh-mah

You need to speak to the school psychologist.
Necesita hablar con el (la) psicólogo (psicóloga) de la escuela.
neh-seh-see-tah ah-blahr kohn ehl (lah) see-koh-loh-goh (see-koh-loh-gah) deh lah ehs-koo-eh-lah

Classroom Fixtures

English	Spanish	Pronunciation
aisle	el pasillo	*ehl pah-see-yoh*
bag	la bolsa	*lah bohl-sah*
bin	el depósito	*ehl deh-poh-see-toh*
box	la caja	*lah kah-hah*
bulletin board	el tablón de anuncios	*ehl tah-blohn deh ah-noon-see-ohs*
cabinet	el gabinete	*ehl gah-bee-neh-teh*
calendar	el calendario	*ehl kah-lehn-dah-ree-oh*
chalkboard	la pizarra	*lah pee-sah-rrah*
chart	el diagrama	*ehl dee-ah-grah-mah*
chest	el baúl	*ehl bah-ool*
computer	la computadora	*lah kohm-poo-tah-doh-rah*
cupboard	el armario	*ehl ahr-mah-ree-oh*

English	Spanish	Pronunciation
desk (student's)	el pupitre	*ehl poo-pee-treh*
door	la puerta	*lah poo-ehr-tah*
drawer	el cajón	*ehl kah-hohn*
easel	el caballete	*ehl kah-bah-yeh-teh*
file	el archivo	*ehl ahr-chee-boh*
flag	la bandera	*lah bahn-deh-rah*
globe	el globo	*ehl gloh-boh*
intercom	el interfono	*ehl een-tehr-foh-noh*
light switch	el interruptor	*ehl een-teh-rroop-tohr*
map	el mapa	*ehl mah-pah*
model	el modelo	*ehl moh-deh-loh*
pole	el palo	*ehl pah-loh*
poster	el cartel	*ehl kahr-tehl*
row	la fila	*lah fee-lah*
screen	la pantalla	*lah pahn-tah-yah*
sign	el letrero	*ehl leh-treh-roh*
stool	el banquillo	*ehl bahn-kee-yoh*
thermostat	el termostato	*ehl tehr-moh-stah-toh*
window	la ventana	*lah behn-tah-nah*
window shade	la persiana	*lah pehr-see-ah-nah*
windowsill	la repisa de la ventana	*lah rreh-pee-sah deh lah behn-tah-nah*

To the Student

The light switch is near the door.
El interruptor está cerca de la puerta.
ehl een-teh-rroop-tohr ehs-tah sehr-kah deh lah poo-ehr-tah

Put the plant on the windowsill.
Ponga [Pon] la planta en la repisa de la ventana.
pohn-gah [pohn] lah plahn-tah ehn lah rreh-pee-sah deh lah behn-tah-nah

Don't touch the thermostat.
No toque [toques] el termostato.
noh toh-keh [toh-kehs] ehl tehr-moh-stah-toh

Open the window with the pole.
Abra [Abre] la ventana con el palo.
ah-brah [ah-breh] lah behn-tah-nah kohn ehl pah-loh

Read the sign on the bulletin board carefully.
Lea [Lee] con cuidado el letrero en el tablón de anuncios.
leh-ah [leh-eh] kohn koo-ee-dah-doh ehl leh-treh-roh ehn ehl tah-blohn deh ah-noon-see-ohs

Look at the map.
Mire [Mira] el mapa.
mee-reh [mee-rah] ehl mah-pah

Put your book on your desk.
Ponga [Pon] el libro en su [tu] pupitre.
pohn-gah [pohn] ehl lee-broh ehn soo [too] poo-pee-treh

Write your homework on the chalkboard.
Escriba [Escribe] la tarea el la pizarra.
ehs-kree-bah [ehs-kree-beh] lah tah-reh-ah ehn lah pee-sah-rrah

Please sit in the first row.
Siéntese [Siéntate] en la primera fila, por favor.
see-ehn-teh-seh [see-ehn-tah-teh] ehn lah pree-meh-rah fee-lah pohr fah-bohr

Don't look out the window.
No mire [mires] por la ventana.
noh mee-reh [mee-rehs] pohr lah behn-tah-nah

Put the toys in the chest.
Ponga [Pon] los juguetes en el baúl.
pohn-gah [pohn] lohs hoo-geh-tehs ehn ehl bah-ool

Look in the box.
Busque [Busca] en la caja.
boos-keh [boos-kah] ehn lah kah-hah

Everyone look at the screen.
Todos miren la pantalla.
toh-dohs mee-rehn lah pahn-tah-yah

Locations

English	Spanish	Pronunciation
attendance office	la oficina de asistencia	*lah oh-fee-see-nah deh ah-sees-tehn-see-ah*
auditorium	el auditorio	*ehl ah-oo-dee-toh-ree-oh*

English	Spanish	Pronunciation
balcony	el balcón	*ehl bahl-kohn*
building	el edificio	*ehl eh-dee-fee-see-oh*
cafeteria	la cafetería	*lah kah-feh-teh-ree-ah*
classroom	el salón de clase	*ehl sah-lohn deh klah-seh*
courtyard	la plaza	*lah plah-sah*
custodian's office	la oficina del guardián (de la guardiana)	*lah oh-fee-see-nah dehl goo-ahr-dee-ahn (deh lah goo-ahr-dee-ah-nah)*
department	el departamento	*ehl deh-pahr-tah-mehn-toh*
door (front)	la puerta (principal)	*lah poo-ehr-tah (preen-see-pahl)*
elevator(s)	el (los) ascensor(es)	*ehl (lohs) ah-sehn-sohr (ah-sehn-soh-rehs)*
entrance	la entrada	*lah ehn-trah-dah*
escalator	la escalera mecánica	*lah ehs-kah-leh-rah meh-kah-nee-kah*
exit	la salida	*lah sah-lee-dah*
fence	la cerca	*lah sehr-kah*
field	el campo	*ehl kahm-poh*
front desk	la recepción	*lah rreh-sehp-see-ohn*
front row	la primera fila	*lah pree-meh-rah fee-lah*
gym	el gimnasio	*ehl heem-nah-see-oh*
hall	el pasillo	*ehl pah-see-yoh*
laboratory	el laboratorio	*ehl lah-boh-rah-toh-ree-oh*
library	la biblioteca	*lah bee-blee-oh-teh-kah*
lobby	el vestíbulo	*ehl behs-tee-boo-loh*
lockers	los armarios	*lohs ahr-mah-ree-ohs*
mailboxes	los buzones	*lohs boo-soh-nehs*
main office	la oficina principal	*lah oh-fee-see-nah preen-see-pahl*
office	la oficina	*lah oh-fee-see-nah*
parking lot	el estacionamiento	*ehl ehs-tah-see-oh-nah-mee-ehn-toh*
playground	el campo de recreo	*ehl kahm-poh deh rreh-kreh-oh*
public phones	los teléfonos públicos	*lohs teh-leh-foh-nohs poo-blee-kohs*
ramp	la rampa	*lah rrahm-pah*

English	Spanish	Pronunciation
restrooms	**los servicios**	*lohs sehr-bee-see-ohs*
sidewalk	**la acera**	*lah ah-seh-rah*
stairway	**la escalera**	*lah ehs-kah-leh-rah*
wall	**la pared**	*lah pah-rehd*
water fountain	**la fuente de agua**	*lah foo-ehn-teh deh ah-goo-ah*
workshop	**el taller**	*ehl tah-yehr*

To the Student

There is a rehearsal in the auditorium.
Hay un ensayo en el auditorio.
ah-ee oon ehn-sah-yoh ehn ehl ah-oo-dee-toh-ree-oh

The team is on the field.
El equipo está en el campo.
ehl eh-kee-poh ehs-tah ehn ehl kahm-poh

We are going to the playground.
Vamos al campo de recreo.
bah-mohs ahl kahm-poh deh rreh-kreh-oh

You may not use the public phones.
No puede[s] usar los teléfonos públicos.
noh poo-eh-deh[s] oo-sahr lohs teh-leh-foh-nohs poo-blee-kohs

Do you have to go to the restroom?
¿Tiene[s] que ir a los servicios?
tee-eh-neh[s] keh eer ah lohs sehr-bee-see-ohs

Go to the dean's office.
Vaya [Ve] a la oficina del decano.
bah-yah (beh) ah lah oh-fee-see-nah dehl deh-kah-noh

Don't run in the hall.
No corra [corras] en el pasillo.
noh ko-rrah [koh-rrahs] ehn ehl pah-see-yoh

The elevators are for the teachers.
Los ascensores son para los profesores (maestros).
lohs ah-sehn-soh-rehs sohn pah-rah los proh-feh-soh-rehs (mah-ehs-trohs)

Giving Directions

English	Spanish	Pronunciation
above	encima de	ehn-see-mah deh
around	alrededor de	ahl-reh-deh-dohr deh
at the bottom of	en la parte inferior de	ehn lah pahr-teh een-feh-ree-ohr deh
at the bottom of	en el fondo de	ehn ehl fohn-doh deh
at the end of	al final de	ahl fee-nahl deh
at the foot of	al pie de	ahl pee-eh deh
at the side of	al lado de	ahl lah-doh deh
at the top of	en lo alto de	ehn loh ahl-toh deh
beneath	debajo de	deh-bah-hoh deh
far	lejos de	leh-hohs deh
forward	adelante	ah-deh-lahn-teh
here	aquí	ah-kee
in	en	ehn
in back of	detrás de	deh-trahs deh
in front of	delante de	deh-lahn-teh deh
in front of	enfrente de	ehn-frehn-teh deh
in the basement	en el sótano	ehn ehl soh-tah-noh
in the middle of	en el centro de	ehn ehl sehn-troh deh
in the middle of	en el medio de	ehn ehl meh-dee-oh deh
inside	adentro	ah-dehn-troh
inside (of)	dentro de	dehn-troh deh
near	cerca de	sehr-kah deh
on	sobre	soh-breh
on the corner of	en la esquina de	ehn lah ehs-kee-nah deh
on the exterior of	en el exterior de	ehn ehl ehks-teh-ree-ohr deh
on the first floor	en el primer piso	ehn ehl pree-mehr pee-soh
on the interior of	en el interior de	ehn ehl een-teh-ree-ohr deh
on the second floor	en el segundo piso	ehn ehl seh-goon-doh pee-soh
on the top floor	en el último piso	ehn ehl ool-tee-moh pee-soh
opposite	enfrente de	ehn-frehn-teh deh
outside	afuera	ah-foo-eh-rah
outside (of)	fuera de	foo-eh-rah deh
over there	allá	ah-yah
straight across	justo al otro lado de	hoos-toh ahl oh-troh lah-doh deh

English	Spanish	Pronunciation
straight ahead	**justo enfrente (todo derecho)**	*hoos-toh ehn-frehn-teh (toh-doh deh-reh-choh)*
there	**allí**	*ah-yee*
to	**hasta, a**	*ahs-tah ah*
to the east	**al este**	*ahl ehs-teh*
to the left of	**a la izquierda de**	*ah lah ees-kee-ehr-dah deh*
to the north	**al norte**	*ahl nohr-teh*
to the right of	**a la derecha de**	*ah lah deh-reh-chah deh*
to the south	**al sur**	*ahl soor*
to the west	**al oeste**	*ahl oh-ehs-teh*
under	**bajo**	*bah-hoh*
up	**arriba**	*ah-rree-bah*
where?	**¿dónde?**	*dohn-deh*

To the Parent

The librarian is not in his (her) office.
El (La) bibliotecario(a) no está en su oficina.
ehl (lah) bee-blee-oh-teh-kah-ree-oh(ah) noh ehs-tah ehn soo oh-fee-see-nah

Here is the main office.
Aquí está la oficina principal.
ah-kee ehs-tah lah oh-fee-see-nah preen-see-pahl

The dean's office is on the first floor.
La oficina del (de la) decano (decana) está en el primer piso.
lah oh-fee-see-nah dehl (deh lah) deh-kah-noh (nah) ehs-tah ehn ehl pree-mehr pee-soh

Take the elevator to the third floor.
Tome el ascensor hasta el tercer piso.
toh-meh ehl ah-sehn-sohr ah-stah ehl tehr-sehr pee-soh

Your child's classroom is near the gym.
El salón de clase de su hijo (hija) está cerca del gimnasio.
ehl sah-lohn deh klah-seh deh soo ee-hoh (ee-hah) ehs-tah sehr-kah dehl heem-nah-see-oh

The library is not far.
La biblioteca no está lejos.
lah bee-blee-oh-teh-kah noh ehs-tah leh-hohs

That office is straight ahead and to the left.
Esa oficina está adelante y a la izquierda.
eh-sah oh-fee-see-nah ehs-tah ah-deh-lahn-teh y ah lah ees-kee-ehr-dah

The bathrooms are downstairs.
Los servicios están abajo.
lohs serh-bee-see-ohs ehs-tahn ah-bah-hoh

That office is next to the art room.
Esa oficina está cerca del salón de arte.
eh-sah oh-fee-see-nah ehs-tah sehr-kah dehl sah-lohn deh ahr-teh

Go to the right.
Vaya a la derecha.
bah-yah ah lah deh-reh-chah

Go down to the basement.
Baje al sótano.
bah-heh ahl soh-tah-noh

Continue straight ahead.
Continúe derecho.
kohn-tee-noo-eh deh-reh-choh

Turn to the left.
Doble a la izquierda.
doh-bleh ah lah ees-kee-ehr-dah

Go to the other side of the building.
Vaya al otro lado del edificio.
bah-yah ahl oh-troh lah-doh dehl eh-dee-fee-see-oh

Pass by the attendance office.
Pase por la oficina de asistencia.
pah-seh pohr lah oh-fee-see-nah deh ah-sees-tehn-see-ah

Continue walking.
Siga caminando.
see-gah kah-mee-nahn-doh

Go up to the second floor.
Suba al segundo piso.
soo-bah ahl seh-goon-doh pee-soh

Cross the courtyard.
Cruce el patio.
kroo-seh ehl pah-tee-oh

Extracurricular Activities

English	Spanish	Pronunciation
baseball team	**el equipo de béisbol**	*ehl eh-kee-poh deh beh-ees-bohl*
basketball team	**el equipo de baloncesto**	*ehl eh-kee-poh deh bah-lohn-sehs-toh*
bowling team	**el equipo de boliche**	*ehl eh-kee-poh deh boh-lee-cheh*
boxing team	**el equipo de boxeo**	*ehl eh-kee-poh deh bohk-seh-oh*
business club	**el club de negocios**	*ehl kloob deh neh-goh-see-ohs*
cheerleader	**animador(a)**	*ah-nee-mah-dohr(ah)*
chess club	**el club de ajedrez**	*ehl kloob deh ah-heh-drehs*
community service	**el trabajo comunitario**	*ehl trah-bah-hoh koh-moo-nee-tah-ree-oh*
computer club	**el club de computadoras**	*ehl kloob deh kohm-poo-tah-doh-rahs*
cooking club	**el club de cocina**	*ehl kloob deh koh-see-nah*
dance club	**el club de baile**	*ehl kloob deh bah-ee-leh*
debate team	**el equipo de debate**	*ehl eh-kee-poh deh deh-bah-teh*
drama club	**el club de drama**	*ehl kloob deh drah-mah*
ecology club	**el club de ecología**	*ehl kloob deh eh-koh-loh-hee-ah*
film club	**el club de películas**	*ehl kloob deh peh-lee-koo-lahs*
football team	**el equipo de fútbol americano**	*ehl eh-kee-poh deh foot-bohl ah-meh-ree-kah-noh*
glee club	**el coro**	*ehl koh-roh*
group	**el grupo**	*ehl groo-poh*
gymnastics team	**el equipo de gimnasia**	*ehl eh-kee-poh deh heem-nah-see-ah*
hockey team (field hockey)	**el equipo de hockey**	*ehl eh-kee-poh deh oh-kee*

English	Spanish	Pronunciation
ice hockey team	el equipo de hockey sobre hielo	*ehl eh-kee-poh deh oh-kee soh-breh ee-eh-loh*
international club	el club internacional	*ehl kloob een-tehr-nah-see-oh-nahl*
lacrosse team	el equipo de lacrosse	*ehl eh-kee-poh deh lah-kroh-seh*
marching band	la banda de marcha	*lah bahn-dah deh mahr-chah*
math club	el club de matemáticas	*ehl kloob deh mah-teh-mah-tee-kahs*
math team	el equipo de matemáticas	*ehl eh-kee-poh deh mah-teh-mah-tee-kahs*
newspaper	el periódico	*ehl peh-ree-oh-dee-koh*
organization	la organización	*lah ohr-gah-nee-sah-see-ohn*
ski club	el club de esquí	*ehl kloob deh ehs-kee*
soccer team	el equipo de fútbol	*ehl eh-kee-poh deh foot-bohl*
softball team	el equipo de sófbol	*ehl eh-kee-poh deh sohf-bohl*
swimming team	el equipo de natación	*ehl eh-kee-poh deh nah-tah-see-ohn*
tennis team	el equipo de tenis	*ehl eh-kee-poh deh teh-nees*
track and field team	el equipo de atletismo	*ehl eh-kee-poh deh aht-leh-tees-moh*
volleyball team	el equipo de voleibol	*ehl eh-kee-poh deh boh-leh-ee-bohl*
wrestling team	el equipo de lucha olímpica	*ehl eh-kee-poh deh loo-chah oh-leem-pee-kah*
yearbook	el anuario	*ehl ah-noo-ah-ree-oh*

To the Parent

Is your child a member of the soccer team?
¿Es su hijo (hija) miembro del equipo de fútbol?
ehs soo ee-hoh (ee-hah) mee-ehm-broh dehl eh-kee-poh deh foot-bohl

Why doesn't your son (daughter) join the debate team?
¿Por qué no ingresa su hijo (hija) en el equipo de debate?
pohr keh noh een-greh-sah soo ee-hoh (ee-hah) ehn ehl eh-kee-poh deh deh-bah-teh

Is your child interested in doing community service?

¿Le interesa a su hijo (hija) hacer trabajo comunitario?

leh een-teh-reh-sah ah soo ee-hoh (ee-hah) ah-sehr trah-bah-hoh koh-moo-nee-tah-ree-oh

All activities take place after school.

Todas las actividades tienen lugar después de las clases.

toh-dahs lahs ahk-tee-bee-dah-dehs tee-eh-nehn loo-gahr dehs-poo-ehs deh lahs klah-sehs

Joining a club will help your child make friends with others.

Hacerse miembro de un club ayudará a su hijo (hija) a crear amistades.

ah-sehr-seh mee-ehm-broh deh oon kloob ah-yoo-dah-rah ah soo ee-hoh (ee-hah) ah kreh-ahr ah-mees-tah-dehs

We need good students for the school newspaper.

Necesitamos buenos (buenas) estudiantes para el periódico de la escuela.

neh-seh-see-tah-mohs boo-eh-nohs (boo-eh-nahs) ehs-too-dee-ahn-tehs pah-rah ehl peh-ree-oh-dee-koh deh lah ehs-koo-eh-lah

To the Student

Would you like to be on the yearbook staff?

¿Quisiera[s] ser parte del personal del anuario?

kee-see-eh-rah[s] sehr pahr-teh dehl pehr-soh-nahl dehl ah-noo-ah-ree-oh

There are many clubs (teams) in the school.

Hay muchos clubes (equipos) en la escuela.

ah-ee moo-chohs kloo-behs (eh-kee-pohs) ehn lah ehs-koo-eh-lah

There is a debate club.

Hay un club de debate.

ah-ee oon kloob deh deh-bah-teh

You can join the tennis team.

Puede[s] hacerse[te] miembro del equipo de tenis.

poo-eh-deh[s] ah-sehr-seh[teh] mee-ehm-broh dehl eh-kee-poh deh teh-nees

Why not form a Spanish club?

¿Por qué no formar un club de español?

pohr keh noh fohr-mahr oon kloob deh ehs-pah-nyohl

Aside from these activities, we also occasionally have _____.
Aparte de estas actividades, tenemos de vez en cuando _____.
ah-pahr-teh deh ehs-tahs ahk-tee-bee-dahd-dehs teh-neh-mohs deh behs ehn
koo-ahn-doh _____

an auction	**una subasta**	*oo-nah soo-bahs-tah*
a banquet	**un banquete**	*oon bahn-keh-teh*
a carnival	**un carnaval**	*oon kahr-nah-bahl*
a concert	**un concierto**	*oon kohn-see-ehr-toh*
a contest	**un concurso**	*oon kohn-koor-soh*
a dance	**un baile**	*oon bah-ee-leh*
a fair	**una feria**	*oo-nah feh-ree-ah*
a festival	**un festival**	*oon fehs-tee-bahl*
a field trip	**una gira**	*oo-nah gee-rah*
a game	**un juego**	*oon hoo-eh-goh*
a match	**un partido**	*oon pahr-tee-doh*
a parade	**un desfile**	*oon dehs-fee-leh*
a performance	**una función**	*oo-nah foon-see-ohn*
a picnic	**un picnic**	*oon peek-neek*
a play	**un drama**	*oon drah-mah*
a program	**un programa**	*oon proh-grah-mah*
a raffle	**un sorteo**	*oon sohr-teh-oh*
a show	**un espectáculo**	*oon ehs-pehk-tah-koo-loh*
a special event	**un evento especial**	*oon eh-behn-toh ehs-peh-see-ahl*
a trip	**un viaje**	*oon bee-ah-heh*

To the Parent

Your child is taking part in a play (a special event).
Su hijo (hija) está participando en un drama (un evento especial).
soo ee-hoh (ee-hah) ehs-tah pahr-tee-see-pahn-doh ehn oon drah-mah (oon eh-behn-toh ehs-peh-see-ahl)

Would you like to come see him (her)?
¿Le gustaría venir a verlo(la)?
leh goos-tah-ree-ah beh-neer ah behr-loh(lah)

It will take place on _____ at _____ o'clock.
Tendrá lugar el _____ a la(s) _____.
tehn-drah loo-gahr ehl _____ ah lah(s) _____

The class is going on a field trip.
Nuestra clase va a hacer una gira.
noo-ehs-trah klah-seh bah ah ah-sehr oo-nah hee-rah

We are going to visit _____.
Vamos a visitar _____.
bah-mohs ah bee-see-tahr _____

The trip is for _____.
La excursión es por _____.
ehl ehk-skoor-see-ohn ehs pohr _____

one day	**un día**	*oon dee-ah*
one night	**una noche**	*oo-nah noh-cheh*
one week	**una semana**	*oo-nah seh-mah-nah*

We need volunteers to come with us.
Necesitamos voluntarios para acompañarnos.
neh-seh-see-tah-mohs boh-loon-tah-ree-ohs pah-rah ah-kohm-pah-nyahr-nohs

Please let me know if you will be available to help.
Favor de informarme si puede ayudarnos con esta actividad.
fah-bohr deh een-fohr-mahr-meh see poo-eh-deh ah-yoo-dahr-nohs kohn ehs-tah ahk-tee-bee-dahd

Please fill out and sign this notice and return it to school.
Por favor, llene y firme este aviso y devuélvalo a la escuela.
pohr fah-bohr yeh-neh ee feer-meh ehs-teh ah-bee-soh ee deh-boo-ehl-bah-loh ah lah ehs-koo-eh-lah

Please send $_____ for the trip.
Por favor, envíe _____ dólares para la excursión.
pohr fah-bohr ehn-bee-eh _____ doh-lah-rehs pah-rah lah ehk-skoor-see-ohn

To the Student

Would you like to see the show?
¿Quisiera[s] ver el espectáculo?
kee-see-eh-rah[s] behr ehl ehs-pehk-tah-koo-loh

Are you interested in the auction?
¿Le [Te] interesa la subasta?
leh [teh] een-teh-reh-sah lah soo-bahs-tah

Are you participating in the match?
¿Va[s] a participar en el partido?
bah[s] ah pahr-tee-see-pahr ehn ehl pahr-tee-doh

There is a festival on Saturday.
Hay un festival el sábado.
ah-ee oon fehs-tee-bahl ehl sah-bah-doh

Would you like to be a volunteer?
¿Quiere[s] ser voluntario(a)?
kee-eh-reh[s] sehr boh-loon-tah-ree-oh(ah)

10

Medical

Note:
1. Letters or words in brackets are used when using the familiar you **[tú]** form.
2. When speaking to more than one adult, **Ud.** (you, singular) becomes **Uds.** (you, plural) and an n is added to the conjugated verb form.
3. The formal you form is expressed in the same way as the third-person singular **él** (he) and **ella** (she) forms.

Parts of the Body

English	Spanish	Pronunciation
ankle	**el tobillo**	*ehl toh-bee-yoh*
arm	**el brazo**	*ehl brah-soh*
back	**la espalda**	*lah ehs-pahl-dah*
body	**el cuerpo**	*ehl koo-ehr-poh*
brain	**el cerebro**	*ehl seh-reh-broh*
cheek	**la mejilla**	*lah meh-hee-yah*
chest	**el pecho**	*ehl peh-choh*
chin	**la barbilla**	*lah bahr-bee-yah*
ear (inner)	**el oído**	*ehl oh-ee-doh*
ear (outer)	**la oreja**	*lah oh-reh-hah*
elbow	**el codo**	*ehl koh-doh*
eye	**el ojo**	*ehl oh-hoh*
face	**la cara**	*lah kah-rah*
finger	**el dedo**	*ehl deh-doh*

English	Spanish	Pronunciation
foot	el pie	*ehl pee-eh*
hair	el pelo	*ehl peh-loh*
hand	la mano	*lah mah-noh*
head	la cabeza	*lah kah-beh-sah*
heart	el corazón	*ehl koh-rah-sohn*
hip	la cadera	*lah kah-deh-rah*
knee	la rodilla	*lah rroh-dee-yah*
leg	la pierna	*lah pee-ehr-nah*
lip	el labio	*ehl lah-bee-oh*
lungs	los pulmones	*lohs pool-moh-nehs*
mouth	la boca	*lah boh-kah*
nail	la uña	*lah oo-nyah*
neck	el cuello	*ehl koo-eh-yoh*
nose	la nariz	*lah nah-rees*
shoulder	el hombro	*ehl ohm-broh*
skin	la piel	*lah pee-ehl*
spine	la espina dorsal	*lah ehs-pee-nah dohr-sahl*
stomach	el estómago	*ehl ehs-toh-mah-goh*
throat	la garganta	*lah gahr-gahn-tah*
toe	el dedo del pie	*ehl deh-doh dehl pee-eh*
tongue	la lengua	*lah lehn-goo-ah*
tooth	el diente	*ehl dee-ehn-teh*
uniform	el uniforme escolar	*ehl oo-nee-fohr-meh ehs-koh-lahr*
wrist	la muñeca	*lah moo-nyeh-kah*

To the Student

Show me where it hurts you.

Muéstreme [Muéstrame] dónde tiene [tienes] dolor (dónde le [te] duele).

moo-ehs-treh-meh [moo-ehs-trah-meh] dohn-deh tee-eh-neh [tee-eh-nehs] doh-lohr (dohn-deh leh [teh] doo-eh-leh)

Show me your left (right) leg.

Muéstreme [Muéstrame] la pierna izquierda (derecha).

moo-ehs-treh-meh [moo-ehs-trah-meh] lah pee-ehr-nah ees-kee-ehr-dah (deh-reh-chah)

Does your arm hurt?
¿Le [Te] duele el brazo?
leh [teh] doo-eh-leh ehl brah-soh

Do your eyes hurt?
¿Le [Te] duelen los ojos?
leh [teh] doo-eh-lehn lohs oh-hohs

To the Parent

He/She hurt his/her wrist.
Se hirió la muñeca.
seh ee-ree-oh lah moo-nyeh-kah

He/She sprained (broke) his/her ankle.
Se torció (rompió) el tobillo.
seh tohr-see-oh (rrohm-pee-oh) ehl toh-bee-yoh

He/She cut his/her finger.
Se cortó el dedo.
seh kohr-toh ehl deh-doh

Accidents

To the Student

How (When, Where) did you hurt yourself?
¿Cómo (¿Cuándo, ¿Dónde) se hirió?
koh-moh (koo-ahn-doh, dohn-deh) seh ee-ree-oh

Who hurt you?
¿Quién lo (la) [te] hirió?
kee-ehn loh (lah) [teh] ee-ree-oh

To the Parent

In case of an accident, whom should we call?
En caso de un accidente, ¿a quién debemos llamar?
ehn kah-soh deh oon ahk-see-dehn-teh ah kee-ehn deh-beh-mohs yah-mahr

Your son (daughter) had an accident _____.
Su hijo (hija) tuvo un accidente _____.
soo ee-hoh (ee-hah) too-boh oon ahk-see-dehn-teh _____

in the cafeteria	**en la cafetería**	*ehn lah kah-feh-teh-ree-ah*
in the classroom	**en el salón de clase**	*ehn ehl sah-lohn deh klah-seh*
in the dormitory	**en el dormitorio**	*ehn ehl dohr-mee-toh-ree-oh*
in the gym	**en el gimnasio**	*ehn ehl heem-nah-see-oh*
in the hallway	**en el pasillo**	*ehn ehl pah-see-yoh*
in the laboratory	**en el laboratorio**	*ehn ehl lah-boh-rah-toh-ree-oh*
in the schoolyard	**en el patio de recreo**	*ehn ehl pah-tee-oh deh rreh-kreh-oh*

He/She fell.
Se cayó.
seh kah-yoh

He/She cut himself/herself.
Se cortó.
seh kohr-toh

He/She burned himself/herself.
Se quemó.
seh keh-moh

He/She has (doesn't have) pain.
(No) Tiene dolor.
(noh) tee-eh-neh doh-lohr

He/She is (not) complaining.
(No) Se está quejando.
(noh) seh ehs-tah keh-hahn-doh

He/She is screaming.
Está gritando.
ehs-tah gree-tahn-doh

He/She is (not) crying.
(No) Está llorando.
(noh) ehs-tah yoh-rahn-doh

He/She is (not) bleeding.
(No) Está sangrando.
(noh) ehs-tah sahn-grahn-doh

He/She is (not) dizzy.
(No) tiene vértigo.
(noh) tee-eh-neh behr-tee-goh

He/She seems to have _____.
Parece tener _____.
pah-reh-seh teh-nehr _____

a broken bone	**un hueso roto**	*oon oo-eh-soh rroh-toh*
a bruise	**una contusión**	*oo-nah kohn-too-see-ohn*
a bump	**una hinchazón**	*oo-nah een-chah-sohn*
a burn	**una quemadura**	*oo-nah keh-mah-doo-rah*
a concussion	**una conmoción cerebral**	*oo-nah kohn-moh-see-ohn seh-reh-brahl*
a cut	**una cortadura**	*oo-nah kohr-tah-doo-rah*
a fever	**una fiebre**	*oo-nah fee-eh-breh*
a lump	**un bulto**	*oon bool-toh*
a pain	**un dolor**	*oon doh-lohr*
a scratch	**un rasguño**	*oon rrahs-goo-nyoh*
a sprain	**una torcedura**	*oo-nah tohr-seh-doo-rah*
a wound	**una herida**	*oo-nah eh-ree-dah*
a swelling	**una inflamación**	*oo-nah een-flah-mah-see-yohn*

He/She is in the nurse's office.
Está en el consultorio de la enfermera.
ehs-tah ehn ehl kohn-sool-toh-ree-oh deh lah ehn-fehr-meh-rah

He/She needs to go to the doctor.
Tiene que ir al médico.
tee-eh-neh keh eer ahl meh-dee-koh

He/She needs to go to the hospital.
Tiene que ir al hospital.
tee-eh-neh keh eer ahl ohs-pee-tahl

He/She needs stitches.
Necesita puntos.
neh-seh-see-tah poon-tohs

He/She needs X-rays.
Necesita rayos equis.
neh-seh-see-tah rrah-yohs eh-kees

He/She needs a tetanus shot.
Necesita una inyección contra el tétanos.
neh-seh-see-tah oo-nah een-yehk-see-ohn kohn-trah ehl teh-tah-nohs

Would you like to speak to him/her?
¿Querría hablarle?
keh-rree-ah ahb-lahr-leh

Can you come to the school immediately?
¿Puede venir a la escuela en seguida?
poo-eh-deh beh-neer ah lah ehs-koo-eh-lah ehn seh-gee-dah

It is (not) an emergency.
(No) Es una urgencia.
(noh) ehs oo-nah oor-hehn-see-ah

The nurse can (not) give him/her _____.
La enfermera (no) puede darle _____.
lah ehn-fehr-meh-rah (noh) poo-eh-deh dahr-leh _____

antibiotics	**los antibióticos**	*lohs ahn-tee-bee-oh-tee-kohs*
an antiseptic	**un antiséptico**	*oon ahn-tee-sehp-tee-koh*
aspirins	**las aspirinas**	*lahs ahs-pee-ree-nahs*
a Band-Aid	**una curita**	*oo-nah koo-ree-tah*
a bandage	**un vendaje**	*oon behn-dah-heh*
cough medicine	**el jarabe para la tos**	*ehl hah-rah-beh pah-rah lah tohs*
ear drops	**las gotas para los oídos**	*lahs goh-tahs pah-rah lohs oh-ee-dohs*
eye drops	**las gotas para los ojos**	*lahs goh-tahs pah-rah lohs oh-hohs*
an ice pack	**una bolsa de hielo**	*oo-nah bohl-sah deh ee-eh-loh*
iodine	**el yodo**	*ehl yoh-doh*
medicine	**la medicina**	*lah meh-dee-see-nah*
pills	**las píldoras**	*lahs peel-doh-rahs*

Illnesses and Medical Conditions

English	Spanish	Pronunciation
acne	el acné	ehl ahk-neh
allergic reaction	una reacción alérgica	oo-nah rreh-ahk-see-yohn ah-lehr-hee-kah
anorexia	la anorexia nerviosa	lah ah-noh-rehk-see-ah nehr-bee-oh-sah
appendicitis	la apendicitis	lah ah-pehn-dee-see-tees
asthma	el asma	ehl ahs-mah
bronchitis	la bronquitis	lah brohn-kee-tees
bulimia	la bulimia	lah boo-lee-mee-ah
cancer	el cáncer	ehl kahn-sehr
chicken pox	la varicela	lah bah-ree-seh-lah
cold	un resfriado	oon rrehs-free-ah-doh
cold	un catarro	oon kah-tah-rroh
conjunctivitis	la conjuntivitis	lah kohn-hoon-tee-bee-tees
constipation	el estreñimiento	ehl ehs-treh-nyee-mee-ehn-toh
chronic disease	una enfermedad crónica	oo-nah ehn-fehr-meh-dahd kroh-nee-kah
degenerative disease	una enfermedad degenerativa	oo-nah ehn-fehr-meh-dahd deh-heh-neh-rah-tee-bah
diabetes	la diabetes	lah dee-ah-beh-tehs
diarrhea	la diarrea	lah dee-ah-rreh-ah
diphtheria	la difteria	lah deef-teh-ree-ah
dysentery	la disentería	lah dee-sehn-teh-ree-ah
eating disorder	un desorden alimenticio	oon dehs-ohr-dehn ah-lee-mehn-tee-see-oh
epilepsy	la epilepsia	lah eh-pee-lehp-see-ah
fleas	las pulgas	lahs pool-gahs
flu	la gripe	lah gree-peh
genetic disease	una enfermedad genética	oo-nah ehn-fehr-meh-dahd heh-neh-tee-kah
German measles	la rubeola	lah rroo-beh-oh-lah
hay fever	la fiebre del heno	lah fee-eh-breh dehl eh-noh
headache	un dolor de cabeza	oon doh-lohr deh kah-beh-sah

English	Spanish	Pronunciation
heart condition	una condición cardíaca	*oo-nah kohn-dee-see-ohn kahr-dee-ah-kah*
heart murmur	un soplo en el corazón	*oon soh-ploh ehn ehl koh-rah-sohn*
hepatitis	la hepatitis	*lah ee-pah-tee-tees*
infection	una infección	*oo-nah een-fehk-see-ohn*
leukemia	la leucemia	*lah leh-oo-seh-mee-ah*
lice	los piojos	*lohs pee-oh-hos*
Lyme's disease	la enfermedad de Lyme	*lah ehn-fehr-meh-dahd deh lah-eem*
measles	el sarampión	*ehl sah-rahm-pee-ohn*
mental disorder	un trastorno mental	*oon trahs-toor-noh mehn-tahl*
mumps	las paperas	*lahs pah-peh-rahs*
neurological disease	una enfermedad neurológica	*oo-nah ehn-fehr-meh-dahd neh-oo-roh-loh-hee-kah*
pneumonia	la pulmonía	*lah pool-moh-nee-yah*
pregnancy	el embarazo	*ehl ehm-bah-rah-soh*
polio	la poliomelitis	*lah poh-lee-oh-meh-lee-tees*
rabies	la rabia	*lah rrah-bee-ah*
scarlet fever	la escarlatina	*lah ehs-kahr-lah-tee-nah*
small pox	la viruela	*lah bee-roo-eh-lah*
stomache ache	un dolor de estómago	*oon doh-lohr deh ehs-toh-mah-goh*
tetanus	el tétanos	*ehl teh-tah-nohs*
ticks	las garrapatas	*lahs gah-rrah-pah-tahs*
tonsilitis	la amigdalitis	*lah ah-meeg-dah-lee-tees*
toothache	un dolor de muelas	*oon doh-lohr deh moo-eh-lahs*
tuberculosis	la tuberculosis	*lah too-behr-koo-loh-sees*
typhoid	la fiebre tifoidea	*lah fee-eh-breh tee-foh-ee-deh-ah*
vertigo	el vértigo	*ehl behr-tee-goh*
whooping cough	la tos ferina	*lah tohs feh-ree-nah*
worms	los gusanos	*lohs goo-sah-nohs*

Speaking about Illnesses and Medical Conditions

Has your child been vaccinated again small pox? When?
**¿Ha recibido su hijo (hija) una vacuna contra la varicela?
¿Cuándo?**
*ah rreh-see-bee-doh soo ee-hoh (ee-hah) oo-nah bah-koo-nah kohn-trah lah
bah-ree-seh-lah koo-ahn-doh*

Your child needs a vaccination against whooping cough.
Su hijo (hija) necesita una vacuna contra la tos ferina.
*soo ee-hoh (ee-hah) neh-seh-see-tah oo-nah bah-koo-nah kohn-trah lah tohs
feh-ree-nah*

What illness does your child have?
¿Qué enfermedad tiene su hijo (hija)?
keh ehn-fehr-meh-dahd tee-eh-neh soo ee-hoh (ee-hah)

Is it a chronic (neurological, degenerative) disease?
¿Es una enfermedad crónica (neurológica, degenerativa)?
*ehs oo-nah ehn-fehr-meh-dahd kroh-nee-kah (neh-oo-roh-loh-hee-kah, deh-
heh-neh-rah-tee-bah)*

How long has your child suffered from diabetes?
¿Desde cuándo sufre de diabetes su hijo (hija)?
dehs-deh koo-ahn-doh soo-freh deh dee-ah-beh-tehs soo ee-hoh (ee-hah)

What treatment is he (she) receiving?
¿Qué tratamiento médico está recibiendo?
keh trah-tah-mee-ehn-toh meh-dee-koh ehs-tah rreh-see-bee-ehn-doh

Does he (she) need dialysis?
¿Necesita diálisis?
neh-seh-see-tah dee-ah-lee-sees

Does your child have hay fever?
¿Es su hijo (hija) alérgico(a) al polen?
ehs soo ee-hoh (ee-hah) ah-lehr-hee-koh(kah) ahl poh-lehn

What medicines does your child take?
¿Qué medicinas toma?
keh meh-dee-see-nahs toh-mah

Is your child depressed?
¿Está deprimido(a) su hijo (hija)?
ehs-tah deh-pree-meeh-doh(dah) soo ee-hoh (ee-hah)

What measures do we have to take?
¿Qué medidas debemos tomar?
keh meh-dee-dahs deh-beh-mohs toh-mahr

Does your child need to take medicine while at school?
¿Tiene que tomar medicinas su hijo (hija) mientras está en la escuela?
tee-eh-neh keh toh-mahr meh-dee-see-nahs soo ee-hoh (ee-hah) mee-ehn-trahs ehs-tah ehn lah ehs-koo-eh-lah

When was your child's last visit to the doctor?
¿Cuándo fue la última visita de su hijo (hija) al médico?
koo-ahn-doh foo-eh lah ool-tee-mah bee-see-tah deh soo ee-hoh (ee-hah) ahl meh-dee-koh

Does your child have an eating disorder? Which one?
¿Tiene su hijo (hija) un desorden alimenticio? ¿Cuál?
tee-eh-neh soo ee-hoh (ee-hah) oon dehs-ohr-dehn ah-lee-mehn-tee-see-oh koo-ahl

What help are you getting for your child's eating disorder?
¿Qué ayuda está recibiendo para el desorden alimenticio de su hijo (hija)?
keh ah-yoo-dah ehs-tah rreh-see-bee-ehn-doh pah-rah ehl dehs-ohr-dehn ah-lee-mehn-tee-see-oh deh soo ee-hoh (ee-hah)

Does anyone in your family have a heart condition?
¿Tiene alguien en su familia una condición cardíaca?
tee-eh-neh ahl-gee-ehn ehn soo fah-mee-lee-ah oo-nah kohn-dee-see-ohn kahr-dee-ah-kah

Your child has a stomachache.
Su hijo (hija) tiene un dolor de estómago.
soo ee-hoh (ee-hah) tee-eh-neh oon doh-lohr deh ehs-toh-mah-goh

Your child is complaining of a toothache.
Su hijo (hija) se está quejando de un dolor de muelas.
soo ee-hoh (ee-hah) seh ehs-tah keh-hahn-doh deh oon doh-lohr deh moo-eh-lahs

How often does your child complain of a headache?
¿Con qué frecuencia se queja su hijo (hija) de un dolor de cabeza?
kohn keh freh-koo-ehn-see-ah seh keh-hah soo ee-hoh (ee-hah) deh oon doh-lohr deh kah-beh-sah

It could be that your child has scarlet fever.
Podría ser que su hijo (hija) tenga la escarlatina.
poh-dree-ah sehr keh soo ee-hoh (ee-hah) tehn-gah lah ehs-kahr-lah-tee-nah

Does your child have any physical (respiratory, visual, hearing) problems?
¿Tiene su hijo (hija) problemas físicos (respiratorios, de la visión, del oído)?
tee-eh-neh soo ee-hoh (ee-hah) proh-bleh-mahs fee-see-kohs (rrehs-pee-rah-toh-ree-ohs, deh lah bee-see-ohn, dehl oh-ee-doh)

Your child needs a blood (urine) test.
Su hijo (hija) necesita un examen de la sangre (orina).
soo ee-hoh (ee-hah) neh-seh-see-tah oon ehk-sah-mehn deh lah sahn-greh (oh-ree-nah)

Check your child for lice.
Verifique si su hijo (hija) tiene piojos.
beh-ree-fee-keh see soo ee-hoh (ee-hah) tee-eh-neh pee-oh-hohs

Your child was bitten by a tick and must see a doctor immediately.
Su hijo (hija) fue picado(a) por una garrapata y tiene que ir al médico en seguida.
soo ee-hoh (ee-hah) foo-eh pee-kah-doh(dah) pohr oo-nah gah-rrah-pah-tah ee tee-eh-neh keh eer ahl meh-dee-koh ehn seh-gee-dah

He/She may have Lyme's disease.
Podría tener la enfermedad de Lyme.
poh-dree-ah teh-nehr lah ehn-fehr-meh-dahd de lah-eem

Your child is sick.
Su hijo (hija) está enfermo(a).
soo ee-hoh (ee-hah) ehs-tah ehn-fehr-moh(mah)

Your child vomited.
Su hijo (hija) vomitó.
soo ee-hoh (ee-hah) boh-mee-toh

Your child has (symptoms of) the flu.
Su hijo (hija) tiene (síntomas de) la gripe.
soo ee-hoh (ee-hah) tee-eh-neh (seen-toh-mahs deh) lah gree-peh

Please come to school to take him (her) home.
Por favor, venga a la escuela para que se lo (la) lleve a casa.
pohr fah-bohr behn-gah ah lah ehs-koo-eh-lah pah-rah keh seh loh (lah) yeh-beh ah kah-sah

Your child should see a doctor.
Su hijo (hija) debe ir al médico.
soo ee-hoh (ee-hah) deh-beh eer ahl meh-dee-koh

Your child should go to the hospital.
Su hijo (hija) debe ir al hospital.
soo ee-hoh (ee-hah) deh-beh eer ahl ohs-pee-tahl

If your daughter is pregnant, she may (not) remain in school.
Si su hija está embarazada, (no) puede quedarse en la escuela.
see soo ee-hah ehs-tah ehm-bah-rah-sah-dah (noh) poo-eh-deh keh-dahr-seh ehn lah ehs-koo-eh-lah

There are several alternative programs.
Hay varios programas alternativos.
ah-ee bah-ree-ohs proh-grah-mahs ahl-tehr-nah-tee-bohs

Does your child see a psychologist (psychiatrist)?
¿Va su hijo (hija) a un psicólogo (psiquiatra)?
bah soo ee-hoh (ee-hah) ah oon see-koh-loh-goh (see-kee-ah-trah)

You can make an appointment with the school psychologist.
Puede hacer una cita con el psicólogo de la escuela.
poo-eh-deh ah-sehr oo-nah see-tah kohn ehl see-koh-loh-goh deh lah ehs-koo-eh-lah

Signs and Symptoms

English	Spanish	Pronunciation
abscess	**un absceso**	*oon ahb-seh-soh*
allergies	**las alergias**	*lahs ah-lehr-hee-ahs*
backache	**un dolor de espalda**	*oon doh-lohr deh ehs-pahl-dah*
blister	**una ampolla**	*oo-nah ahm-poh-yah*
bruise	**una contusión**	*oo-nah kohn-too-see-ohn*

English	Spanish	Pronunciation
chills	**los escalofríos**	*lohs ehs-kah-loh-free-ohs*
convulsions	**las convulsiones**	*lahs kohn-bool-see-oh-nehs*
cough	**una tos**	*oo-nah tohs*
dizziness	**los mareos**	*lohs mah-reh-ohs*
fever	**la fiebre**	*lah fee-eh-breh*
hiccups	**el hipo**	*ehl ee-poh*
insect bite	**una picadura de insecto**	*oo-nah pee-kah-doo-rah deh een-sehk-toh*
itching	**la picazón**	*lah pee-kah-sohn*
lump	**un bulto**	*oon bool-toh*
migraine	**la jaqueca**	*lah hah-keh-kah*
nausea	**la náusea**	*lah nah-oo-seh-ah*
numbness	**el adormecimiento**	*ehl ah-dohr-meh-see-mee-ehn-toh*
phlegm	**la flema**	*lah fleh-mah*
seizures	**los ataques**	*lohs ah-tah-kehs*
stomach cramps	**las retortijones de vientre**	*lahs rreh-tohr-tee-hoh-nehs deh bee-ehn-treh*
swelling	**la hinchazón**	*lah een-chah-sohn*

Speaking about Symptoms

How often does your child have a fever?
¿Con qué frecuencia tiene fiebre su hijo (hija)?
kohn keh freh-koo-ehn-see-ah tee-eh-neh fee-eh-breh soo ee-hoh (ee-hah)

Does your child often have the hiccups?
¿Tiene hipo a menudo su hijo (hija)?
tee-eh-neh ee-poh ah meh-noo-doh soo ee-hoh (ee-hah)

Your child is coughing (sneezing) a lot.
Su hijo (hija) está tosiendo (estornudando) mucho.
soo ee-hoh (ee-hah) ehs-tah toh-see-ehn-doh (ehs-tohr-noo-dahn-doh) moo-choh

Has your child had a seizure before?
¿Ha tenido ataques su hijo (hija) anteriormente?
ah teh-nee-doh ah-tah-kehs soo ee-hoh (ee-hah) ahn-teh-ree-ohr-mehn-teh

How often?
¿Con qué frecuencia?
kohn keh freh-koo-ehn-see-ah

Your child has the symptoms of epilepsy.
Su hijo (hija) tiene síntomas de epilepsia.
soo ee-hoh (ee-hah) tee-eh-neh seen-toh-mahs deh eh-pee-lehp-see-ah

For how long has your child complained of dizziness?
¿Desde cuándo se queja su hijo (hija) de mareos?
dehs-deh koo-ahn-doh seh keh-hah soo ee-hoh (ee-hah) deh mah-reh-ohs

What does your child take for his (her) allergies?
¿Qué toma su hijo (hija) para las alergias?
keh toh-mah soo ee-hoh (ee-hah) pah-rah lahs ah-lehr-hee-ahs

Is your child allergic to dust (mold)?
¿Es alérgico(a) al polvo (moho) su hijo (hija)?
ehs ah-lehr-hee-koh(kah) ahl pohl-boh (moh-oh) soo ee-hoh (ee-hah)

Is your child allergic to insect bites?
¿Es alérgico(a) a las picaduras de insectos su hijo (hija)?
ehs ah-lehr-hee-koh(kah) ah lahs pee-kah-doo-rahs deh een-sehk-tohs soo ee-hoh (ee-hah)

Your child needs medical attention.
Su hijo (hija) necesita atención médica.
soo ee-hoh (ee-hah) neh-seh-see-tah ah-tehn-see-ohn meh-dee-kah

Do you have medical insurance?
¿Tiene Ud. seguro médico?
tee-eh-neh oo-stehd seh-goo-roh meh-dee-koh

Abuse

To the Student

Why do you have so many black-and-blue marks?
¿Por qué tiene(s) tantos moretones?
pohr keh tee-eh-neh(s) tahn-tohs moh-reh-toh-nehs

Does someone hit (hurt) you? Who?
¿Alguien le [te] está pegando (haciendo daño)? ¿Quién(es)?
ahl-gee-ehn leh [teh] ehs-tah peh-gahn-doh (ah-see-ehn-doh dah-nyoh) kee-ehn(ehs)

Does someone touch you where they shouldn't?
¿Alguien lo (la) [te] toca donde no debe?
ahl-gee-ehn loh (lah) [teh] toh-kah dohn-deh noh deh-beh

You can show (tell) me where they touch you.
Puede[s] mostrarme (decirme) dónde lo (la) [te] tocan.
poo-eh-deh[s] mohs-trahr-meh (deh-seer-meh) dohn-deh loh (lah) [teh] toh-kahn

Have you told your parents?
¿Se lo ha[s] dicho a sus [tus] padres?
seh lo ah[s] dee-choh ah soos [toos] pah-drehs

Do you want to speak to a counselor (nurse, doctor)?
¿Quiere[s] hablar con un(a) consejero(a) (enfermero(a), médico(a))?
kee-eh-reh[s] ah-blahr kohn oon(oo-nah) kohn-seh-heh-roh(rah) (ehn-fehr-meh-roh(rah), meh-dee-koh(kah))

Everything you say is strictly confidential.
Todo lo que diga[s] es completamente confidencial.
toh-doh loh keh dee-gah[s] ehs kohm-pleh-tah-mehn-teh kohn-fee-dehn-see-ahl

To the Parent

This is a very serious matter.
Es un asunto muy serio.
ehs oon ah-soon-toh moo-ee seh-ree-oh

Someone is abusing your child.
Alguien está maltratando a su hijo (hija).
ahl-gee-ehn ehs-tah mahl-trah-tahn-doh ah soo ee-hoh (ee-hah)

Are you aware of this?
¿Es Ud. consciente de ésto?
ehs oos-tehd kohn-see-ehn-teh deh ehs-toh

Do you have any idea whom that may be?
¿Sabe quién puede ser?
sah-beh kee-ehn poo-eh-deh sehr

Your child needs help.
Su hijo (hija) necesita ayuda.
soo ee-hoh (ee-hah) neh-seh-see-tah ah-yoo-dah

He (She) needs professional counseling.
Necesita consejos profesionales.
neh-seh-see-tah koh-seh-hohs proh-feh-see-oh-nah-lehs

I am obligated to report this matter to the authorities.
Estoy obligado(a) a informar a las autoridades sobre este asunto.
ehs-toh-ee oh-blee-gah-doh(dah) ah een-fohr-mahr ah lahs ah-oo-toh-ree-dah-dehs soh-breh ehs-teh ah-soon-toh

Nutritional Requirements

English	Spanish	Pronunciation
apple	la manzana	*lah mahn-sah-nah*
banana	la banana	*lah bah-nah-nah*
beef	la carne de vaca	*lah kahr-neh deh bah-kah*
bread	el pan	*ehl pahn*
cake	el pastel	*ehl pahs-tehl*
carrot	la zanahoria	*lah sah-nah-oh-ree-ah*
cheese	el queso	*ehl keh-soh*
cherry	la cereza	*lah seh-reh-sah*
chicken	el pollo	*ehl poh-yoh*
coffee	el café	*ehl kah-feh*
cookie	la galletita	*lah gah-yeh-tee-tah*
corn	el maíz	*ehl mah-ees*
dessert	el postre	*ehl pohs-treh*
eggs	los huevos	*lohs oo-eh-bohs*
fish	el pescado	*ehl pehs-kah-doh*
fruit	la fruta	*lah froo-tah*
grape	la uva	*lah oo-bah*
green beans	los ejotes	*lohs eh-hoh-tehs*
ham	el jamón	*ehl hah-mohn*
hamburger	la hamburguesa	*lah ahm-boor-geh-sah*
ice cream	el helado	*ehl eh-lah-doh*
jam	la mermelada	*lah mehr-meh-lah-dah*
juice	el jugo	*ehl hoo-goh*
ketchup	la salsa de tomate	*lah sahl-sah deh toh-mah-teh*
lemon	el limón	*ehl lee-mohn*
lemonade	la limonada	*lah lee-moh-nah-dah*
lettuce	la lechuga	*lah leh-choo-gah*

English	Spanish	Pronunciation
milk	**la leche**	*lah leh-cheh*
nuts	**las nueces**	*lahs noo-eh-sehs*
orange	**la naranja**	*lah nah-rahn-hah*
peach	**el melocotón**	*ehl meh-loh-koh-tohn*
peanut	**el cacahuete**	*ehl kah-kah-hoo-eh-teh*
peanut	**el maní**	*ehl mah-nee*
pear	**la pera**	*lah peh-rah*
peas	**los guisantes**	*lohs gee-sahn-tehs*
pepper	**la pimienta**	*lah pee-mee-ehn-tah*
pineapple	**la piña**	*lah pee-nyah*
pork	**el cerdo**	*ehl sehr-doh*
potatoes	**las papas**	*lahs pah-pahs*
pudding	**el pudín**	*ehl poo-deen*
rice	**el arroz**	*ehl ah-rrohs*
roll	**el panecillo**	*ehl pah-neh-see-yoh*
salad	**la ensalada**	*lah ehn-sah-lah-dah*
salt	**la sal**	*lah sahl*
sandwich	**el sándwich**	*ehl sahnd-weech*
seafood	**los mariscos**	*lohs mah-rees-kohs*
soda	**la gaseosa**	*lah gah-seh-oh-sah*
soup	**la sopa**	*lah soh-pah*
strawberry	**la fresa**	*lah freh-sah*
tea	**el té**	*ehl teh*
tomato	**el tomate**	*ehl toh-mah-teh*
turkey	**el pavo**	*ehl pah-boh*
vegetable	**la verdura**	*lah behr-doo-rah*
watermelon	**la sandía**	*lah sahn-dee-ah*
yogurt	**el yogur**	*ehl yoh-goor*

Referring to Foods and Meals

Is your child allowed to eat meat?
¿Deja que su hijo (hija) coma carne?
deh-hah keh soo ee-hoh (ee-hah) koh-mah kahr-neh

Is your child a vegetarian?
¿Es vegetariano(a) su hijo (hija)?
ehs beh-heh-tah-ree-ah-noh(nah) soo ee-hoh (ee-hah)

Can your child eat dairy products?
¿Puede tolerar los productos lácteos su hijo (hija)?
poo-eh-deh toh-leh-rahr lohs proh-dook-tohs lahk-teh-ohs soo ee-hoh (ee-hah)

Does your child have any dietary restrictions?
¿Tiene su hijo (hija) restricciones alimenticias?
tee-eh-neh soo ee-hoh (ee-hah) rrehs-treek-see-oh-nehs ah-lee-mehn-tee-see-ahs

What are they?
¿Cuáles son?
koo-ah-lehs sohn

Does your child follow a special diet?
¿Sigue un régimen especial su hijo (hija)?
see-geh oon rreh-hee-mehn ehs-peh-see-ahl soo ee-hoh (ee-hah)

For what reason?
¿Por qué?
pohr keh

Is your child's sugar (fat) intake limited?
¿Está limitado el consumo de azúcar (grasa) de su hijo (hija)?
eh-stah lee-mee-tah-doh ehl kohn-soo-moh deh ah-soo-kahr (grah-sah) deh soo ee-hoh (ee-hah)

Does your child eat breakfast in the morning?
¿Toma su hijo (hija) el desayuno por la mañana?
toh-mah soo ee-hoh (ee-hah) ehl deh-sah-yoo-noh pohr lah mah-nyah-nah

He/She should eat a good breakfast.
Debe tomar un buen desayuno.
deh-beh toh-mahr oon boo-ehn deh-sah-yoo-noh

What does he/she eat?
¿Qué come?
keh koh-meh

What does your child normally eat for lunch?
¿Qué toma su hijo (hija) generalmente de almuerzo?
keh toh-mah soo ee-hoh (ee-hah) heh-neh-rahl-mehn-teh deh ahl-moo-ehr-soh

Is your child allergic to any food(s)? Which one(s)?
¿Es alérgico(a) a algún comestible su hijo (hija)? ¿A cuál(es)?
ehs ah-lehr-gee-koh(kah) ah ahl-goon koh-meh-stee-bleh soo ee-hoh (ee-hah) ah koo-ahl(koo-ah-lehs)

Is your child allergic to shellfish?
¿Es alérgico(a) a los mariscos su hijo (hija)?
ehs ah-lehr-gee-koh(kah) ah lohs mah-rees-kohs soo ee-hoh (ee-hah)

Does your child require a gluten-free diet?
¿Necesita su hijo (hija) un régimen libre de gluten?
neh-seh-see-tah soo ee-hoh (ee-hah) oon rreh-hee-mehn lee-breh deh gloo-tehn

Does your child like fruits (vegetables)?
¿Le gustan a su hijo (hija) las frutas (verduras)?
leh goo-stahn ah soo ee-hoh (ee-hah) lahs froo-tahs (behr-doo-rahs)

Does your child drink enough milk?
¿Toma suficiente leche su hijo (hija)?
toh-mah soo-fee-see-ehn-teh leh-cheh soo ee-hoh (ee-hah)

Does your child take vitamins?
¿Toma vitaminas su hijo (hija)?
toh-mah bee-tah-mee-nahs soo ee-hoh (ee-hah)

Quantities

English	Spanish	Pronunciation
a bag of	un saco de	*oon sah-koh deh*
a bar of	una tableta de	*oo-nah tah-bleh-tah deh*
	(una barra de)	*(oo-nah bah-rrah deh)*
a bottle of	una botella de	*oo-nah boh-teh-yah deh*
a box of	una caja de	*oo-nah kah-hah de*
a can of	una lata de	*oo-nah lah-tah deh*
a cup of	una taza de	*oo-nah tah-sah deh*
a glass of	un vaso de	*oon bah-soh deh*
a handful of	un puñado de	*oon poo-nyah-doh deh*
a jar of	un pomo de	*oon poh-moh deh*
	(un frasco de)	*(oon frahs-koh deh)*
a liter of	un litro de	*oon lee-troh deh*
a lot	mucho (mucha)	*moo-choh (moo-chah)*
a mouthful of	un bocado de	*oon boh-kah-doh deh*
a package of	un paquete de	*oon pah-keh-teh deh*
a piece of	un trozo de	*oon troh-soh deh*
a pound of	quinientos	*kee-nee-ehn-tohs*
	gramos de	*grah-mohs deh*
a quart of	un cuartillo de	*oon koo-ahr-tee-yoh deh*

English	Spanish	Pronunciation
a slice of	**un trozo de**	*oon troh-soh de*
a tablespoon of	**una cucharada de**	*oo-nah koo-chah-rah-dah deh*
a teaspoon of	**una cucharadita de**	*oo-nah koo-chah-rah-dee-tah deh*
enough	**bastante (suficiente)**	*bahs-tahn-teh (soo-fee-see-ehn-teh)*
little	**poco (poca)**	*poh-koh (poh-kah)*
too much	**demasiado(a)**	*deh-mah-see-ah-doh(dah)*

Does your child eat enough vegetables?
¿Come su hijo (hija) suficientes verduras?
koh-meh soo ee-hoh (ee-hah) soo-fee-see-ehn-tehs behr-doo-rahs

How much milk does your child drink per day?
¿Cuánta leche bebe su hijo (hija) diariamente?
koo-ahn-tah leh-cheh beh-beh soo ee-hoh (ee-hah) dee-ah-ree-ah-mehn-teh

Your child eats too many sweets.
Su hijo (hija) come demasiados dulces.
soo ee-hoh (ee-hah) koh-meh deh-mah-see-ah-dohs dool-sehs

Does your child take a teaspoon or a tablespoon of his (her) medicine?
¿Toma su hijo (hija) una cucharadita o una cucharada de medicina?
toh-mah soo ee-hoh (ee-hah) oo-nah koo-chah-rah-dee-tah oh oo-nah koo-chah-rah-dah deh meh-dee-see-nah

You child eats very little in school.
Su hijo (hija) come muy poco en la escuela.
soo ee-hoh (ee-hah) koh-meh moo-ee poh-koh ehn lah ehs-koo-eh-lah

Your child swallowed a mouthful of pills.
Su hijo (hija) se tragó un bocado de píldoras.
soo ee-hoh (ee-hah) seh trah-goh oon boh-kah-doh deh peel-doh-rahs

Emergencies

Your child has had an accident, but he (she) is fine now.
Su hijo (hija) tuvo un accidente, pero está bien ahora.
soo ee-hoh (ee-hah) too-boh oon ahk-see-dehn-teh peh-roh ehs-tah bee-ehn ah-oh-rah

Please come to school immediately.
Venga a la escuela en seguida, por favor.
behn-gah ah lah ehs-koo-eh-lah ehn seh-gee-dah pohr fah-bohr

He/She wants to go home.
Quiere irse a casa.
kee-eh-reh eer-seh ah kah-sah

We had (didn't have) to call 911.
(No) Tuvimos que llamar al nueve-uno-uno.
(noh) too-bee-mohs keh yah-mahr ahl noo-eh-beh-oo-noh-oo-noh

An ambulance is on its way.
Una ambulancia está en camino.
oo-nah ahm-boo-lahn-see-ah ehs-tah ehn kah-mee-noh

The paramedics gave first aid on the scene.
Los paramédicos le dieron los primeros auxilios en el lugar del accidente.
lohs pah-rah-meh-dee-kohs leh dee-eh-rohn lohs pree-meh-rohs ah-oo-see-lee-ohs ehn ehl loo-gahr dehl ahk-see-dehn-teh

An ambulance took him (her) to the hospital.
Una ambulancia lo (la) llevó al hospital.
oo-nah ahm-boo-lahn-see-ah loh (lah) yeh-boh ahl ohs-pee-tahl

11

Content Areas

Note:
1. Letters or words in brackets are used when using the familiar you **[tú]** form.
2. When speaking to more than one adult, **Ud.** (you, singular) becomes **Uds.** (you, plural) and an n is added to the conjugated verb form.
3. The formal you form is expressed in the same way as the third-person singular **él** (he) and **ella** (she) forms.

School Subjects

English	Spanish	Pronunciation
algebra	el álgebra	*ehl ahl-heh-brah*
art	el arte	*ehl ahr-teh*
band	la banda	*lah bahn-dah*
biology	la biología	*lah bee-oh-loh-gee-ah*
calculus	el cálculo	*ehl kahl-koo-loh*
chemistry	la química	*lah kee-mee-kah*
Chinese	el chino	*ehl chee-noh*
chorus	el coro	*ehl koh-roh*
computer science	la informática	*lah een-fohr-mah-tee-kah*
drama	el drama	*ehl drah-mah*
drawing	el diseño	*ehl dee-seh-nyoh*
driver's education	la clase de conducir	*lah klah-seh deh kohn-doo-seer*
earth science	la geología	*lah heh-oh-loh-hee-ah*

143

English	Spanish	Pronunciation
economics	**la economía**	*lah eh-kohh-noh-mee-ah*
English	**el inglés**	*ehl een-glehs*
English as a Second Language	**el inglés como segundo idioma**	*ehl een-glehs koh-moh seh-goon-doh ee-dee-oh-mah*
foreign language	**el idioma extranjero**	*ehl ee-dee-oh-mah ehks-trahn-heh-roh*
French	**el francés**	*ehl frahn-sehs*
geography	**la geografía**	*lah heh-oh-grah-fee-ah*
geometry	**la geometría**	*lah heh-oh-meh-tree-ah*
German	**el alemán**	*ehl ah-leh-mahn*
global studies	**los estudios globales**	*lohs ehs-too-dee-ohs gloh-bah-lehs*
health	**la salud**	*lah sah-lood*
history	**la historia**	*lah ees-toh-ree-ah*
industrial arts	**las artes industriales**	*lahs ahr-tehs een-doos-tree-ah-lehs*
Italian	**el italiano**	*ehl ee-tah-lee-ah-noh*
Japanese	**el japonés**	*ehl hah-poh-nehs*
journalism	**el periodismo**	*ehl peh-ree-oh-dees-moh*
Latin	**el latín**	*ehl lah-teen*
literature	**la literatura**	*lah lee-teh-rah-too-rah*
mathematics	**las matemáticas**	*lahs mah-teh-mah-tee-kahs*
music	**la música**	*lah moo-see-kah*
orchestra	**la orquesta**	*lah ohr-kehs-tah*
penmanship	**la caligrafía**	*lah kah-lee-grah-fee-ah*
physical education	**la educación física**	*lah eh-doo-kah-see-ohn fee-see-kah*
physics	**la física**	*lah fee-see-kah*
Portuguese	**el portugués**	*ehl pohr-too-gehs*
psychology	**la psicología**	*lah see-koh-loh-hee-ah*
reading	**la lectura**	*lah lehk-too-rah*
religion	**la religión**	*lah rreh-lee-hee-ohn*
science	**la ciencia**	*lah see-ehn-see-ah*
social studies	**los estudios sociales**	*lohs ehs-too-dee-ohs soh-see-ah-lehs*
special education	**la educación especial**	*lah eh-doo-kah-see-ohn ehs-peh-see-ahl*
speech	**el discurso**	*ehl dees-koor-soh*

English	Spanish	Pronunciation
spelling	la ortografía	*lah ohr-toh-grah-fee-ah*
technology	la tecnología	*lah tehk-noh-loh-hee-ah*
trigonometry	la trigonometría	*lah tree-goh-noh-meh-tree-ah*
U.S. history	la historia de los Estados Unidos	*lah ees-toh-ree-ah deh lohs ehs-tah-dohs oo-nee-dohs*
word processing	el procesamiento de textos	*ehl proh-seh-sah-mee-ehn-toh deh tehks-tohs*
world history	la historia mundial	*lah ees-toh-ree-ah moon-dee-ahl*
writing	la escritura	*lah ehs-kree-too-rah*

To the Parent

What subjects does your child like?
¿Qué materias le gustan a su hijo (hija)?
keh mah-teh-ree-ahs leh goos-tahn ah soo ee-hoh (ee-hah)

Does your child like science?
¿Le gusta la ciencia a su hijo (hija)?
leh goos-tah lah see-ehn-see-ah ah soo ee-hoh (ee-hah)

Your child continues to make progress in writing.
Su hijo (hija) sigue progresando en la escritura.
soo ee-hoh (ee-hah) see-geh proh-greh-sahn-doh ehn lah ehs-kree-too-rah

Your child is making satisfactory (excellent) progress in English.
Su hijo (hija) está progresando satisfactoriamente (excelente-mente) en inglés.
soo ee-hoh (ee-hah) ehs-tah proh-greh-sahn-doh sah-tees-fahk-toh-ree-ah-mehn-teh (ehk-seh-lehn-teh-mehn-teh) ehn een-glehs

Your child has improved in chemistry.
Su hijo (hija) ha mejorado en química.
soo ee-hoh (ee-hah) ah meh-hoh-rah-doh ehn kee-mee-kah

Your child is (not) passing world history.
Su hijo (hija) (no) está aprobando la historia mundial.
soo ee-hoh (ee-hah) (noh) ehs-tah ah-proh-bahn-doh lah ees-toh-ree-ah moon-dee-ahl

Your child is having difficulty with English.
Su hijo (hija) tiene dificultad con el inglés.
soo ee-hoh (ee-hah) tee-eh-neh dee-fee-kool-tahd kohn ehl een-glehs

Your child needs help with biology.
Su hijo (hija) necesita ayuda con la biología.
soo ee-hoh (ee-hah) neh-seh-see-tah ah-yoo-dah kohn lah bee-oh-loh-hee-ah

Your child is failing algebra.
Su hijo (hija) está reprobando la clase de álgebra.
soo ee-hoh (ee-hah) ehs-tah rreh-proh-bahn-doh lah klah-seh deh ahl-heh-brah

Can you help your child with math?
¿Puede ayudar a su hijo (hija) con las matemáticas?
poo-eh-deh ah-yoo-dahr ah soo ee-hoh (ee-hah) kohn lahs mah-teh-mah-tee-kahs

Do you know anyone who could help your child with reading?
¿Conoce a alguien que pueda ayudar a su hijo (hija) con la lectura?
koh-noh-seh ah ahl-gee-ehn keh poo-eh-dah ah-yoo-dahr ah soo ee-hoh (ee-hah) kohn lah lehk-too-rah

Your child should attend extra help sessions after school.
Su hijo (hija) debería asistir a las clases remediativas después de la escuela.
soo ee-hoh (ee-hah) deh-beh-ree-ah ah-sees-teer ah lahs klah-sehs rreh-meh-dee-ah-tee-bahs dehs-poo-ehs deh lah ehs-koo-eh-lah

Your child excels in foreign languages.
Su hijo (hija) sobresale en lenguas extranjeras.
soo ee-hoh (ee-hah) soh-breh-sah-leh ehn lehn-goo-ahs ehks-trahn-heh-rahs

Your child needs one credit of science to graduate from high school.
Su hijo (hija) necesita un crédito de ciencia para obtener el título de bachiller.
soo ee-hoh (ee-hah) neh-seh-see-tah oon kreh-dee-toh deh see-ehn-see-ah pah-rah ohb-teh-nehr ehl tee-too-loh deh bah-chee-yehr

To the Student

Why aren't you doing well in English?
¿Por qué no está[s] saliendo bien en inglés?
pohr keh noh ehs-tah[s] sah-lee-ehn-doh bee-ehn ehn een-glehs

Who can help you with your work?
¿Quién puede ayudarlo [ayudarte] con su [tu] trabajo?
kee-ehn poo-eh-deh ah-yoo-dahr-loh [ah-yoo-dahr-teh] kohn soo [too]
trah-bah-hoh

What do you have to do to pass Spanish?
¿Qué tiene[s] que hacer parar salir bien en español?
keh tee-eh-neh[s] keh ah-sehr pah-rah sah-leer bee-ehn ehn ehs-pah-nyohl

You are making progress in physics.
Está[s] progresando en física.
ehs-tah[s] proh-greh-sahn-doh ehn fee-see-kah

You have improved in French.
Ha[s] mejorado en francés.
ah[s] meh-hoh-rah-doh ehn frahn-sehs

In English Class

Your sentence needs a/an _____.
Su [Tu] frase necesita _____.
soo [too] frah-seh neh-seh-see-tah _____

We are going to study (to do, to read) _____.
Vamos a estudiar (hacer, leer) _____.
bah-mohs ah ehs-too-dee-ahr (ah-sehr, leh-ehr) _____

You must use _____.
Debe[s] usar _____.
deh-beh[s] oo-sahr _____

What is _____?
¿Qué es _____?
keh ehs _____

Begin your sentence with _____.
Empiece [Empieza] su [tu] frase con _____.
ehm-pee-eh-seh [ehm-pee-eh-sah] soo [too] frah-seh kohn _____

What is the meaning of that word?
¿Qué significa esa palabra?
keh seeg-nee-fee-kah eh-sah pah-lah-brah

English	Spanish	Pronunciation
adjective	un adjetivo	oon ahd-heh-tee-boh
adverb	un adverbio	oon ahd-behr-bee-oh
antonym	un antónimo	oon ahn-toh-nee-moh
capital letter	una letra mayúscula	oo-nah leh-trah mah-yoos-koo-lah
comma	una coma	oo-nah koh-mah
consonant	una consonante	oo-nah kohn-soh-nahn-teh
exercise	un ejercicio	oon eh-hehr-see-see-oh
future	el futuro	ehl foo-too-roh
grammar	la gramática	lah grah-mah-tee-kah
literature	la literatura	lah lee-teh-rah-too-rah
lowercase letter	una letra minúscula	oo-nah leh-trah mee-noo-skoo-lah
meaning	el significado	ehl seeg-nee-fee-kah-doh
noun	un sustantivo	oon soos-tahn-tee-boh
novel	una novela	oo-nah noh-beh-lah
object	un objeto	oon ohb-heh-toh
participle (present, past)	un participio (presente, pasado)	oon pahr-tee-see-pee-oh (preh-sehn-teh, pah-sah-doh)
past tense	el pasado	ehl pah-sah-doh
period	un punto	oon poon-toh
play	una obra dramática	oo-nah oh-brah drah-mah-tee-kah
poem	un poema	oon poh-eh-mah
present	el presente	ehl preh-sehn-teh
pronoun	un pronombre	oon proh-nohm-breh
sentence	una frase	oo-nah frah-seh
short story	un cuento	oon koo-ehn-toh
subject	el sujeto	ehl soo-heh-toh
symbol	el símbolo	ehl seem-boh-loh
synonym	un sinónimo	oon see-noh-nee-moh
tense	el tiempo	ehl tee-ehm-poh
theme	el tema	ehl teh-mah
verb	el verbo	ehl behr-boh
vocabulary	el vocabulario	ehl boh-kah-boo-lah-ree-oh
vowel	la vocal	lah boh-kahl
word	la palabra	lah pah-lah-brah
writing	la escritura	lah ehs-kree-too-rah

About Bilingual Education and ESL

In a bilingual class, academic subjects are taught in Spanish and in English.

En una clase bilingüe las materias se enseñan en español y en inglés.

ehn oo-nah klah-seh bee-leen-goo-eh lahs mah-teh-ree-ahs seh ehn-seh-nyahn ehn ehs-pah-nyohl ee ehn een-glehs

In an English as a Second Language (ESL) class, your child (you) learn to speak, read, and write English.

En una clase de inglés como segundo idioma, su hijo (hija, Ud.) aprende a hablar, leer, y escribir en inglés.

ehn oo-nah klah-seh deh een-glehs koh-moh seh-goon-doh ee-dee-oh-mah soo ee-hoh (ee-hah, oo-stehd) ah-prehn-deh ah ah-blahr, leh-ehr ee ehs-kree-beer ehn een-glehs

Instruction is entirely in English.

La instrucción es totalmente en inglés.

lah een-strook-see-ohn ehs toh-tahl-mehn-teh ehn een-glehs

Placement depends upon test results.

La colocación depende de los resultados de un examen.

lah koh-loh-kah-see-ohn deh-pehn-deh deh lohs rreh-sool-tah-dohs deh oon ehk-sah-men

Standards for ESL students are not as strict for testing and promotion.

Los estudiantes de inglés como segundo idioma están sujetos a criterios menos estrictos para los exámenes y la promoción.

lohs ehs-too-dee-ahn-tehs deh een-glehs koh-moh seh-goon-doh ee-dee-oh-mah ehs-tahn soo-heh-tohs ah kree-teh-ree-ohs meh-nohs ehs-treek-tohs pah-rah lohs ehk-sah-meh-nehs ee lah proh-moh-see-ohn

In History and Geography Class

Let's talk about _____.

Hablemos de _____.

ah-bleh-mohs deh _____

Let's study _____.

Estudiemos _____.

ehs-too-dee-eh-mohs _____

English	Spanish	Pronunciation
ancestor	el antepasado	*ehl ahn-teh-pah-sah-doh*
army	el ejército	*ehl eh-hehr-see-toh*
battle	la batalla	*lah bah-tah-yah*
border	la frontera	*lah frohn-teh-rah*
candidate	el candidato	*ehl kahn-dee-dah-toh*
capitalism	el capitalismo	*ehl kah-pee-tah-lees-moh*
century	el siglo	*ehl see-gloh*
civilization	la civilización	*la see-bee-lee-sah-see-ohn*
colony	la colonia	*lah koh-loh-nee-ah*
communism	el comunismo	*ehl koh-moo-nees-moh*
congress	el congreso	*ehl kohn-greh-soh*
conquest	la conquista	*lah kohn-kees-tah*
continent	el continente	*ehl kohn-tee-nehn-teh*
country	el país	*ehl pah-ees*
culture	la cultura	*lah kool-too-rah*
custom	la costumbre	*lah kohs-toom-breh*
democracy	la democracia	*lah deh-moh-krah-see-ah*
development	el desarrollo	*ehl deh-sah-rroh-yoh*
dictator	el dictador	*ehl deek-tah-dohr*
dictatorship	la dictadura	*lah deek-tah-doo-rah*
discovery	el descubrimiento	*ehl dehs-koo-bree-mee-ehn-toh*
dynasty	la dinastía	*lah dee-nahs-tee-ah*
economy	la economía	*lah eh-koh-noh-mee-ah*
election	la elección	*la eh-lehk-see-ohn*
empire	el imperio	*ehl eem-peh-ree-oh*
equality	la igualdad	*lah ee-goo-ahl-dahd*
exploration	la exploración	*lah ehks-ploh-rah-see-ohn*
fascism	el fascismo	*ehl fah-sees-moh*
freedom	la libertad	*lah lee-behr-tahd*
government	el gobierno	*ehl goh-bee-ehr-noh*
governor	el (la) gobernador (gobernadora)	*ehl (lah) goh-behr-nah-dohr (goh-behr-nah-doh-rah)*
independence	la independencia	*lah een-deh-pehn-dehn-see-ah*
invasion	la invasión	*lah een-bah-see-ohn*
justice	la justicia	*lah hoos-tee-see-ah*
king	el rey	*ehl rreh-ee*
lake	el lago	*ehl lah-goh*

English	Spanish	Pronunciation
law	la ley	*lah leh-ee*
mayor	el (la) alcalde (alcaldesa)	*ehl (lah) ahl-kahl-deh (ahl-kahl-deh-sah)*
monarchy	la monarquía	*lah moh-nahr-kee-ah*
mountain	la montaña	*lah mohn-tah-nyah*
nation	la nación	*lah nah-see-ohn*
origin	el origen	*ehl oh-ree-hehn*
peace	la paz	*lah pahs*
political parties	los partidos políticos	*lohs pahr-tee-dohs poh-lee-tee-kohs*
politics	la política	*lah poh-lee-tee-kah*
population	la población	*lah poh-blah-see-ohn*
press	la prensa	*lah prehn-sah*
queen	la reina	*lah rreh-ee-nah*
reign	el reino	*ehl rreh-ee-noh*
republic	la república	*lah rreh-poo-blee-kah*
revolution	la revolución	*lah rreh-boh-loo-see-ohn*
rights (human)	los derechos (humanos)	*lohs deh-reh-chohs (oo-mah-nohs)*
river	el río	*ehl rree-oh*
senate	el senado	*ehl seh-nah-doh*
senator	el (la) senador (senadora)	*ehl (lah) seh-nah-dohr (seh-nah-doh-rah)*
state	el estado	*ehls ehs-tah-doh*
strike	la huelga	*lah oo-ehl-gah*
tax	el impuesto	*ehl eem-poo-ehs-toh*
territory	el territorio	*ehl teh-rree-toh-ree-oh*
trade	el comercio	*ehl koh-mehr-see-oh*
treaty	el tratado	*ehl trah-tah-doh*
vote	el voto	*ehl boh-toh*
war	la guerra	*lah geh-rrah*
world	el mundo	*ehl moon-doh*

In Math Class

What is the _____?
¿Cuál es _____?
koo-ahl ehs _____

You must draw _____.
Debe [Debes] dibujar _____.
deh-beh [deh-behs] dee-boo-hahr _____

Look at _____.
Mire [Mira] _____.
mee-reh [mee-rah] _____

Measure _____.
Mida [Mide] _____.
mee-dah [mee-deh] _____

English	Spanish	Pronunciation
angle	el ángulo	*ehl ahn-goo-loh*
arc	el arco	*ehl ahr-koh*
area	el área	*ehl ah-reh-ah*
average	el promedio	*ehl proh-meh-dee-oh*
center	el centro	*ehl sehn-troh*
circle	el círculo	*ehl seer-koo-loh*
circumference	la circunferencia	*lah seer-koon-feh-rrehn-see-ah*
cone	el cono	*ehl koh-noh*
cylinder	el cilindro	*ehl see-leen-droh*
decimal	el decimal	*ehl deh-see-mahl*
degree	el grado	*ehl grah-doh*
denominator	el denominador	*ehl deh-noh-mee-nah-dohr*
diagram	el diagrama	*ehl dee-ah-grah-mah*
diameter	el diámetro	*ehl dee-ah-meh-troh*
difference	la diferencia	*lah dee-feh-rehn-see-ah*
digit	el dígito	*ehl dee-hee-toh*
dimension	la dimensión	*lah dee-mehn-see-ohn*
distance	la distancia	*lah dees-tahn-see-ah*
equation	la ecuación	*lah eh-koo-ah-see-ohn*
equivalent	el equivalente	*ehl eh-kee-bah-lehn-teh*
example	el ejemplo	*ehl eh-hehm-ploh*
exponent	el exponente	*ehl ehks-poh-nehn-teh*
figure	la figura	*lah fee-goo-rah*
formula	la fórmula	*lah fohr-moo-lah*
fraction	la fracción	*lah frahk-see-ohn*
height	la altura	*lah ahl-too-rah*
length	la longitud	*lah lohn-hee-tood*
line	la línea	*lah lee-neh-ah*
mode	el modo	*ehl moh-doh*

English	Spanish	Pronunciation
numeral	**el numeral**	*ehl noo-meh-rahl*
numerator	**el numerador**	*ehl noo-meh-rah-dohr*
percent	**el porcentaje**	*ehl pohr-sehn-tah-heh*
perimeter	**el perímetro**	*ehl peh-ree-meh-troh*
point	**el punto**	*ehl poon-toh*
probability	**la probabilidad**	*lah proh-bah-bee-lee-dahd*
product	**el producto**	*ehl proh-dook-toh*
quadrant	**el cuadrante**	*ehl koo-ah-drahn-teh*
quotient	**el cociente**	*ehl koh-see-ehn-teh*
radius	**el radio**	*ehl rrah-dee-oh*
rate	**la tasa**	*lah tah-sah*
ratio	**la proporción**	*lah proh-pohr-see-ohn*
remainder	**el residuo**	*ehl rreh-see-doo-oh*
side	**el lado**	*ehl lah-doh*
solution	**la solución**	*lah soh-loo-see-ohn*
square	**el cuadro**	*ehl koo-ah-droh*
statistic	**la estadística**	*lah ehs-tah-dees-tee-kah*
sum	**la suma**	*lah soo-mah*
surface	**la superficie**	*lah soo-pehr-fee-see-eh*
total	**el total**	*ehl toh-tahl*
triangle	**el triángulo**	*ehl tree-ahn-goo-loh*
unit	**la unidad**	*lah oo-nee-dahd*
value	**el valor**	*ehl bah-lohr*

We are going to solve some problems.
Vamos a resolver algunos problemas.
bah-mohs ah rreh-sohl-behr ahl-goo-nohs proh-bleh-mahs

Are the lines parallel (perpendicular)?
¿Son paralelas (perpendiculares) las líneas?
sohn pah-rah-leh-lahs (pehr-pehn-dee-koo-lah-rehs) lahs lee-neh-ahs

English	Spanish	Pronunciation
and	**y**	*ee*
divided by	**dividido por**	*dee-bee-dee-doh pohr*
minus	**menos**	*meh-nohs*
multiplied by	**multiplicado por**	*mool-tee-plee-kah-doh pohr*
parallel	**paralelo**	*pah-rah-leh-loh*
perpendicular	**perpendicular**	*pehr-pehn-dee-koo-lahr*
plus	**más**	*mahs*

Two and two are four.
Dos y (más) dos son cuatro.
dohs ee (mahs) dohs sohn koo-ah-troh

Twelve divided by four is three.
Doce dividido por cuatro son tres.
doh-seh dee-bee-dee-doh pohr koo-ah-troh sohn trehs

Twenty minus eleven is nine.
Veinte menos once son nueve.
beh-een-teh meh-nohs ohn-seh sohn noo-eh-beh

Five times six is thirty.
Cinco multiplicado por seis son treinta.
seen-koh mool-tee-plee-kah-doh pohr seh-ees sohn treh-een-tah

You must _____.
Debe(s) _____.
deh-beh(s)

English	Spanish	Pronunciation
to add	**sumar**	*soo-mahr*
to calculate	**calcular**	*kahl-koo-lahr*
to change	**cambiar**	*kahm-bee-ahr*
to divide	**dividir**	*dee-bee-deer*
to factor	**factorizar**	*fahk-toh-ree-sahr*
to measure	**medir**	*meh-deer*
to multiply	**multiplicar**	*mool-tee-plee-kahr*
to reduce	**reducir**	*rreh-doo-seer*
to round off	**redondear**	*rreh-dohn-deh-ahr*
to simplify	**simplificar**	*seem-plee-fee-kahr*
to solve	**resolver**	*rreh-sohl-behr*
to subtract	**restar**	*rrehs-tahr*

In Science Class

We are going to study _____.
Vamos a estudiar _____.
bah-mohs ah ehs-too-dee-ahr

What is important is _____.
Lo importante es _____.
loh eem-pohr-tahn-teh ehs

English	Spanish	Pronunciation
atmosphere	**la atmósfera**	*lah aht-mohs-feh-rah*
comet	**el cometa**	*ehl koh-meh-tah*
energy	**la energía**	*lah eh-nehr-hee-ah*
environment	**el ambiente**	*ehl ahm-bee-ehn-teh*
gas	**el gas**	*ehl gahs*
gravity	**la gravedad**	*lah grah-beh-dahd*
heat	**el calor**	*ehl kah-lohr*
human body	**el cuerpo humano**	*ehl koo-ehr-poh oo-mah-noh*
light	**la luz**	*lah loos*
liquid	**el líquido**	*ehl lee-kee-doh*
machine	**la máquina**	*lah mah-kee-nah*
matter	**la materia**	*lah mah-teh-ree-ah*
moon	**la luna**	*lah loo-nah*
motion	**el movimiento**	*ehl moh-bee-mee-ehn-toh*
planet	**el planeta**	*ehl plah-neh-tah*
plants	**las plantas**	*lahs plahn-tahs*
powder	**el polvo**	*ehl pohl-boh*
power	**la potencia**	*lah poh-tehn-see-ah*
rock	**la roca**	*lah rroh-kah*
solar system	**el sistema solar**	*ehl sees-teh-mah soh-lahr*
solid	**el sólido**	*ehl soh-lee-doh*
sound	**el sonido**	*ehl soh-nee-doh*
speed	**la velocidad**	*lah beh-loh-see-dahd*
star	**la estrella**	*lah ehs-treh-yah*
sun	**el sol**	*ehl sohl*
temperature	**la temperatura**	*lah tehm-peh-rah-too-rah*
universe	**el universo**	*ehl oo-nee-behr-soh*
weather	**el clima**	*ehl klee-mah*
weight	**el peso**	*ehl peh-soh*

Laboratory Items

Item	Spanish	Pronunciation
beaker	**la cubeta**	*lah koo-beh-tah*
burner	**el quemador**	*ehl keh-mah-dohr*
candle	**la vela**	*lah beh-lah*
faucet	**el grifo**	*ehl gree-foh*
filter paper	**el papel de filtro**	*ehl pah-pehl deh feel-troh*
flask	**el frasco**	*ehl frahs-koh*

Item	Spanish	Pronunciation
forceps	**las tenazas**	*lahs teh-nah-sahs*
funnel	**el embudo**	*ehl ehm-boo-doh*
lens	**el lente**	*ehl lehn-teh*
magnet	**el imán**	*ehl ee-mahn*
magnifying glass	**la lupa**	*lah loo-pah*
match	**el fósforo**	*ehl fohs-foh-roh*
microscope	**el microscopio**	*ehl mee-krohs-koh-pee-oh*
prism	**el prisma**	*ehl prees-mah*
Petri dish	**el platito de muestras**	*ehl plah-tee-toh deh moo-ehs-trahs*
safety goggles	**los lentes de seguridad**	*lohs lehn-tehs deh seh-goo-ree-dahd*
scale	**la balanza**	*lah bah-lahn-sah*
slide	**la transparencia**	*lah trahns-pah-rehn-see-ah*
telescope	**el telescopio**	*ehl teh-lehs-koh-pee-oh*
(test) tube	**el tubo (de ensayo)**	*ehl too-boh (deh ehn-sah-yoh)*

To the Student

We are going to use microscopes.
Vamos a usar microscopios.
bah-mohs ah oo-sahr mee-krohs-koh-pee-ohs

Don't play with the scale.
No juegue [juegues] con la balanza.
noh hoo-eh-geh [hoo-eh-gehs] kohn lah bah-lahn-sah

Pay attention to the slide.
Ponga [Pon] atención a la transparencia.
pohn-gah [pohn] ah-tehn-see-ohn ah lah trahns-pah-rehn-see-ah

Use a funnel.
Emplee [Emplea] un embudo.
ehm-pleh-eh [ehm-pleh-ah] oon ehm-boo-doh

Wear your safety goggles at all times.
Lleve [Lleva] sus [tus] lentes de seguridad todo el tiempo.
yeh-beh [yeh-bah] soos [toos] lehn-tehs deh seh-goo-ree-dahd toh-doh ehl tee-ehm-poh

Turn off the faucet.
Apague [Apaga] el grifo.
ah-pah-geh [ah-pah-gah] ehl gree-foh

Look at the beaker.
Mire [Mira] la cubeta.
mee-reh [mee-rah] lah koo-beh-tah

In Computer Science

You need _____.
Necesita[s] _____.
neh-seh-see-tah[s] _____

Look at _____.
Mire [Mira] _____.
mee-reh [mee-rah] _____

Use _____.
Emplee [Emplea] _____.
ehm-pleh-eh [ehm-pleh-ah] _____

English	Spanish	Pronunciation
address	**la dirección**	*lah dee-rehk-see-ohn*
computer science	**la informática**	*lah een-fohr-mah-tee-kah*
database	**la base de datos**	*lah bah-seh deh dah-tohs*
drive	**la disquetera**	*lah dees-keh-teh-rah*
e-mail	**el correo electrónico**	*ehl koh-rreh-oh eh-lehk-troh-nee-koh*
key	**la tecla**	*lah tehk-lah*
keyboard	**el teclado**	*ehl tehk-lah-doh*
laptop	**la computadora portátil**	*lah kohm-poo-tah-doh-rah pohr-tah-teel*
memory	**la memoria**	*lah meh-moh-ree-ah*
monitor	**el monitor**	*ehl moh-nee-tohr*
mouse	**el ratón**	*ehl rrah-tohn*
network	**la red**	*la rrehd*
printer	**la impresora**	*lah eem-preh-soh-rah*
scanner	**el escáner**	*ehl ehs-kah-nehr*
screen	**la pantalla**	*lah pahn-tah-yah*

English	Spanish	Pronunciation
search engine	**el buscador**	*ehl boos-kah-dohr*
server	**el servidor**	*ehl sehr-bee-dohr*
spell check	**el verificador de ortografía**	*ehl beh-ree-fee-kah-dohr deh ohr-toh-grah-fee-ah*
spreadsheet	**la hoja de cálculo electrónica**	*lah oh-hah deh kahl-koo-loh eh-lehk-troh-nee-kah*
system	**el sistema**	*ehl sees-teh-mah*
thesaurus	**el diccionario de sinónimos**	*ehl deek-see-oh-nah-ree-oh deh see-noh-nee-mohs*
word processor	**el procesador de textos**	*ehl proh-seh-sah-dohr deh tehks-tohs*

In Art Class

Would you like to make _____?
¿Le [Te] gustaría hacer _____?
leh [teh] goos-tah-ree-ah ah-sehr _____

design	**un diseño**	*oon dee-seh-nyoh*
drawing	**un dibujo**	*oon dee-boo-hoh*
painting	**una pintura**	*oo-nah peen-too-rah*
sculpture	**una escultura**	*oo-nah ehs-kool-too-rah*

In Music Class

Do you play in the band (the orchestra)?
¿Toca[s] en la banda (la orquesta)?
toh-kah[s] ehn lah bahn-dah (lah ohr-kehs-tah)

Do you play _____?
¿Toca[s] _____?
toh-kah[s] _____

the cello	**el violoncelo**	*ehl bee-oh-lohn-seh-loh*
the clarinet	**el clarinete**	*ehl klah-ree-neh-teh*
the drum	**el tambor**	*ehl tahm-bohr*
the flute	**la flauta**	*lah flah-oo-tah*
the guitar	**la guitarra**	*la gee-tah-rrah*
the oboe	**el oboe**	*ehl oh-boh-eh*

the piano	**el piano**	*ehl pee-ah-noh*
the piccolo	**el piccolo**	*ehl pee-koh-loh*
the saxophone	**el saxofón**	*ehl sahk-soh-fohn*
the trombone	**el trombón**	*ehl trohm-bohn*
the trumpet	**la trompeta**	*lah trohm-peh-tah*
the violin	**el violín**	*ehl bee-oh-leen*

In Physical Education Class

We are going to _____.

Vamos a _____.

bah-mohs ah _____

do exercises	**hacer ejercicios**	*ah-sehr eh-hehr-see-see-ohs*
lift weights	**levantar pesos**	*leh-bahn-tahr peh-sohs*
play sports	**practicar deportes**	*prahk-tee-kahr deh-pohr-tehs*
run	**correr**	*koh-rrehr*
swim	**nadar**	*nah-dahr*

Academic Skills

English	Spanish	Pronunciation
adding	**sumar**	*soo-mahr*
calculating (percentages)	**calcular (porcentajes)**	*kahl-koo-lahr (pohr-sehn-tah-hehs)*
counting	**contar**	*kohn-tahr*
dividing	**dividir**	*dee-bee-deer*
expressing himself/herself	**expresarse**	*ehks-preh-sahr-seh*
identifying coins	**identificar monedas**	*ee-dehn-tee-fee-kahr moh-neh-dahs*
identifying patterns	**identificar patrones**	*ee-dehn-tee-fee-kahr pah-troh-nehs*
identifying words	**identificar palabras**	*ee-dehn-tee-fee-kahr pah-lah-brahs*
memorizing facts	**aprender de memoria datos**	*ah-preh-dehr deh meh-moh-ree-ah dah-tohs*

English	Spanish	Pronunciation
multipying	**multiplicar**	*mool-tee-plee-kahr*
processing new information	**procesar datos nuevos**	*proh-seh-sahr dah-tohs noo-eh-bohs*
reading	**leer**	*leh-ehr*
recognizing basic shapes	**reconocer las figuras básicas**	*rreh-koh-noh-sehr lahs fee-goo-rahs bah-see-kahs*
recognizing	**reconocer**	*rreh-koh-noh-sehr*
recognizing words	**reconocer las palabras**	*rreh-koh-noh-sehr lahs pah-lah-brahs*
speaking	**hablar**	*ah-blahr*
subtracting	**restar**	*rrehs-tahr*
telling time	**leer la hora**	*leh-ehr lah oh-rah*
understanding (the vocabulary, grammar)	**comprender (el vocabulario, la gramática)**	*kohm-prehn-dehr (ehl boh-kah-boo-lah-ree-oh, lah grah-mah-tee-kah)*
using fractions	**usar fracciones**	*oo-sahr frahk-see-oh-nehs*
writing	**escribir**	*ehs-kree-beer*

Your child has difficulty understanding grammar.
Su hijo (hija) tiene dificultad con la gramática.
soo ee-hoh (ee-hah) tee-eh-neh dee-fee-kool-tahd kohn lah grah-mah-tee-kah

Your child shows progress in subracting numbers.
Su hijo (hija) está progresando en la resta.
soo ee-hoh (ee-hah) ehs-tah proh-greh-sahn-doh ehn lah rrehs-tah

Your child excels at using fractions.
Su hijo (hija) sobresale en el uso de las fracciones.
soo ee-hoh (ee-hah) soh-breh-sah-leh ehn ehl oo-soh deh lahs frahk-see-oh-nehs

Your child needs more practice recognizing words.
Su hijo (hija) necesita más práctica reconociendo palabras.
soo ee-hoh (ee-hah) neh-seh-see-tah mahs prahk-tee-kah rreh-koh-noh-see-ehn-doh pah-lah-brahs

Your child shows improvement in reading.
Su hijo (hija) ha mejorado en lectura.
soo ee-hoh (ee-hah) ah meh-hoh-rah-doh ehn lehk-too-rah

Can you help your child with telling time?
¿Puede ayudar a su hijo (hija) a leer la hora?
poo-eh-deh ah-yoo-dahr ah soo ee-hoh (ee-hah) ah leh-ehr lah oh-rah

School Supplies

English	Spanish	Pronunciation
atlas	un atlas	*oon aht-lahs*
backpack	una mochila	*oo-nah moh-chee-lah*
ballpoint pen	un bolígrafo	*oon boh-lee-grah-foh*
book	un libro	*oon lee-broh*
book cover	una cubierta	*oo-nah koo-bee-ehr-tah*
bookbag	una bolsa para libros	*oo-nah bohl-sah pah-rah lee-brohs*
calculator	una calculadora	*oo-nah kahl-koo-lah-doh-rah*
chalk	una tiza	*oo-nah tee-sah*
crayons	crayones	*krah-yoh-nehs*
dictionary (bilingual)	un diccionario (bilingüe)	*oon deek-see-oh-nah-ree-oh (bee-leen-goo-eh)*
encyclopedia	una enciclopedia	*oo-nah ehn-see-kloh-peh-dee-ah*
eraser	una goma de borrar	*oo-nah goh-mah deh boh-rrahr*
folder	una carpeta	*oo-nah kahr-peh-tah*
glue stick	una barra de pegamento	*oo-nah bah-rrah deh peh-gah-mehn-toh*
labels	etiquetas	*eh-tee-keh-tahs*
map	un mapa	*oon mah-pah*
markers (felt-tipped)	marcadores (de punta de fieltro)	*mahr-kah-doh-rehs (deh poon-tah deh fee-ehl-troh)*
notebook	un cuaderno	*oon koo-ah-dehr-noh*
paper (wide-ruled, graph, unruled)	papel (con líneas, cuadriculado, sin líneas)	*pah-pehl (kohn lee-neh-ahs, koo-ah-dree-koo-lah-doh, seen lee-neh-ahs)*
pen	una pluma	*oo-nah ploo-mah*
pencil (colored pencils)	un lápiz (lápices de colores)	*oon lah-pees (lah-pee-sehs deh koh-loh-rehs)*
reinforcements	refuerzos	*rreh-foo-ehr-sohs*
ruler	una regla	*oo-nah rreh-glah*
school supplies	útiles escolares	*oo-tee-lehs ehs-koh-lah-rehs*
scissors (a pair of)	(un par de) tijeras	*(oon pahr deh) tee-heh-rahs*

English	Spanish	Pronunciation
textbook	**un libro de texto**	*oon lee-broh deh tehks-toh*
three-ring binder	**una carpeta de tres anillos**	*oo-nah kahr-peh-tah deh trehs ah-nee-yohs*

Your child must have all necessary school supplies by Friday.
Su hijo (hija) debe tener todos los útiles escolares necesarios para el viernes.
soo ee-hoh (ee-hah) deh-beh teh-nehr toh-dohs lohs oo-tee-lehs ehs-koh-lah-rehs neh-seh-sah-ree-ohs pah-rah ehl bee-ehr-nehs

Your child must cover all of his (her) books.
Su hijo (hija) tiene que forrar todos sus libros.
soo ee-hoh (ee-hah) tee-eh-neh keh foh-rrahr toh-dohs soos lee-brohs

Your child needs a box of twenty-four crayons.
Su hijo (hija) necesita una caja de veinticuatro crayones.
soo ee-hoh (ee-hah) neh-seh-see-tah oo-nah kah-hah deh beh-een-tee-koo-ah-troh krah-yoh-nehs

Your child needs graph paper for our math class.
Su hijo (hija) necesita papel cuadriculado para la clase de matemáticas.
soo ee-hoh (ee-hah) neh-seh-see-tah pah-pehl koo-ah-dree-koo-lah-doh pah-rah lah klah-seh deh mah-teh-mah-tee-kahs

Please buy a three-ring binder for your child.
Por favor, compre una carpeta de tres anillos para su hijo (hija).
pohr fah-bohr kohm-preh oo-nah kahr-peh-tah deh trehs ah-nee-yohs pah-rah soo ee-hoh (ee-hah)

Please tell your child to bring a pen to school every day.
Por favor, dígale a su hijo (hija) que traiga un bolígrafo a la escuela todos los días.
pohr fah-bohr, dee-gah-leh ah soo ee-hoh (ee-hah) keh trah-ee-gah oon boh-lee-grah-foh ah lah ehs-koo-eh-lah toh-dohs lohs dee-ahs

Your child must write in blue or black ink.
Su hijo (hija) debe escribir con tinta azul o negra.
soo ee-hoh (ee-hah) deh-beh ehs-kree-beer kohn teen-tah ah-sool oh neh-grah

Your child may correct his (her) work in red ink (with a red pencil).
Su hijo (hija) puede corregir su trabajo con tinta roja (con un lápiz rojo).
soo ee-hoh (ee-hah) poo-eh-deh koh-rreh-heer soo trah-bah-hoh kohn teen-tah rroh-hah (kohn oon lah-pees rroh-hoh)

Does your child have an atlas at home?
¿Tiene su hijo (hija) un atlas en casa?
tee-eh-neh soo ee-hoh (ee-hah) oon aht-lahs ehn kah-sah

Your child must buy a bilingual dictionary.
Su hijo (hija) tiene que comprar un diccionario bilingüe.
soo ee-hoh (ee-hah) tee-eh-neh keh kohm-prahr oon deek-see-oh-nah-ree-oh bee-leen-goo-eh

Your child often forgets to bring a pencil to class.
Su hijo (hija) se olvida a menudo de traer un lápiz a la clase.
soo ee-hoh (ee-hah) seh ohl-bee-dah ah meh-noo-doh deh trah-ehr oon lah-pees ah lah klah-seh

If your child loses his (her) textbook, he/she must pay for it (replace it).
Si su hijo (hija) pierde su libro de texto, tiene que pagarlo (reemplazarlo).
see soo ee-hoh (ee-hah) pee-ehr-deh soo lee-broh deh tehks-toh tee-eh-neh keh pah-gahr-loh (rreh-ehm-plah-sahr-loh)

Your child would benefit from having an encyclopedia at home.
Su hijo (hija) sacaría provecho de tener una enciclopedia en casa.
soo ee-hoh (ee-hah) sah-kah-ree-ah proh-beh-choh deh teh-nehr oo-nah ehn-see-kloh-peh-dee-ah ehn kah-sah

12

Expectations and Consequences

Note:
1. Letters or words in brackets are used when using the familiar you **[tú]** form.
2. When speaking to more than one adult, **Ud.** (you, singular) becomes **Uds.** (you, plural) and an n is added to the conjugated verb form.
3. The formal you form is expressed in the same way as the third-person singular **él** (he) and **ella** (she) forms.

Dress Codes

Clothing

English	Spanish	Pronunciation
bathing suit	el traje de baño	*ehl trah-heh deh bah-nyoh*
belt	el cinturón	*ehl seen-too-rohn*
boots	las botas	*lahs boh-tahs*
gloves	los guantes	*lohs goo-ahn-tehs*
hat	el sombrero	*ehl sohm-breh-roh*
jacket	la chaqueta	*lah chah-keh-tah*
jeans	los jeans, los vaqueros	*lohs geens, lohs bah-keh-rohs*

English	Spanish	Pronunciation
jogging suit	el traje de trotar, la sudadera	*ehl trah-heh deh troh-tahr, lah soo-dah-deh-rah*
overcoat	el abrigo	*ehl ah-bree-goh*
pants	los pantalones	*lohs pahn-tah-loh-nehs*
raincoat	el impermeable	*ehl eem-pehr-meh-ah-bleh*
sandals	las sandalias	*lahs sahn-dah-lee-ahs*
scarf	la bufanda	*lah boo-fahn-dah*
shoes	los zapatos	*lohs sah-pah-tohs*
shorts	los pantalones cortos	*lohs pahn-tah-loh-nehs kohr-tohs*
sneakers	los tenis	*lohs teh-nees*
socks	los calcetines	*lohs kahl-seh-tee-nehs*
sweater	el suéter	*ehl soo-eh-tehr*
sweatshirt	la sudadera	*lah soo-dah-deh-rah*
tie	la corbata	*lah kohr-bah-tah*
T-shirt	la camiseta, la playera	*lah kah-mee-seh-tah, lah plah-yeh-rah*
uniform	el uniforme escolar	*ehl oo-nee-fohr-meh ehs-koh-lahr*
umbrella	el paraguas	*ehl pah-rah-goo-ahs*
wallet	la cartera	*lah kahr-teh-rah*

Colors

English	Spanish	Pronunciation
beige	beige	*beh-ee-heh*
black	negro	*neh-groh*
blue	azul	*ah-sool*
brown	marrón, pardo	*mah-rrohn, pahr-doh*
gray	gris	*grees*
green	verde	*behr-deh*
orange	anaranjado	*ah-nah-rahn-hah-doh*
pink	rosado	*rroh-sah-doh*
purple	púrpura, morado	*poor-poo-rah, moh-rah-doh*
red	rojo	*rroh-hoh*
white	blanco	*blahn-koh*
yellow	amarillo	*ah-mah-ree-yoh*

Note:

To describe a color as light, add the word **claro** (klah-roh) after the color: **azul claro** (ah-sool klah-roh) = light blue. To describe a color as dark, add the word **oscuro** (ohs-koo-roh) after the color: **azul oscuro** (ah-sool ohs-koo-roh) = dark blue.

To the Student

You need two red pens.
Necesita[s] dos bolígrafos rojos.
neh-seh-see-tah[s] dohs boh-lee-grah-fohs rroh-hohs

You must write in blue or black ink.
Debe[s] escribir con tinta azul o negra.
deh-beh[s] ehs-kree-beer kohn teen-tah ah-sool oh neh-grah

You must wear a white shirt to assembly.
Tiene[s] que llevar una camisa blanca a la asamblea.
tee-eh-neh[s] keh yeh-bahr oo-nah kah-mee-sah blahn-kah ah lah ah-sahm-bleh-ah

What color is the umbrella that you lost?
¿De qué color es el paraguas que perdió [perdiste]?
deh keh koh-lohr ehs ehl pah-rah-goo-ahs keh pehr-dee-oh [pehr-dees-teh]

You are not permitted to wear shorts to school.
No se permite llevar pantalones cortos en la escuela.
noh seh pehr-mee-teh yeh-bahr pahn-tah-loh-nehs kohr-tohs ehn lah ehs-koo-eh-lah

There is a dress code.
Hay normas sobre la indumentaria.
ah-ee nohr-mahs soh-breh lah een-doo-mehn-tah-ree-ah

Please take off your hat.
Por favor, quítese [quítate] el sombrero.
pohr fah-bohr kee-teh-seh (kee-tah-teh) ehl sohm-breh-roh

To the Parents

Your child must be appropriately dressed for school.
Su hijo (hija) tiene que llevar ropa apropiada a la escuela.
soo ee-hoh (ee-hah) tee-eh-neh keh yeh-bahr rroh-pah ah-proh-pee-ah-dah ah lah ehs-koo-eh-lah

The school uniform is gray and blue.
El uniforme escolar es gris y azul.
ehl oo-nee-fohr-meh ehs-koh-lahr ehs grees ee ah-sool

Your child needs black pants for our program.
Su hijo (hija) necesita pantalones negros para nuestro programa.
soo ee-hoh (ee-hah) neh-seh-see-tah pahn-tah-loh-nehs neh-grohs pah-rah noo-ehs-troh proh-grah-mah

Your child got his (her) coat dirty.
Su hijo (hija) ensució su abrigo.
soo ee-hoh (ee-hah) ehn-soo-see-oh soo ah-bree-goh

Your child spilled red paint on his (her) shirt.
Su hijo (hija) derramó pintura roja en su camisa.
soo ee-hoh (ee-hah) deh-rrah-moh peen-too-rah rroh-hah ehn soo kah-mee-sah

Your child tore his (her) jacket.
Su hijo (hija) desgarró su chaqueta.
soo ee-hoh (ee-hah) dehs-gah-rroh soo chah-keh-tah

Your child left his (her) hat at school.
Su hijo (hija) dejó el sombrero en la escuela.
soo ee-hoh (ee-hah) deh-hoh ehl sohm-breh-roh ehn lah ehs-koo-eh-lah

Your child lost his (her) scarf.
Su hijo (hija) perdió la bufanda.
soo ee-hoh (ee-hah) pehr-dee-oh lah boo-fahn-dah

Your child can't find his (her) wallet.
Su hijo (hija) no puede encontrar la cartera.
soo ee-hoh (ee-hah) noh poo-eh-deh ehn-kohn-trahr lah kahr-teh-rah

Sneakers must be worn in the gym.
Hay que llevar tenis en el gimnasio.
ah-ee keh yeh-bahr teh-nees ehn ehl heem-nah-see-oh

Wearing a hat to class is prohibited.
Se prohibe llevar sombrero en la clase.
seh proh-ee-beh yeh-bahr sohm-breh-roh ehn lah klah-seh

Class Participation

Your son (daughter) is (You are) [You are] a very conscientious
student.
**Su hijo (hija, Ud.) es [Tú eres] un(a) estudiante muy concien-
zudo(a).**
*soo ee-hoh (ee-hah, oo-stehd) es [eh-rehs] oon (oo-nah) ehs-too-dee-ahn-teh
moo-ee kohn-see-ehn-soo-doh(dah)*

He (She) has (You have) [You have] made many fine contributions
to our class.
Ha[s] contribuido mucho a la clase.
ah[s] kohn-tree-boo-ee-doh moo-choh ah lah klah-seh

He (She) is (You are) [You are] an inspiration to his (her) (your)
classmates.
Inspira[s] a todos sus [tus] compañeros.
een-spee-rah[s] ah toh-dohs soos [toos] kohm-pah-nyeh-rohs

He (She) is (You are) [You are] enthusiastic about participating.
Le [Te] encanta participar.
leh [teh] ehn-kahn-tah pahr-tee-see-pahr

His (Her, Your [Your]) class participation is excellent.
Su [Tu] participación en clase es excelente.
soo [too] pahr-tee-see-pah-see-yohn ehn klah-seh ehs ehk-seh-lehn-teh

He (She) makes (You make) [You make] fine contributions to
classroom discussions.
Su [Tu] contribución en las discusiones en clase es excelente.
*soo [too] kohn-tree-boo-see-ohn ehn lahs dees-koo-see-oh-nehs ehn klah-seh
ehs ehk-seh-lehn-teh*

He (She) has (You have) [You have] interesting ideas.
Tiene[s] ideas interesantes.
tee-eh-neh[s] ee-deh-ahs een-teh-reh-sahn-tehs

He (She) doesn't (You don't) [You don't] volunteer often but he (she) does (you do) [you do] his (her) (your) [your] classwork.
No se [te] ofrece[s] frecuentemente como voluntario(a) pero hace[s] todo su [tu] trabajo en clase.
noh seh [teh] oh-freh-seh[s] freh-koo-ehn-teh-mehn-teh koh-moh boh-loon-tah-ree-oh(ah) peh-roh ah-seh[s] toh-doh soo [too] trah-bah-hoh ehn klah-seh

He (She, You) [You] rarely (often) participate(s).
Participa[s] rara vez (frecuentemente).
pahr-tee-see-pah[s] rrah-rah behs (freh-koo-ehn-teh-mehn-teh)

He (She) needs (You need) [You need] to participate (raise his/her/your hand) more in class.
Necesita[s] participar (levantar la mano) más frecuentemente en clase.
neh-seh-see-tah[s] pahr-tee-see-pahr (leh-bahn-tahr lah mah-noh) mahs freh-koo-ehn-teh-mehn-teh ehn klah-seh

He (She) needs (You need) [You need] to take a more active part in class discussion.
Necesita[s] tomar parte más activa en las discusiones en clase.
neh-seh-see-tah[s] toh-mahr pahr-teh mahs ahk-tee-bah ehn lahs dees-koo-see-oh-nehs ehn klah-seh

He (She) doesn't (You don't) [You don't] participate. Why?
No participa[s]. ¿Por qué?
noh pahr-tee-see-pah[s] pohr-keh

Class participation counts for 20 percent of his/her/your final grade.
La participación en clase representa veinte por ciento de la nota final.
lah pahr-tee-see-pah-see-ohn ehn klah-seh rreh-preh-sehn-tah beh-een-teh pohr see-ehn-toh deh lah noh-tah fee-nahl

What can I do to help him (her, you [you]) participate more frequently?
¿Qué puedo hacer para ayudarlo (ayudarla, ayudarle a Ud. [ayudarte]) a participar más frecuentemente?
keh poo-eh-doh ah-sehr pah-rah ah-yoo-dahr-loh (ah-yoo-dahr-lah, ah-yoo-dahr-leh ah oo-stehd [ah-yoo-dahr-teh]) ah pahr-tee-see-pahr mahs freh-koo-ehn-teh-mehn-teh

Lateness

Your child (You) [You] must arrive to school on time every day.
Su hijo (hija) (Ud.) [Tú] tiene[s] que llegar a tiempo a la escuela todos los días.
soo ee-hoh (ee-hah) (oo-stehd) [too] tee-eh-neh[s] keh yeh-gahr ah tee-ehm-poh ah lah ehs-koo-eh-lah toh-dohs lohs dee-ahs

He (She) is (You are) [You are] often late (by ten minutes or more).
Llega[s] tarde frecuentemente (con diez minutos de atraso o más).
yeh-gah[s] tahr-deh freh-koo-ehn-teh-mehn-teh (kohn dee-ehs mee-noo-tohs deh ah-trahs oh mahs)

This disturbs the other students.
Esto disturba a los demás alumnos.
ehs-toh dees-toor-bah ah lohs deh-mahs ah-loom-nohs

Why is he (she) (are you) [are you] late?
¿Por qué llega[s] tarde?
pohr keh yeh-gah[s] tahr-deh

Does he (she, you) [you] have an excuse?
¿Tiene[s] una excusa?
tee-eh-neh[s] oo-nah ehks-koo-sah

What is the reason?
¿Cuál es la razón?
koo-ahl ehs lah rrah-sohn

Does he (she) (Do you [you]) live far from the school?
¿Vive[s] lejos de la escuela?
bee-beh[s] leh-hohs deh lah ehs-koo-eh-lah

Are there transportation problems?
¿Hay problemas de transporte?
ah-ee proh-bleh-mahs deh trahns-pohr-teh

Where is his (her) (are your) [are your] late slips?
¿Dónde están sus [tus] notas de tardanza?
dohn-deh ehs-tahn soos [toos] noh-tahs deh tahr-dahn-sah

This is negatively affecting his (her, your [your]) grade.
Esto afecta negativamente su [tu] nota.
ehs-toh ah-fehk-tah neh-gah-tee-bah-mehn-teh soo [too] noh-tah

Perhaps he (she, you [you]) can wake up earlier.
Quizás podrá[s] despertarse [despertarte] más temprano.
kee-sahs poh-drah[s] dehs-pehr-tahr-seh [dehs-pehr-tahr-teh] mahs tehm-prah-noh

He (She, You, [You]) should go to bed earlier.
Tiene[s] que acostarse [acostarte] más temprano.
tee-eh-neh[s] keh ah-kohs-tahr-seh [ah-kohs-tahr-teh] mahs tehm-prah-noh

He (She, You [You]) should prepare himself (herself, yourself) for school the night before.
Tiene[s] que prepararse [prepararte] la noche anterior para ir a la escuela.
tee-eh-neh[s] keh preh-pah-rahr-seh [preh-pah-rahr-teh] lah noh-cheh ahn-teh-ree-ohr pah-rah eer ah lah ehs-koo-eh-lah

Please speak to your child (do something) about this problem.
Por favor, háblele a su hijo (hija) (haga algo acerca) de este problema.
pohr fah-bohr ah-bleh-leh ah soo ee-hoh (ee-hah) (ah-gah ahl-goh ah-sehr-kah) deh ehs-teh proh-bleh-mah

Excessive Absence

Your child (You) [You] must come to school every day.
Su hijo (hija) (Ud.) [Tú] tiene[s] que asistir a la escuela todos los días.
soo ee-hoh (ee-hah) [oo-stehd] [too] tee-eh-neh[s] keh ah-sees-teer ah lah ehs-koo-eh-lah toh-dohs lohs dee-ahs

He (She) is (You are [You are]) often absent. Why?
Está[s] ausente frecuentemente. ¿Por qué?
ehs-tah[s] ah-oo-sehn-teh freh-koo-ehn-teh-mehn-teh pohr keh

Why was (was [were]) he (she) [you] absent yesterday?
¿Por qué estuvo [estuviste] ausente ayer?
pohr keh ehs-too-boh [ehs-too-bee-steh] ah-oo-sehn-teh ah-yehr

He (She) was (You were [You were]) absent _____ times this marking period (month, year) [this week].
Estuvo [Estuviste] ausente _____ veces este semestre (mes, año) [esta semana].
ehs-too-boh [eh-stoo-bee-steh] ah-oo-sehn-teh _____ beh-sehs ehs-teh seh-mehs-treh (mehs, ah-nyoh) [ehs-tah seh-mah-nah]

His (Her, Your [Your]) frequent absences are negatively affecting his (her, your) grade.

Sus [Tus] ausencias frecuentes están afectando negativamente su [tu] nota.

soos [toos] ah-oo-sehn-see-ahs freh-koo-ehn-tehs ehs-tahn ah-fehk-tahn-doh neh-gah-tee-bah-mehn-teh soo [too] noh-tah

The quality of his (her, your [your]) work is suffering.

La calidad de su [tu] trabajo está sufriendo.

lah kah-lee-dahd de soo [too] trah-bah-hoh ehs-tah soo-free-ehn-doh

His (Her, Your [Your]) frequent absences make it difficult for him (her, you [you]) to keep up with the other students.

Sus [Tus] ausencias frecuentes le [te] impiden mantenerse [mantenerte] a la par con los demás alumnos.

soos [toos] ah-oo-sehn-see-ahs freh-koo-ehn-tehs leh [teh] eem-pee-dehn mahn-teh-nehr-teh [mahn-teh-gahr-teh] ah lah pahr kohn lohs deh-mahs ah-loom-nohs

His (Her, Your [Your]) frequent absences are causing problems.

Sus [Tus] ausencias frecuentes están causando problemas.

soos [toos] ah-oo-sehn-see-ahs freh-koo-ehn-tehs ehs-tahn kah-oo-sahn-doh proh-bleh-mahs

He (She, You [You]) cannot learn if you aren't here.

No puede[s] aprender si no está[s] aquí.

noh poo-eh-deh[s] ah-prehn-dehr see noh ehs-tah[s] ah-kee

He (She, You [You]) must make up the work you've missed.

Tiene[s] que completar el trabajo que debe[s].

tee-eh-neh[s] keh kohm-pleh-tahr ehl trah-bah-hoh keh deh-beh[s]

He (She, You [You]) will receive a lower grade because the work is late.

Recibirá[s] una nota más baja porque la tarea está atrasada.

rreh-see-bee-rah[s] oo-nah noh-tah mahs bah-hah pohr-keh lah tah-reh-ah ehs-tah ah-trah-sah-dah

Absence is not an excuse for not doing (handing in) the work.

Una ausencia no justifica no hacer (entregar) el trabajo.

oo-nah ah-oo-sehn-see-ah noh hoos-tee-fee-kah noh ah-sehr (ehn-treh-gahr) ehl trah-bah-hoh

When he (she) is (you are [you are]) absent, he (she, you) must bring a doctor's note or a note from one of his (her, your) parents.

Cuando esté[s] ausente, tiene[s] que traer una nota del doctor o de uno de sus [tus] padres.

koo-ahn-doh ehs-teh[s] ah-oo-sehn-teh tee-eh-neh[s] keh trah-ehr oo-nah noh-tah dehl dohk-tohr oh deh oo-noh deh soos [toos] pah-drehs

Where is his/her/your doctor's note?

¿Dónde está la nota del doctor?

dohn-deh ehs-tah lah noh-tah dehl dohk-tohr

I cannot accurately evaluate his/her/your [your] progress due to his/her/your [your] frequent absences.

No puedo evaluar exactamente su [tu] progreso debido a sus [tus] ausencias frecuentes.

noh poo-eh-doh eh-bah-loo-ahr ehk-sahk-tah-mehn-teh soo [too] proh-greh-soh deh-bee-doh ah soos [toos] ah-oo-sehn-see-ahs freh-koo-ehn-tehs

Does he/she (Do you [Do you]) have a special medical condition I should know about?

¿Tiene[s] una condición médica especial de la cual debo ser consciente?

tee-eh-neh[s] oo-nah kohn-dee-see-ohn meh-dee-kah ehs-peh-see-ahl deh lah koo-ahl deh-boh sehr kohn-see-ehn-teh

Is he/she (Are you [Are you]) in poor health?

¿Es delicada su [tu] salud?

ehs deh-lee-kah-dah soo [too] sah-lood

What problem(s) does he/she (you [you]) have?

¿Qué problema(s) tiene[s]?

keh proh-bleh-mah(s) tee-eh-neh[s]

I would like to have a conference with you as soon as possible about his/her frequent absences.

Quisiera reunirme con Ud. lo antes posible para hablar de sus ausencias frecuentes.

kee-see-eh-rah rreh-oo-neer-meh kohn oo-stehd loh ahn-tehs poh-see-bleh pah-rah ah-blahr deh soos ah-oo-sehn-see-ahs freh-koo-ehn-tehs

To check your child's attendance you must go to (call) the attendance office.

Para verificar la asistencia de su hijo (hija) Ud. tiene que ir (telefonear) a la oficina de asistencia.

pah-rah beh-ree-fee-kahr lah ah-sees-tehn-see-ah deh soo ee-hoh (ee-hah) oo-stehd tee-eh-neh keh eer (teh-leh-foh-neh-ahr) ah lah oh-fee-see-nah deh ah-sees-tehn-see-ah

The attendance office number is _____.

El número de teléfono de la oficina de asistencia es _____.

ehl noo-meh-roh deh teh-leh-foh-noh deh lah oh-fee-see-nah deh ah-sees-tehn-see-ah ehs _____

Cutting Class

Your child plays (You play [You play]) hooky from school.

Su hijo (hija, Ud.) hace [Tú haces] novillos.

soo ee-hoh (ee-hah, oo-stehd) ah-seh [too ah-sehs] noh-bee-yohs

He/She is (You are [You are]) coming to school but he/she is (you are [you are]) not attending his/her (your) _____ class.

Viene[s] a la escuela, pero no asiste[s] a su [tu] clase de _____.

bee-eh-neh[s] ah lah ehs-koo-eh-lah peh-roh noh ah-sees-teh[s] ah soo [too] klah-seh deh _____

This is unacceptable behavior.

Su [Tu] conducta es inaceptable.

soo [too] kohn-dook-tah ehs een-ah-sehp-tah-bleh

He/She (You) will fail any class that he/she does (you do [you do]) not attend on a regular basis.

Reprobará[s] en las clases a las cuales falta[s] con regularidad.

rreh-proh-bah-rah[s] ehn lahs klah-sehs ah lahs koo-ah-lehs fahl-tah[s] kohn rreh-goo-lah-ree-dahd

He (She, You [You]) will be (severely) penalized for unexcused absences.

Lo (La) [Te] penalizarán (severamente) por ausencias sin excusa.

loh (lah) [teh] peh-nah-lee-sah-rahn (seh-beh-rah-mehn-teh) pohr ah-oo-sehn-see-ahs seen ehks-koo-sah

Please speak to your son (daughter) about this.
Por favor, hable con su hijo (hija) acerca de ésto.
pohr fah-bohr ah-bleh kohn soo ee-hoh (ee-hah) ah-sehr-kah deh ehs-toh

This is a very serious problem.
Es un problema muy serio.
ehs oon proh-bleh-mah moo-ee seh-ree-oh

You may call your child's teacher regarding his (her) daily attendance.
Ud. puede telefonear al profesor (a la profesora) de su hijo (hija) acerca de su asistencia diaria.
oos-tehd poo-eh-deh teh-leh-foh-neh-ahr ahl proh-feh-sohr (ah lah proh-feh-soh-rah) deh soo ee-hoh (ee-hah) ah-sehr-kah deh soo ah-sees-tehn-see-ah dee-ah-ree-ah

If he (she, you [you]) continues to miss class, he (she, you [you]) will fail the course and will have to repeat it.
Si continúa[s] a faltar a la clase, reprobará[s] el curso y tendrá[s] que repetirlo.
see kohn-tee-noo-ah[s] ah fahl-tahr ah lah klah-seh rreh-proh-bah-rah[s] ehl koor-soh ee tehn-drah[s] keh rreh-peh-teer-loh

Homework

Your child (You [You]) do a very good job on your homework.
Su hijo (hija, Ud. [Tú]) hace[s] muy bien sus [tus] tareas.
soo ee-hoh (ee-hah, oo-stehd [too]) ah-seh[s] moo-ee bee-ehn soos [toos] tah-reh-ahs

He (She) works (You work [You work]) hard on your assignments.
Se aplica [Te aplicas] mucho en sus [tus] tareas.
seh ah-plee-kah [teh ah-plee-kahs] moo-choh ehn soos [toos] tah-reh-ahs

The quality of his (her, your) assignments reflects the amount of effort put into them.
La calidad de sus [tus] tareas refleja el esfuerzo que hace[s].
lah kah-lee-dahd deh soos [toos] tah-reh-ahs rreh-fleh-hah ehl ehs-foo-ehr-soh keh ah-seh[s]

I recommend that you set aside a specific time each afternoon or evening when your child (you) can concentrate on his (her, your) homework.

Le recomiendo a Ud. que reserve una hora determinada cada tarde o cada noche para que su hijo (hija, Ud. [tú]) pueda[s] concentrarse en sus [tus] tareas.

leh rreh-koh-mee-ehn-doh oo-stehd keh rreh-sehr-beh oo-nah oh-rah deh-tehr-mee-nah-dah kah-dah tahr-deh oh kah-dah noh-cheh pah-rah keh soo ee-hoh (ee-hah) oo-stehd [too] poo-eh-dah[s] kohn-sehn-trahr-seh ehn soos [toos] tah-reh-ahs

Your child needs (You need [You need]) to do his (her, your) home-work more carefully.

Su hijo (hija, Ud. [Tú]) necesita[s] hacer sus [tus] tareas más cuidadosamente.

soo ee-hoh (ee-hah, oo-stehd) [too] neh-seh-see-tah[s] ah-sehr soos [toos] tah-reh-ahs mahs koo-ee-dah-doh-sah-mehn-teh

His (Her, Your [Your]) homework is poorly done.

Hace[s] sus [tus] tareas descuidadamente.

ah-seh[s] soos [toos] tah-reh-ahs dehs-koo-ee-dah-dah-mehn-teh

He (She, You [You]) must pay more attention when doing his (her, your) homework.

Tiene[s] que prestar más atención cuando hace[s] sus [tus] tareas.

tee-eh-neh[s] keh prehs-tahr mahs ah-tehn-see-ohn koo-ahn-doh ah-seh[s] soos [toos] tah-reh-ahs

He (She, You [You]) should check his (her, your) answers before handing in his (her, your) homework.

Debe[s] verificar sus [tus] respuestas antes de entregar sus [tus] tareas.

deh-beh[s] beh-ree-fee-kahr soos [toos] rrehs-poo-ehs-tahs ahn-tehs deh ehn-treh-gahr soos [toos] tah-reh-ahs

He (She) is (You are [You are]) missing _____ homeworks.

Le (Te) faltan _____ tareas.

leh (teh) fahl-tahn _____ tah-reh-ahs

Why didn't (he, she, you [you]) do your homework?

¿Por qué no hizo [hiciste] su [tu] tarea?

pohr keh noh ee-soh [ee-sees-teh] soo [too] tah-reh-ah

Is there a good reason for this?

¿Tiene[s] una buena razón para explicar ésto?

tee-eh-neh[s] oo-nah boo-eh-nah rrah-sohn pah-rah ehks-plee-kahr ehs-toh

If all his (her, your [your]) homeworks are not handed in, your grade will be lowered.

Si no entrega[s] todas sus [tus] tareas, recibirá[s] una nota más baja.

see noh ehn-treh-gah[s] toh-dahs soos [toos] tah-reh-ahs rreh-see-bee-rah[s] oo-nah noh-tah mahs bah-hah

Behavior and Interaction with Peers

Your child's behavior is excellent.

El comportamiento de su hijo (hija) es excelente.

ehl kohm-pohr-tah-mee-ehn-toh deh soo ee-hoh (ee-hah) ehs ehk-seh-lehn-teh

It is a pleasure to have your child in my class.

Es un placer tener a su hijo (hija) en mi clase.

ehs oon plah-sehr teh-nehr ah soo ee-hoh (ee-hah) ehn mee klah-seh

He (She) is always well-mannered and behaved.

Siempre es bien educado(a) y se comporta bien.

see-ehm-preh ehs bee-ehn eh-doo-kah-doh(dah) ee seh kohm-pohr-tah bee-ehn

He/She is easy to get along with.

Es tratable.

ehs trah-tah-bleh

He/She works well in a group.

Trabaja bien en grupo.

trah-bah-hah bee-ehn ehn groo-poh

He/She tries to behave in class.

Trata de portarse bien en clase.

trah-tah deh pohr-tahr-seh bee-ehn ehn klah-seh

His/Her behavior is improving.

Su comportamiento sigue mejorando.

soo kohm-pohr-tah-mee-ehn-toh see-geh meh-hoh-rahn-doh

His/Her behavior affects his/her grades (work).

Su comportamiento afecta sus notas (estudios).

soo kohm-pohr-tah-mee-ehn-toh ah-fehk-tah soos noh-tahs (ehs-too-dee-ohs)

He/She is learning more self-control (self-discipline).
Está aprendiendo a dominarse más (a tener más autodisciplina).
ehs-tah ah-prehn-dee-ehn-doh ah doh-mee-nahr-seh mahs (ah teh-nehr mahs ah-oo-toh-dee-see-plee-nah)

He/She has shown improvement with his/her behavior problems.
Demuestra progreso con sus problemas de conducta.
deh-moo-ehs-trah proh-greh-soh kohn soos proh-bleh-mahs deh kohn-dook-tah

He (She) is well-liked by his (her) peers.
Es muy querido(a) por sus compañeros.
ehs moo-ee keh-ree-doh(dah) pohr soos kohm-pah-nyeh-rohs

He/She (doesn't get) gets along well with others.
(No) Se lleva bien con los demás.
(noh) seh yeh-bah bee-ehn kohn lohs deh-mahs

He/She often talks out loud.
Muchas veces habla en voz alta.
moo-chahs beh-sehs ah-blah ehn bos ahl-tah

He/She often disturbs the entire class.
Muchas veces disturba a toda la clase.
moo-chahs beh-sehs dees-toor-bah ah toh-dah lah klah-seh

He/She often needs to be reminded of the rules.
Hay que recordarle frecuentemente las reglas.
ah-ee keh rreh-kohr-dahr-leh freh-koo-ehn-teh-mehn-teh lahs rreh-glahs

He/She is too interested in his/her classmates' work.
Se interesa demasiado en el trabajo de sus compañeros.
seh een-teh-reh-sah deh-mah-see-ah-doh ehn ehl trah-bah-hoh deh soos kohm-pah-nyeh-rohs

He (She) is talkative.
Es hablador(a).
ehs ah-blah-dohr(doh-rah)

He (She) isn't attentive.
No es atento(a).
noh ehs ah-tehn-toh(tah)

He/She talks too much to his (her) friends.
Habla demasiado con sus amigos (amigas).
ah-blah deh-mah-see-ah-doh kohn soos ah-mee-gohs (ah-mee-gahs)

He (She) needs to be more considerate.
Necesita ser más considerado(a).
neh-seh-see-tah sehr mahs kohn-see-deh-rah-doh(dah)

Your child disturbs others.
Su hijo (hija) disturba a los demás.
soo ee-hoh (ee-hah) dees-toor-bah ah lohs deh-mahs

He/She must learn to wait his/her turn.
Debe aprender a esperar su turno.
deh-beh ah-preh-dehr ah ehs-peh-rahr soo toor-noh

He/She doesn't listen (follow the rules).
No escucha (sigue las reglas).
noh ehs-koo-chah (see-geh lahs rreh-glahs)

He/She often has to be reminded to cooperate.
Necesito recordarle frecuentemente que tiene que cooperar.
*neh-seh-see-toh rreh-kohr-dahr-leh freh-koo-ehn-teh-mehn-teh keh tee-eh-neh
keh koh-oh-peh-rahr.*

He/She is too involved in other students' business.
Se interesa demasiado en los asuntos de los demás alumnos.
*seh een-teh-reh-sah deh-mah-see-ah-doh ehn lohs ah-soon-tohs deh lohs deh-
mahs ah-loom-nohs*

He/She has difficulties in his/her relationships with peers.
Tiene dificultades en sus relaciones con los demás alumnos.
*tee-eh-neh dee-fee-kool-tah-dehs ehn soos rreh-lah-see-oh-nehs kohn lohs deh-
mahs ah-loom-nohs*

He/She is often in trouble with the other children.
Frecuentemente se mete en líos con los demás niños.
freh-koo-ehn-teh-mehn-teh seh meh-teh ehn lee-ohs kohn lohs deh-mahs nee-nyohs

Attitude

Your child has a/an excellent (good, poor) attidude.
Su hijo (hija) tiene una actitud excelente (buena, mala).
*soo ee-hoh (ee-hah) tee-eh-neh oo-nah ahk-tee-tood ehk-seh-lehn-teh
(boo-eh-nah, mah-lah)*

His/Her attitude has improved (gotten worse).
Su actitud ha mejorado (empeorado).
soo ahk-tee-tood ah meh-hoh-rah-doh (ehm-peh-oh-rah-doh)

I am pleased with this improvement.
Estoy contento(a) con esta mejora.
ehs-toh-ee kohn-tehn-toh(tah) kohn ehs-tah meh-hoh-rah

Your child is very mature (immature).
Su hijo (hija) es muy maduro(a) (inmaduro)(a).
soo ee-hoh (ee-hah) ehs moo-ee mah-doo-roh(rah) (een-mah-doo-roh)(rah)

He/She is trying to improve his/her attitude.
Está tratando de mejorar su actitud.
eh-stah trah-tahn-doh deh meh-hoh-rahr soo ahk-tee-tood

He/She is applying himself/herself more (less).
Se está aplicando más (menos).
seh ehs-tah ah-plee-kahn-doh mahs (meh-nohs)

He (She) is uncooperative (argumentative, hostile, stubborn).
Es poco colaborador(a) (discutidor(a), hostil, testarudo(a)).
*ehs poh-koh koh-lah-boh-rah-dohr (doh-rah) (dees-koo-tee-dohr (doh-rah),
ohs-teel, tehs-tah-roo-doh(dah))*

Work Habits

Your child works well (poorly).
Su hijo (hija) trabaja bien (mal).
soo ee-hoh (ee-hah) trah-bah-hah bee-ehn (mahl)

He (She) is hard-working.
Es muy aplicado(a).
ehs moo-ee ah-plee-kah-doh(dah)

He/She does his/her best.
Hace lo mejor que puede.
ah-seh loh meh-hohr keh poo-eh-deh

He/She is enthusiastic.
Es entusiasta.
ehs ehn-too-see-ahs-tah

He/She is proud of doing his/her work well.
Se enorgullece de hacer bien sus tareas.
seh eh-nohr-goo-yeh-seh deh ah-sehr bee-ehn soos tah-reh-ahs

He/She shows initiative.
Demuestra iniciativa.
deh-moo-ehs-trah ee-nee-see-ah-tee-bah

He/She does neat work.
Hace sus tareas con esmero.
ah-seh soos tah-reh-ahs kohn ehs-meh-roh

His/Her work habits have improved.
Sus hábitos de estudio han mejorado.
soos ah-bee-tohs deh ehs-too-dee-oh ahn meh-hoh-rah-doh

He/She does (not) use his/her time efficiently.
(No) aprovecha su tiempo eficazmente.
(noh) ah-proh-beh-chah soo tee-ehm-poh eh-fee-kahs-mehn-teh

He/She always (never) finishes his/her work.
Siempre (Nunca) termina su trabajo.
see-ehm-preh (noon-kah) tehr-mee-nah soo trah-bah-hoh

His/Her work habits are inconsistent.
Sus hábitos de estudio son inconsistentes.
soos ah-bee-tohs deh ehs-too-dee-oh sohn een-kohn-sees-tehn-tehs

He/She is easily distracted.
Se distrae fácilmente.
seh dees-trah-eh fah-seel-mehn-teh

He (She) is careless.
Es descuidado(a).
ehs dehs-koo-ee-dah-doh(dah)

He/She wastes a lot of time.
Pierde mucho tiempo.
pee-ehr-deh moo-choh tee-ehm-poh

He/She needs to put in more effort.
Necesita esforzarse más.
neh-seh-see-tah ehs-fohr-sahr-seh mahs

He/She needs to improve his/her work habits.
Necesita mejorar sus hábitos de estudio.
neh-seh-see-tah meh-hoh-rahr soos ah-bee-tohs deh ehs-too-dee-oh

He (She) has trouble working alone.
Tiene dificultad trabajando solo(a).
tee-eh-neh dee-fee-kool-tahd trah-bah-hahn-doh soh-loh(lah)

He/She doesn't finish his/her work because he/she is constantly talking to others.
No termina su trabajo porque pasa demasiado tiempo conversando con los demás.
noh tehr-mee-nah soo trah-bah-hoh pohr-keh pah-sah deh-mah-see-ah-doh tee-ehm-poh kohn-behr-sahn-doh kohn lohs deh-mahs

He/She daydreams a lot.
Está frecuentemente en las nubes.
ehs-tah freh-koo-ehn-teh-mehn-teh ehn lahs noo-behs

He/She is not working up to his/her ability.
No trabaja a toda capacidad.
noh trah-bah-hah ah toh-dah kah-pah-see-dahd

He/She is capable of better work.
Tiene el potencial para ser mejor estudiante.
tee-eh-neh ehl-poh-tehn-see-ahl pah-rah sehr meh-hohr ehs-too-dee-ahn-teh

He/She has difficulty concentrating.
Tiene dificultad para concentrarse.
tee-eh-neh dee-fee-kool-tahd pah-rah kohn-sehn-trahr-seh

He/She requires constant supervision.
Requiere supervisión continua.
rreh-kee-eh-reh soo-pehr-bee-see-ohn kohn-tee-noo-ah

Discipline

Your child was (You were [You were]) caught _____.
Su hijo (hija, Ud.) [tu] fue [fuiste] sorprendido _____.
soo ee-hoh (ee-hah, oo-stehd) foo-eh [foo-ees-teh] sohr-prehn-dee-doh _____

carrying a dangerous weapon	**llevando un arma peligrosa**	*yeh-bahn-doh oon ahr-mah peh-lee-groh-sah*

carrying a gun (explosives)	**portando un arma de fuego (explosivos)**	pohr-tahn-doh oon ahr-mah deh foo-eh-goh (ehks-ploh-see-bohs)
cheating on a test	**copiándose**	koh-pee-ahn-doh-seh
defying authority	**resistiendo la autoridad**	rreh-sees-tee-ehn-doh lah ah-oo-toh-ree-dahd
disobeying the rules	**desobedeciendo las reglas**	deh-soh-beh-deh-see-ehn-doh lahs rreh-glahs
fighting	**peleando**	peh-leh-ahn-doh
harassing a classmate (teacher)	**acosando a un (una) compañero(a) (profesor(a))**	ah-kohs-ahn-doh ah oon (oo-nah) kohm-pah-nyeh-roh (kohm-pah-nyeh-rah) (proh-feh-sohr) (proh-feh-soh-rah)
littering	**tirando basura**	tee-rahn-doh bah-soo-rah
pulling the fire alarms	**haciendo sonar las alarmas de fuego**	ah-see-ehn-doh soh-nahr lahs ah-lahr-mahs deh foo-eh-goh
setting a fire	**prendiendo un fuego**	prehn-dee-ehn-doh oon foo-eh-goh
spraying the fire extinguisher	**usando el extinguidor de incendios**	oo-sahn-doh ehl ehks-teen-goo-ee-dohr deh een-sehn-dee-ohs
stealing from someone	**robándole a alguien**	rroh-bahn-doh-leh ah ahl-gee-ehn
threatening a classmate (teacher)	**amenazando a un (una) compañero(a) (profesor(a))**	ah-mehn-ah-sahn-doh ah oon (oo-nah) kohm-pah-nyeh-roh (kohm-pah-nyeh-rah) (proh-feh-sohr) (proh-feh-soh-rah)
throwing things	**tirando cosas**	tee-rahn-doh koh-sahs
using alcohol (drugs)	**usando alcohol (drogas)**	oo-sahn-doh ahl-koh-ohl (droh-gahs)
using gang signs	**haciendo las señas de una pandilla**	ah-see-ehn-doh lahs seh-nyahs deh oo-nah pahn-dee-yah
writing graffiti	**escribiendo grafiti**	ehs-kree-bee-ehn-doh grah-fee-tee

This is disruptive behavior.
Su [Tu] comportamiento crea desorden.
soo [too] kohm-pohr-tah-mee-ehn-toh kreh-ah dehs-ohr-dehn

He (She, You [You]) must be punished.
Debe[s] recibir un castigo.
deh-beh[s] rreh-see-beer oon kahs-tee-goh

He (She, You [You]) must serve detention.
Debe[s] quedarse [quedarte] en la escuela después de las clases.
deh-beh[s] keh-dahr-seh [keh-dahr-teh] ehn lah ehs-koo-eh-lah dehs-poo-ehs
deh lahs klah-sehs

He (She, You [You]) must remain in the social worker's (principal's, guidance) office.
Tiene[s] que quedarse [quedarte] en la oficina del (de la) trabajador(a) social (del (de la) director(a), del (de la) consejero(a)).
tee-eh-neh[s] keh keh-dahr-seh [keh-dahr-teh] ehn lah oh-fee-see-nah dehl
(deh lah) trah-bah-hah-dohr(doh-rah) soh-see-ahl dehl (deh lah) dee-rehk-
tohr(toh-rah), dehl deh lah kohn-seh-heh-roh (kohn-seh-heh-rah)

This is serious.
Es serio.
ehs seh-ree-oh

A reprimand is (not) enough.
Un regaño (no) es suficiente.
oon rreh-gah-nyoh (noh) ehs soo-fee-see-ehn-teh

Students can be suspended from school if they are considered dangerous to themselves or others.
Los estudiantes pueden ser suspendidos de la escuela si se consideran peligrosos para sí mismos o los demás.
lohs ehs-too-dee-ahn-tehs poo-eh-dehn sehr soos-pehn-dee-dohs deh lah ehs-
koo-eh-lah see seh kohn-see-deh-rahn peh-lee-groh-sohs pah-rah see mees-mohs
oh lohs deh-mahs

You can read the rules on student behavior in this pamphlet.
Ud. puede leer las reglas de comportamiento estudiantil en este folleto.
oo-stehd poo-eh-deh leh-ehr lahs rreh-glahs deh kohm-pohr-tah-mee-ehn-toh
ehs-too-dee-ahn-teel ehn ehs-teh foh-yeh-toh

He (She) is (You are [You are]) suspended from school for _____ day(s) (week(s)).

Está[s] suspendido (suspendida) de la escuela por _____ día(s) (semana(s)).

ehs-tah[s] soos-pehn-dee-doh(dah) deh lah ehs-koo-eh-lah pohr _____ dee-ah(s) (seh-mah-nah(s))

In case of a suspension, you have the right to be notified of the specific charges immediately.

En caso de suspensión, tiene[s] derecho a recibir notificación inmediata de los cargos específicos.

ehn kah-soh deh soos-pehn-see-ohn tee-eh-neh[s] deh-reh-choh ah rreh-see-beer noh-tee-fee-kah-see-ohn een-meh-dee-ah-tah deh lohs kahr-gohs ehs-peh-see-fee-kohs

You are also entitled to all documentary evidence against him (her, you).

También tiene[s] derecho a recibir toda la evidencia documen-tada en contra de él (ella, Ud.) [tu].

tahm-bee-ehn tee-eh-neh[s] deh-reh-choh ah rreh-see-beer toh-dah lah eh-bee-dehn-see-ah doh-koo-mehn-tah-dah ehn kohn-trah deh ehl (eh-yah, oo-stehd)[too]

You have the right to legal counsel during the suspension hearing.

Tiene[s] derecho a representación legal durante la audiencia de suspensión.

tee-eh-neh[s] deh-reh-choh ah rreh-preh-sehn-tah-see-ohn leh-gahl doo-rahn-teh lah ah-oo-dee-ehn-see-ah deh soos-pehn-see-ohn

Students have the right to receive all homework, classwork, and alternative instruction during the period of suspension.

Los estudiantes tienen derecho a recibir todas las tareas, tra-bajo de clase, e instrucción alternativa durante la suspensión.

lohs ehs-too-dee-ahn-tehs tee-eh-nehn deh-reh-choh ah rreh-see-beer toh-dahs lahs tah-reh-ahs, trah-bah-hoh deh klah-seh eh een-strook-see-ohn ahl-tehr-nah-tee-bah doo-rahn-teh lah soos-pehn-see-ohn

Your child (You [You]) may be transferred from the school.

Su hijo (hija) (Ud.) [Tú] puedes ser trasladado(a) de la escuela.

soo ee-hoh (ee-hah oo-stehd) [too] poo-eh-deh[s] sehr trahs-lah-dah-doh[dah] deh lah ehs-koo-eh-lah

For security reasons, he (she, you [you]) will be transferred.
Por razones de seguridad, será[s] trasladado(a).
poh rrah-soh-nehs deh seh-goo-ree-dahd seh-rah[s] trahs-lah-dah-doh(dah)

You may request a safety transfer to another school.
Puede[s] pedir un traslado a otra escuela por razones de seguridad.
poo-eh-deh[s] peh-deer oon trahs-lah-doh ah oh-trah ehs-koo-eh-lah pohr rrah-soh-nehs deh seh-goo-ree-dahd

Grades and Promotion

Your child's grades are good (satisfactory, excellent, poor).
Las notas de su hijo (hija) son buenas (satisfactorias, excelentes, malas).
lahs noh-tahs deh soo ee-hoh (ee-hah) sohn boo-eh-nahs (sah-tees-fahk-toh-ree-ahs, ehk-seh-lehn-tehs, mah-lahs)

He (She) excels in _____.
Sobresale en _____.
soh-breh-sah-leh ehn _____

Your child's grades are improving (getting lower).
Las notas de su hijo (hija) están mejorando (bajando).
lahs noh-tahs deh soo ee-hoh (ee-hah) ehs-tahn meh-hoh-rahn-doh (bah-hahn-doh)

He/She is (not) getting good grades.
(No) Saca buenas notas.
(noh) sah-kah boo-eh-nahs noh-tahs

He/She has made excellent (good) progress.
Ha hecho progresos excelentes (buenos).
ah eh-choh proh-greh-sohs ehk-seh-lehn-tehs (boo-eh-nohs)

He/She has shown improvement in his/her academic work.
Muestra progreso en sus estudios académicos.
moo-ehs-trah proh-greh-soh ehn soos ehs-too-dee-ohs ah-kah-deh-mee-kohs

He/She is working at grade level.
Su trabajo corresponde al nivel de su grado.
soo trah-bah-hoh koh-rrehs-pohn-deh ahl nee-behl deh soo grah-doh

He/She is passing (failing) his/her _____ class.
Está aprobando (reprobando) la clase de _____.
ehs-tah ah-proh-bahn-doh (rreh-proh-bahn-doh) lah klah-seh deh _____

Have you seen his/her report card?
¿Ha visto sus calificaciones?
ah bees-toh soos kah-lee-fee-kah-see-oh-nehs

He/She is capable of receiving better grades.
Tiene el potencial para recibir notas más altas.
tee-eh-neh ehl poh-tehn-see-ahl pah-rah rreh-see-beer noh-tahs mahs ahl-tahs

He (She) will (not) be promoted to the next grade.
(No) Será ascendido(a) al grado superior.
(noh) seh-rah ah-sehn-dee-doh(dah) ahl grah-doh soo-peh-ree-ohr

He (She) is not ready for the next grade.
No está listo(a) para pasar al próximo grado.
noh ehs-tah lees-toh(tah) pah-rah pah-sar ahl prohk-see-moh grah-doh

His/Her work is below grade-level standards.
Su trabajo es inferior al nivel de su grado.
soo trah-bah-hoh ehs een-feh-ree-ohr ahl nee-behl deh soo grah-doh

He/She needs more time to complete this grade.
Necesita más tiempo para terminar los estudios de este grado.
neh-seh-see-tah mahs tee-ehm-poh pah-rah tehr-mee-nahr lohs ehs-too-dee-ohs deh ehs-teh grah-doh

His/Her achievements are (not) high enough to go on to the next grade.
Su aprovechamiento (no) es suficiente para pasar al próximo grado.
soo ah-proh-beh-chah-mee-ehn-toh (noh) ehs soo-fee-see-ehn-teh pah-rah pah-sahr ahl prohk-see-moh grah-doh

He/She doesn't work up to his/her ability.
No trabaja al nivel de su capacidad.
noh trah-bah-hah ahl nee-behl deh soo kah-pah-see-dahd

If he/she repeats this grade, he/she will do better next year.
Si repite el grado, saldrá mejor el año próximo.
see rreh-pee-teh ehl grah-doh sahl-drah meh-hohr ehl ah-nyoh prohk-see-moh

He/She must attend night (summer) school if he/she wants to graduate on time.

Debe asistir a la escuela nocturna (de verano) si quiere gra-duarse a tiempo.

deh-beh ah-sees-teer ah lah ehs-koo-eh-lah nohk-toor-nah (deh beh-rah-noh) see kee-eh-reh grah-doo-ahr-seh ah tee-ehm-poh

Conferences

Would you be able to visit our class soon?

¿Podría visitar nuestra clase pronto?

poh-dree-ah bee-see-tahr noo-ehs-trah klah-seh prohn-toh

I would like a conference with you as soon as possible to speak about _____.

Deseo reunirme con Ud. lo antes posible para hablar de _____.

deh-seh-oh rreh-oo-neer-meh kohn oo-stehd loh ahn-tehs poh-see-bleh pah-rah ah-blahr deh _____

Is Monday at three o'clock (after classes) convenient for you?

¿Puede venir el lunes, a las tres de la tarde (después de las clases)?

poo-eh-deh beh-neer ehl loo-nehs ah lahs trehs deh lah tahr-deh (dehs-poo-ehs deh lahs klah-sehs)

Would you call the office to make an appointment for a conference?

¿Puede telefonear a la oficina para hacer una cita?

poo-eh-deh teh-leh-foh-neh-ahr ah lah oh-fee-see-nah pah-rah ah-sehr oo-nah see-tah

Please feel free to call me at any time.

Por favor, llámeme a cualquier hora.

pohr fah-bohr yah-meh-meh ah koo-ahl-kee-ehr oh-rah

It would be helpful to have a conference with you concerning your child.

Sería beneficioso reunirnos para hablar de su hijo (hija).

seh-ree-ah beh-neh-fee-see-oh-soh rreh-oo-neer-nohs pah-rah ah-blahr deh soo ee-hoh (ee-hah)

Thank you for coming to speak to me about your child.
Le agradezco haber venido a la escuela para hablar de su hijo (hija).
leh ah-grah-dehs-koh ah-behr beh-nee-doh ah lah ehs-koo-eh-lah pah-rah ah-blahr deh soo ee-hoh (ee-hah)

It is a pleasure to talk to you about your child's progress.
Es un placer hablarle sobre el progreso de su hijo (hija).
ehs oon plah-sehr ah-blahr-leh soh-breh ehl proh-greh-soh deh soo ee-hoh (ee-hah)

How can we help him/her develop better work habits?
¿Cómo podemos ayudarle a desarrollar mejores hábitos de estudio?
koh-moh poh-deh-mohs ah-yoo-dahr-leh ah deh-sah-rroh-yair meh-hoh-rehs ah-bee-tohs deh ehs-too-dee-oh

He/She has the potential to do better.
Tiene el potencial para ser mejor estudiante.
tee-eh-neh ehl poh-tehn-see-ahl pah-rah sehr meh-hohr ehs-too-dee-ahn-teh

He (She) is proud of his (her) work.
Se siente muy orgulloso(a) de su trabajo.
seh see-ehn-teh moo-ee ohr-goo-yoh soh(sah) deh soo trah-bah-hoh

He/She tries hard.
Se esfuerza.
seh ehs-foo-ehr-sah

He/She has a problem.
Tiene un problema.
tee-eh-neh oon proh-bleh-mah

Perhaps you could speak to him/her about it.
Quizás Ud. podría hablarle de esto.
kee-sahs oo-stehd poh-dree-ah ah-blahr-leh deh ehs-toh

He/She needs all the help and encouragement we can give him/her.
Necesita toda la ayuda y estímulo que podamos darle.
neh-seh-see-tah toh-dah lah ah-yoo-dah ee ehs-tee-moo-loh keh poh-dah-mohs dahr-leh

Together we can help your child.
Juntos (Juntas) podemos ayudar a su hijo (hija).
hoon-tohs (hoon-tahs) poh-deh-mohs ah-yoo-dahr ah soo ee-hoh (ee-hah)

Thank you for your visit (cooperation).
Muchas gracias por su visita (cooperación).
moo-chahs grah-see-ahs pohr soo bee-see-tah (koh-oh-peh-rah-see-ohn)

On the Phone

Hello, may I speak to Mr. (Mrs., Miss) _____?
¿Aló, puedo hablar con el señor (la señora, la señorita) _____?
ah-loh poo-eh-doh ah-blahr kohn ehl seh-nyohr (lah seh-nyoh-rah, lah seh-nyoh-ree-tah) _____

With whom am I speaking?
¿Con quién hablo?
kohn kee-ehn ah-bloh

This is _____.
Habla _____.
ah-blah _____

I'm calling about _____.
Estoy llamando acerca de _____.
ehs-toh-ee yah-mahn-doh ah-sehr-kah deh _____

When can I call him/her back?
¿Cuándo puedo devolver la llamada?
koo-ahn-doh poo-eh-doh deh-bohl-behr lah yah-mah-dah

My number is _____.
Mi número es _____.
mee noo-meh-roh ehs _____

I can't hear.
No puedo oír.
noh poo-eh-doh oh-eer

Speak louder (more slowly), please.
Hable más alto (despacio), por favor.
ah-bleh mahs ahl-toh (dehs-pah-see-oh) pohr fah-bohr

Could you please repeat that?
¿Puede repetir eso, por favor?
poo-eh-deh rreh-peh-teer eh-soh pohr fah-bohr

Wait a minute.
Espere un momento, por favor.
ehs-peh-reh oon moh-mehn-toh pohr fah-bohr

Don't hang up.
No cuelgue.
noh koo-ehl-geh

Can I call him (her, you) later?
¿Puedo llamarlo (llamarla) más tarde?
poo-eh-doh yah-mahr-loh (lah) mahs tahr-deh

Can you call me later?
¿Puede llamarme más tarde?
poo-eh-deh yah-mahr-meh mahs tahr-deh

I would like to leave a message.
Quisiera dejar un recado.
kee-see-eh-rah deh-hahr oon rreh-kah-doh

Please tell him (her) that I called to speak about his (her) child.
Dígale por favor que telefoneé para hablarle de su hijo (hija).
dee-gah-leh pohr fah-bohr keh teh-leh-foh-neh-eh pah-rah ah-blahr-leh deh soo ee-hoh (ee-hah)

It is very important (urgent).
Es muy importante (urgente).
ehs moo-ee eem-pohr-tahn-teh (oor-gehn-teh)

Your child's teacher isn't here right now.
El profesor (La profesora) de su hijo (hija) no está aquí en este momento.
ehl proh-feh-sohr (lah proh-feh-soh-rah) deh soo ee-hoh (ee-hah) noh ehs-tah ah-kee ehn ehs-teh moh-mehn-toh

He/She can't come to the phone.
No puede contestar la llamada.
noh poo-eh-deh kohn-tehs-tahr lah yah-mah-dah

Do you want to leave a message?
¿Quiere dejar un recado?
kee-eh-reh deh-hahr oon rreh-kah-doh

I will give him/her your message.
Voy a darle su mensaje.
boh-ee ah dahr-leh soo mehn-sah-heh

Dial this number to speak to the principal (counselor).
Marque este número para hablar con el (la) director(a) (consejero(a)).
mahr-keh ehs-teh noo-meh-roh pah-rah ah-blahr kohn ehl (lah) dee-rehk-tohr (toh-rah) (kohn-seh-heh-roh (rah))

I'll transfer you.
Voy a transferirlo (transferirla).
boh-ee ah trahns-feh-reer-loh(lah)

Ask for this number.
Pida este número.
pee-dah ehs-teh noo-meh-roh

You have the wrong number.
Tiene el número equivocado.
tee-eh-neh ehl noo-meh-roh eh-kee-boh-kah-doh

13

The Special-Needs Student

Note:

1. Letters or words in brackets are used when using the familiar you **[tú]** form.
2. When speaking to more than one adult, **Ud.** (you, singular) becomes **Uds.** (you, plural) and an n is added to the conjugated verb form.
3. The formal you form is expressed in the same way as the third-person singular **él** (he) and **ella** (she) forms.

Special Needs

Does your child have special needs?
¿Requiere su hijo (hija) atención especial?
rreh-kee-eh-reh soo ee-hoh (ee-hah) ah-tehn-see-ohn ehs-peh-see-ahl

Why? Is he/she _____?
¿Por qué? ¿Es _____?
pohr keh ehs _____

blind	**ciego(a)**	*see-eh-goh(gah)*
deaf	**sordo(a)**	*sohr-doh(dah)*
develop-	**atrasado(a)**	*ah-trah-sah-doh(dah)*
mentally	**en el**	*ehn ehl*
challenged	**desarrollo**	*deh-sah-rroh-yoh*
mute	**mudo(a)**	*moo-doh(dah)*
physically handicapped	**minusválido(a)**	*mee-noos-bah-lee-doh(dah)*

Why? Is he/she _____?
¿Por qué? ¿Tiene _____?
pohr keh tee-eh-neh _____

emotionally handicapped	**problemas emocionales**	*proh-bleh-mahs eh-moh-see-oh-nah-les*
hearing impaired	**problemas de audición**	*proh-bleh-mahs deh ah-oo-dee-see-ohn*
learning disabled	**problemas de aprendizaje**	*proh-bleh-mahs deh ah-prehn-dee-sah-heh*
mentally handicapped	**problemas psicológicos**	*proh-bleh-mahs see-koh-loh-hee-kohs*
visually impaired	**problemas de la vista**	*proh-bleh-mahs deh lah bees-tah*

Is he (she) toilet trained?
¿Está acostumbrado(a) a ir solo(a) al baño?
ehs-tah ah-kohs-toom-brah-doh(dah) ah eer soh-loh(lah) ahl bah-nyoh

What is (are) his (her) problems?
¿Cuál(es) es (son) su(s) problema(s)?
koo-ah-leh(s) ehs (sohn) soo(s) proh-bleh-mah(s)

Does he/she suffer from _____?
¿Sufre _____?
soo-freh _____

AIDS	**de SIDA**	*deh see-dah*
allergies	**de alergias**	*deh ah-lehr-gee-ahs*
an auditory deficiency	**de un defecto auditivo**	*deh oon deh-fehk-toh ah-oo-dee-tee-boh*
asthma	**del asma**	*dehl ahs-mah*
attention deficit disorder (with hyperactivity)	**de un desorden de déficit de atención (con hiperactividad)**	*deh oon dehs-ohr-dehn deh deh-fee-seet deh ah-tehn-see-ohn (kohn ee-pehr-ahk-tee-bee-dahd)*
auditory processing problems	**de problemas de procesamiento auditorio**	*deh proh-bleh-mahs deh proh-seh-sah-mee-ehn-toh ah-oo-dee-toh-ree-oh*
autism	**de autismo**	*deh ah-oo-tees-moh*
bipolar disorder	**de trastorno bipolar**	*deh trahs-tohr-noh bee-poh-lahr*

cancer	**de cáncer**	*deh kahn-sehr*
cerebral palsy	**de parálisis cerebral**	*deh pah-rah-lee-sees seh-reh-brahl*
a chemical sensitivity	**de una susceptibilidad química**	*deh oo-nah soo-sehp-tee-bee-lee-dahd kee-mee-kah*
a chronic disease	**de una enfermedad crónica**	*deh oo-nah ehn-fehr-meh-dahd kroh-nee-kah*
cystic fibrosis	**de fibrosis cística**	*deh fee-broh-sees sees-tee-kah*
a degenerative disease	**de una enfermedad degenerativa**	*deh oo-nah ehn-fehr-meh-dahd deh-geh-neh-rah-tee-bah*
depression	**de depresión**	*deh deh-preh-see-ohn*
Down's syndrome	**del síndrome de Down**	*dehl seen-droh-meh deh down*
dyslexia	**de dislexia**	*deh dees-lehk-see-ah*
epilepsy	**de epilepsia**	*deh eh-pee-lehp-see-ah*
a genetic disease	**de una enfermedad genética**	*deh oo-nah ehn-fehr-meh-dahd heh-neh-tee-kah*
hyperactivity	**de hiperactividad**	*deh ee-pehr-ahk-tee-bee-dahd*
juvenile diabetes	**de diabetes infantil**	*deh dee-ah-beh-tehs een-fahn-teel*
leukemia	**de leucemia**	*deh leh-oo-seh-mee-ah*
Lyme disease	**de la enfermedad de Lyme**	*deh lah ehn-fehr-meh-dahd deh lyme*
multiple sclerosis	**de esclerosis múltiple**	*deh ehs-kleh-roh-sees mool-tee-pleh*
muscular dystrophy	**de distrofia muscular**	*deh dees-troh-fee-ah moos-koo-lahr*
a neurological disease	**de una enfermedad neurológica**	*deh oo-nah ehn-fehr-meh-dahd neh-oo-roh-loh-hee-kah*
a personality disorder	**de un trastorno de la personalidad**	*deh oon trahs-tohr-noh deh lah pehr-soh-nah-lee-dahd*
polio	**de polio**	*deh poh-lee-oh*

Tourette's syndrome	**del síndrome de Tourette**	*dehl seen-droh-meh deh tourette*
a visual deficiency	**de un defecto visual**	*deh oon deh-fehk-toh bee-soo-ahl*
visual processing problems	**de problemas de procesamiento visual**	*deh proh-bleh-mahs deh proh-seh-sah-mee-ehn-toh bee-soo-ahl*

How is his/her problem manifested?
¿Cómo se manifesta su problema?
koh-moh seh mah-nee-fehs-tah soo proh-bleh-mah

How long has he/she had this problem?
¿Desde cuándo sufre de este problema?
dehs-deh koo-ahn-doh soo-freh deh ehs-teh proh-bleh-mah

Does he/she have sensory issues?
¿Tiene problemas sensoriales?
tee-eh-neh proh-bleh-mahs sehn-soh-ree-ah-lehs

Can he/she _____?
¿Puede _____?
poo-eh-deh _____

breathe easily	**respirar fácilmente**	*rrehs-pee-rahr fah-seel-mehn-teh*
calculate	**calcular**	*kahl-koo-lahr*
concentrate	**concentrarse**	*kohn-sehn-trahr-seh*
go to the bathroom alone	**ir al baño solo(a)**	*eer ahl bah-nyoh soh-loh(lah)*
hear	**oír**	*oh-eer*
learn	**aprender**	*ah-prehn-dehr*
listen attentively	**escuchar atentamente**	*ehs-koo-chahr ah-tehn-tah-mehn-teh*
move his/her arms (legs)	**mover los brazos (las piernas)**	*moh-behr lohs brah-sohs (lahs pee-ehr-nahs)*
run	**correr**	*koh-rrehr*
see (without glasses, contact lenses)	**ver (sin lentes, lentes de contacto)**	*behr (seen lehn-tehs, lehn-tehs deh kohn-tahk-toh)*

speak	**hablar**	*ah-blahr*
spell	**deletrear**	*deh-leh-treh-ahr*
think clearly	**pensar**	*pehn-sahr*
	claramente	*klah-rah-mehn-teh*
walk	**caminar**	*kah-mee-nahr*

If not, he/she is learning disabled.
Si no, tiene problemas de aprendizaje.
see noh tee-eh-neh proh-bleh-mahs deh ah-prehn-dee-sah-heh

Does he/she need _____?
¿Necesita _____?
neh-seh-see-tah _____

audiobooks	**libros en**	*lee-brohs ehn*
	formato audio	*fohr-mah-toh ah-oo-dee-oh*
books written	**libros escritos**	*lee-brohs ehs-kree-tohs*
in Braille	**en Braille**	*ehn Braille*
a cane	**un bastón**	*oon bahs-tohn*
crutches	**muletas**	*moo-leh-tahs*
elevator	**acceso al**	*ahk-seh-soh ahl*
access	**ascensor**	*ah-sehn-sohr*
a hearing aid	**un audífono**	*oon ah-oo-dee-foh-noh*
large-type	**libros escritos**	*lee-brohs ehs-kree-tohs*
books	**con letra grande**	*kohn leh-trah grahn-deh*
a wheelchair	**una silla de**	*oo-nah see-yah deh*
	ruedas	*rroo-eh-dahs*

School Offerings

We offer _____.
Ofrecemos _____.
oh-freh-seh-mohs _____

behavioral	**análisis del**	*ah-nah-lee-sees dehl*
analysis	**comportamiento**	*kohm-pohr-tah-mee-ehn-toh*
bilingual	**enseñanza**	*ehn-seh-nyahn-sah*
instruction	**bilingüe**	*bee-leen-goo-eh*
counseling	**consejería**	*kohn-seh-heh-ree-ah*
feeding	**programas de**	*proh-grah-mahs deh*
programs	**alimentación**	*ah-lee-mehn-tah-see-ohn*
home	**enseñanza**	*ehn-seh-nyahn-sah*
instruction	**en casa**	*ehn kah-sah*

individualized instruction	**enseñanza individualizada**	ehn-seh-nyahn-sah een-dee-bee-doo-ah-lee-sah-dah
sign-language services	**servicio de lenguaje por señas**	sehr-bee-see-oh deh lehn-goo-ah-heh pohr seh-nyahs
special services	**servicios especiales**	sehr-bee-see-ohs ehs-peh-see-ah-lehs
tutoring	**servicios de tutoría**	sehr-bee-see-ohs deh too-toh-ree-ah

Our school is completely handicapped accessible.

Nuestra escuela es completamente accesible a personas con impedimentos.

noo-ehs-trah ehs-koo-eh-lah ehs kohm-pleh-tah-mehn-teh ah-seh-see-bleh ah pehr-soh-nahs kohn eem-peh-dee-mehn-tohs

We have ramps outside of exits _____, _____, and _____.

Tenemos rampas en las salidas _____, _____, y _____.

teh-neh-mohs rrahm-pahs ehn lahs sah-lee-dahs _____, _____, ee _____

Your child will be accompanied by an aid (paraprofessional, sign-language specialist) at all times.

Un(a) asistente (paraprofesional, especialista en lenguaje por señas) acompañará a su hijo (hija) todo el tiempo.

oon (oo-nah) ah-sees-tehn-teh (pah-rah-proh-feh-see-oh-nahl, ehs-peh-see-ah-lees-tah ehn lehn-goo-ah-heh pohr seh-nyahs) ah-kohm-pah-nyah-rah ah soo ee-hoh (ee-hah) toh-doh ehl tee-ehm-poh

His/Her name is _____.

Se llama _____.

seh yah-mah _____

Special Education

A student cannot be recommended for a special-education class because he (she) doesn't speak English.

Un(a) estudiante no puede ser recomendado(a) para una clase de educación especial por no hablar inglés.

oon (oo-nah) ehs-too-dee-ahn-teh noh poo-eh-deh sehr rreh-koh-mehn-dah-doh(dah) pah-rah oo-nah klah-seh deh eh-doo-kah-see-ohn ehs-peh-see-ahl pohr noh ah-blahr een-glehs

Your child needs to be evaluated.
Tenemos que evaluar a su hijo (hija).
teh-neh-mohs keh eh-bah-loo-ahr ah soo ee-hoh (ee-hah)

This is a free service.
Es un servicio gratis.
ehs oon sehr-bee-see-oh grah-tees

If the evaluation indicates a disability, your child can receive services.
Si la evaluación indica un impedimento, su hijo (hija) puede recibir servicios.
see lah eh-bah-loo-ah-see-ohn een-dee-kah oon eem-peh-dee-mehn-toh soo ee-hoh (ee-hah) poo-eh-deh rreh-see-beer sehr-bee-see-ohs

Before considering a special-education class, we will try to give him/her _____.
Antes de considerar una clase de educación especial, trataremos de darle _____.
ahn-tehs deh kohn-see-deh-rahr oo-nah klah-seh deh eh-doo-kah-see-ohn ehs-peh-see-ahl trah-tah-reh-mohs deh dahr-leh _____

an administrative meeting to develop a plan	**una reunión administrativa para desarrollar un plan**	*oo-nah rreh-oo-nee-ohn ahd-mee-nee-strah-tee-bah pah-rah deh-sah-rroh-yahr oon plahn*
after-school programs	**programas extracurriculares**	*proh-grah-mahs ehks-trah-koo-rree-koo-lah-rehs*
behavioral strategies	**estrategias de comportamiento**	*ehs-trah-tah-hee-ahs deh kohm-pohr-tah-mee-ehn-toh*
a change of class	**un cambio de clase**	*oon kahm-bee-oh deh klah-seh*
counseling	**consejería**	*kohn-seh-heh-ree-ah*
ESL classes	**clases de inglés como segundo idioma**	*klah-sehs deh een-glehs koh-moh seh-goon-doh ee-dee-oh-mah*
tutoring	**tutoría**	*too-toh-ree-ah*

The law protects students whose physical or mental disabilities substantially limit their activities.
La ley protege a estudiantes cuyos impedimentos físicos o mentales limitan sus actividades.
lah leh-ee proh-teh-heh ah ehs-too-dee-ahn-tehs koo-yohs eem-peh-dee-mehn-tohs fee-see-kohs oh mehn-tah-lehs lee-mee-tahn soos ahk-tee-bee-dah-dehs

Your child needs the services of the resource room (a special education class).
Su hijo (hija) necesita los servicios del salón de recursos (una clase de educación especial).
soo ee-hoh (ee-hah) neh-seh-see-tah lohs sehr-bee-see-ohs dehl sah-lohn deh
rreh-koor-sohs (oo-nah klah-seh deh eh-doo-kah-see-ohn ehs-peh-see-ahl)

Special education is a series of services.
La educación especial es una serie de servicios.
lah eh-doo-kah-see-ohn ehs-peh-see-ahl ehs oo-nah seh-ree-eh deh
sehr-bee-see-ohs

It is specialized instruction for students with disabilities that make learning difficult.
Es una instrucción especializada para estudiantes con impedimentos que complican el aprendizaje.
ehs oo-nah eens-trook-see-ohn ehs-peh-see-ah-lee-sah-dah pah-rah ehs-too-dee-
ahn-tehs kohn eem-peh-dee-mehn-tohs keh kohm-plee-kahn ehl ah-prehn-dee-
sah-heh

It may include general classroom aids, services, and support such as _____.
Puede incluir asistencia general en el salón, servicios, y apoyo como _____.
poo-eh-deh een-kloo-eer ah-sees-tehn-see-ah heh-neh-rahl ehn ehl sah-lohn,
sehr-bee-see-ohs ee ah-poh-yoh koh-moh _____

additional time for tests	**tiempo adicional para tomar exámenes**	*tee-ehm-poh ah-dee-see-oh-nahl pah-rah toh-mahr ehk-sah-meh-nehs*
assistive technology	**tecnología auxiliar**	*tehk-noh-loh-hee-ah ah-oo-see-lee-ahr*
computer-assisted devices	**aparatos auxiliares computarizados**	*ah-pah-rah-tohs ah-oo-see-lee-ah-rehs kohm-poo-tah-ree-sah-dohs*
counseling	**consejería**	*kohn-seh-heh-ree-ah*
curriculum modifications	**modificaciones en el currículo**	*moh-dee-fee-kah-see-oh-nehs ehn ehl koo-ree-koo-loh*
help from an expert in special education	**ayuda de un(a) especialista experto(a) en educación especial**	*ah-yoo-dah deh oon (oo-nah) ehs-peh-see-ah-lees-tah ehks-pehr-toh(tah) ehn eh-doo-kah-see-ohn ehs-peh-see-ahl*

home visits	**visitas a domicilio**	*bee-see-tahs ah doh-mee-see-lee-oh*
individualized para-professional help	**ayuda individual por paraprofesio-nales**	*ah-yoo-dah een-dee-bee-doo-ahl pohr pah-rah-proh-feh-see-oh-nah-lehs*
lesson modifications	**modificaciones en lecciones**	*moh-dee-fee-kah-see-oh-nehs ehn lehk-see-oh-nehs*
modified gym participation	**participación modificada en las actividades físicas**	*pahr-tee-see-pah-see-ohn moh-dee-fee-kah-dah ehn lahs ahk-tee-bee-dah-dehs fee-see-kahs*
music therapy	**terapia musical**	*teh-rah-pee-ah moo-see-kahl*
a note taker	**un escritor de apuntes**	*oon ehs-kree-tohr deh ah-poon-tehs*
occupational therapy	**terapia ocupacional**	*teh-rah-pee-ah oh-koo-pah-see-oh-nahl*
physical therapy	**terapia física**	*teh-rah-pee-ah fee-see-kah*
preferred seating	**un asiento de preferencia**	*oon ah-see-ehn-toh deh preh-feh-rehn-see-ah*
a reader	**un(a) lector(a)**	*oon (oo-nah) lehk-tohr (toh-rah)*
resource room	**salón de recursos**	*sah-lohn deh rreh-koor-sohs*
small-group tutoring	**tutoría para grupos pequeños**	*too-toh-ree-ah pah-rah groo-pohs peh-keh-nyohs*
special curriculum	**currículo especial**	*koo-rree-koo-loh ehs-peh-see-ahl*
special services	**servicios especiales**	*sehr-bee-see-ohs ehs-peh-see-ah-lehs*
speech therapy	**terapia del habla**	*teh-rah-pee-ah dehl ah-blah*
supplementary support	**apoyo suplementario**	*ah-poh-yoh soo-pleh-mehn-tah-ree-oh*
training for regular-education teachers	**entrenamiento para profesores de educación general**	*ehn-treh-nah-mee-ehn-toh pah-rah proh-feh-soh-rehs deh eh-doo-kah-see-ohn heh-neh-rahl*
use of a calculator	**uso de una calculadora**	*oo-soh deh oo-nah kahl-koo-lah-doh-rah*

use of a nebulizer	**uso de un nebulizador**	*oo-soh deh oon neh-boo-lee-sah-dohr*
use of a tape recorder	**uso de una grabadora**	*oo-soh deh oo-nah grah-bah-doh-rah*
use of the elevator	**uso del ascensor**	*oo-soh dehl ah-sehn-sohr*

Other services include but are not limited to _____.
Otros servicios incluyen pero no están limitados a _____.
oh-trohs sehr-bee-see-ohs een-kloo-yehn peh-roh noh ehs-tahn lee-mee-tah-dohs ah _____

receiving blood tests to determine blood-sugar level	**recibir pruebas de sangre para determinar el nivel de azúcar en la sangre**	*rreh-see-beer proo-eh-bahs deh sahn-greh pah-rah deh-tehr-mee-nahr ehl nee-behl deh ah-soo-kahr ehn lah sahn-greh*
receiving medicine during the school day	**recibir medicinas durante el día escolar**	*rreh-see-beer meh-dee-see-nahs doo-rahn-teh ehl dee-ah ehs-koh-lahr*
taking a test in a quiet location	**tomar un examen en un lugar tranquilo**	*toh-mahr oon ehk-sah-meh ehn oon loo-gahr trahn-kee-loh*

Students can also receive these services in a separate classroom for handicapped students.
Los estudiantes también pueden recibir estos servicios en un aula separada para estudiantes con impedimentos.
lohs ehs-too-dee-ahn-tehs tahm-bee-ehn poo-eh-dehn rreh-see-beer ehs-tohs sehr-bee-see-ohs ehn oon ah-oo-lah seh-pah-rah-dah pah-rah ehs-too-dee-ahn-tehs kohn eem-peh-dee-mehn-tohs

A modification is a change in class, schedule, or instruction that allows him/her to participate fully in school activities.
Una modificación es un cambio de clase, horario, o instrucción que le permite participar completamente en las actividades de la escuela.
oo-nah moh-dee-fee-kah-see-ohn ehs oon kahm-bee-oh deh klah-seh, oh-rah-ree-oh, oh eens-trook-see-ohn keh le pehr-mee-teh pahr-tee-see-pahr kohm-pleh-tah-mehn-teh ehn lahs ahk-tee-bee-dah-dehs deh lah ehs-koo-eh-lah

The law requires that disabled students receive special education in the "least restrictive environment."

La ley exige que los estudiantes con impedimentos reciban educación especial en el "ambiente menos restrictivo."

lah leh-ee ehk-see-heh keh lohs ehs-too-dee-ahn-tehs kohn eem-peh-dee-mehn-tohs rreh-see-bahn eh-doo-kah-see-ohn ehs-peh-see-ahl ehn ehl ahm-bee-ehn-teh meh-nohs rrehs-treek-tee-boh

The "least restrictive environment" permits a disabled student to be educated with students without disability in regular classes.

El "ambiente menos restrictivo" le permite a los estudiantes con incapacidades educarse en clases regulares con estudiantes sin incapacidades.

ehl ahm-bee-ehn-teh meh-nohs rreh-streek-tee-boh leh pehr-mee-teh ah lohs eh-stoo-dee-ahn-tehs kohn een-kah-pah-see-dah-dehs eh-doo-kahr-seh ehn klah-sehs rreh-goo-lah-rehs kohn ehs-too-dee-ahn-tehs seen een-kah-pah-see-dah-dehs

"Being mainstreamed" means that a student spends his day learning together with students without disabilities in a general-education class.

"Normalizar" quiere decir que un estudiante pasa el día junto con estudiantes sin incapacidades, en una clase de educación general.

nohr-mah-lee-sahr kee-eh-reh deh-seer keh oon ehs-too-dee-ahn-teh pah-sah ehl dee-ah hoon-toh kohn ehs-too-dee-ahn-tehs seen een-kah-pah-see-dah-dehs ehn oo-nah klah-seh deh eh-doo-kah-see-ohn heh-neh-rahl

The student's placement is based on his/her specific needs.

La colocación de un estudiante está basada en sus necesidades específicas.

lah koh-loh-kah-see-ohn deh oon ehs-too-dee-ahn-teh ehs-tah bah-sah-dah ehn soos neh-seh-see-dah-dehs ehs-peh-see-fee-kahs

The evaluation includes _____.

La evaluación incluye _____.

lah eh-bah-loo-ah-see-ohn een-kloo-yeh _____

an educational evaluation	**una evaluación académica**	*oo-nah eh-bah-loo-ah-see-ohn ah-kah-deh-mee-kah*
observations	**observaciones**	*ohb-sehr-bah-see-oh-nehs*

a physical exam	**un examen físico**	*oon ehk-sah-mehn fee-see-koh*
a pyschological evaluation	**una evaluación psicológica**	*oo-nah eh-bah-loo-ah-see-ohn see-koh-loh-hee-kah*
a social history	**un historial social**	*oon ees-toh-ree-ahl soh-see-ahl*

The Individualized Education Program (IEP) indicates _____.
El Programa Individualizado de Educación indica _____.
ehl proh-grah-mah een-dee-bee-doo-ah-lee-sah-doh deh eh-doo-kah-see-ohn een-dee-kah _____

his/her yearly educational goals	**sus metas académicas anuales**	*soos meh-tahs ah-kah-deh-mee-kahs ah-noo-ah-lehs*
methods to reach these goals	**los métodos necesarios para lograr estas metas**	*los meh-toh-dohs neh-seh-sah-ree-ohs pah-rah loh-grahr ehs-tahs meh-tahs*
the ratio of teachers to students	**la proporción entre profesores y estudiantes**	*lah proh-pohr-see-ohn ehn-treh proh-feh-soh-rehs ee ehs-too-dee-ahn-tehs*
the services to which he/she is entitled	**todos los servicios a que tiene derecho**	*toh-dohs lohs sehr-bee-see-ohs ah keh tee-eh-neh deh-reh-choh*
your child's needs	**las necesidades de su hijo (hija)**	*lahs neh-seh-see-dah-dehs deh soo ee-hoh (ee-hah)*
your child's placement	**la colocación de su hijo (hija)**	*lah koh-loh-kah-see-ohn deh soo ee-hoh (ee-hah)*

An Individualized Education Program (IEP) must include an explanation of why a student cannot be included in a general class.
Un Programa Individualizado de Educación debe incluir la razón por la cual un(a) estudiante no puede ser incluido(a) en una clase general.
oon proh-grah-mah een-dee-bee-doo-ah-lee-sah-doh deh eh-doo-kah-see-ohn deh-beh een-kloo-eer lah rrah-sohn pohr lah koo-ahl oon (oo-nah) ehs-too-dee-ahn-teh noh poo-eh-deh sehr een-kloo-ee-doh(dah) ehn oo-nah klah-seh heh-neh-rahl

As a parent or guardian, you are an important member of the
Individualized Education Program (IEP) team.
**Como padre, madre, o encargado(a), Ud. es un miembro
importante del IEP team.**
*koh-moh pah-dreh, mah-dreh oh ehn-kahr-gah-doh(dah) oo-stehd ehs oon
mee-ehm-broh eem-pohr-tahn-teh dehl eh-kee-poh IEP*

The other team members include _____.
Los otros miembros del equipo incluyen _____.
lohs oh-trohs mee-ehm-brohs dehl eh-kee-poh een-kloo-yehn _____

at least one	**por lo menos**	*pohr loh meh-nohs ah*
regular-	**a un(a)**	*oon (oo-nah) proh-feh-sohr*
education	**profesor(a)**	*(pro-feh-soh-rah) deh*
teacher	**de educación**	*eh-doo-kah-see-ohn*
	general	*heh-neh-rahl*
at least one	**por lo menos**	*pohr loh meh-nohs*
special-	**a un(a)**	*ah oon (oo-nah)*
education	**profesor(a)**	*proh-feh-sohr (proh-feh-soh-*
teacher	**de educación**	*rah) deh eh-doo-kah-see-ohn*
	especial	*ehs-peh-see-ahl*
a district	**a un(a)**	*ah oon (oo-nah) rreh-preh-*
representative	**representante**	*sehn-tahn-teh dehl*
	del distrito	*dees-tree-toh*
someone to	**a alguien que**	*ah ahl-ghee-ehn keh*
interpret the	**interprete las**	*een-tehr-preh-teh lahs*
evaluations	**evaluaciones**	*eh-bah-loo-ah-see-oh-nehs*

A physican may participate.
Un médico puede participar.
oon meh-dee-koh poo-eh-deh pahr-tee-see-pahr

A parent or guardian can invite _____.
Un padre, madre, o encargado(a) puede invitar a _____.
*oon pah-dreh mah-dreh oh ehn-kahr-gah-doh(dah) poo-eh-deh een-bee-tahr
ah _____*

a family friend	**un(a) amigo(a)**	*oon (oo-nah) ah-mee-*
	de la familia	*goh(gah) deh lah fah-*
		mee-lyah
a social worker	**un(a) asistente**	*oon (oo-nah) ah-sees-tehn-*
	social	*teh soh-see-ahl*
an advocate	**un(a) defensor(a)**	*oon (oo-nah) deh-fehn-sohr*
		(deh-fehn-soh-rah)

an independent evaluator	**un(a) evaluador(a) independiente**	*oon (oo-nah) eh-bah-loo-ah-dohr (eh-bah-loo-ah-doh-rah) een-deh-pehn-dee-ehn-teh*

The IEP may change the standards of promotion and graduation for a special-education student.
El IEP puede modificar los estándares de promoción y de graduación para un estudiante de educación especial.
ehl IEP poo-eh-deh moh-dee-fee-kahr lohs ehs-tahn-dah-rehs deh proh-moh-see-ohn ee deh grah-doo-ah-see-ohn pah-rah oon ehs-too-dee-ahn-teh deh eh-doo-kah-see-ohn eh-speh-see-ahl

A student is transferred to another class or school only when his (her) disabilty is so severe that he (she) cannot learn in a regular class, despite the use of supplementary support and services.
Un(a) estudiante es trasladado(a) a otra clase o escuela sola-mente cuando su incapacidad es tan severa que le impide aprender en una clase regular, a pesar del uso de apoyos y servicios suplementarios.
oon (oo-nah) ehs-too-dee-ahn-teh ehs trahs-lah-dah-doh(dah) ah oh-trah klah-seh oh ehs-koo-eh-lah soh-lah-mehn-teh koo-ahn-doh soo een-kah-pah-see-dahd ehs tahn seh-beh-rah keh leh eem-pee-deh ah-prehn-dehr ehn oo-nah klah-seh rreh-goo-lahr ah peh-sahr dehl oo-soh deh ah-poh-yohs ee sehr-bee-see-ohs soo-pleh-mehn-tah-ree-ohs

A student may be transferred if his (her) behavior is so bad that it negatively affects the instruction of the others.
Un(a) estudiante puede ser trasladado(a) si su comportamiento es tan malo que afecta negativamente el aprendizaje de los demás.
oon (oo-nah) ehs-too-dee-ahn-teh poo-eh-deh sehr trahs-lah-dah-doh(dah) see soo kohm-pohr-tah-mee-ehn-toh ehs tahn mah-loh keh ah-fehk-tah neh-gah-tee-bah-mehn-teh ehl ah-prehn-dee-sah-heh deh lohs deh-mahs

Special-education teachers have up-to-date, comprehensive training.
Los profesores de educación especial han recibido un entre-namiento actualizado y comprensivo.
lohs proh-feh-soh-rehs deh eh-doo-kah-see-ohn ehs-peh-see-ahl ahn rreh-see-bee-doh oon ehn-treh-nah-mee-ehn-toh ahk-too-ah-lee-sah-doh ee kohm-prehn-see-boh

Parents' Rights

You have the right to have all documents, evaluations, and notifications regarding special education translated into Spanish.

Ud. tiene derecho a tener todos los documentos, evaluaciones, y notificaciones concernientes a la educación especial traducidos en español.

oo-stehd tee-eh-neh deh-reh-choh ah teh-nehr toh-dohs lohs doh-koo-mehn-tohs, eh-bah-loo-ah-see-oh-nehs ee noh-tee-fee-kah-see-oh-nehs kohn-sehr-nee-ehn-tehs ah lah eh-doo-kah-see-ohn ehs-peh-see-ahl trah-doo-see-dohs ehn ehs-pah-nyohl

You can ask in writing to have your child recommended and evaluated for special education.

Ud. puede pedir por escrito que su hijo (hija) sea recomendado(a) y evaluado(a) para el programa de educación especial.

oo-stehd poo-eh-deh peh-deer pohr ehs-kree-toh keh soo ee-hoh (ee-hah) seh-ah rreh-koh-mehn-dah-doh(dah) ee eh-bah-loo-ah-doh(dah) pah-rah ehl proh-grah-mah deh eh-doo-kah-see-ohn ehs-peh-see-ahl

No child can be evaluated for special education without the consent of his (her) parents.

Ningún (Ninguna) niño(a) puede ser evaluado(a) para el programa de educación especial sin el consentimiento de sus padres.

neen-goon (neen-goo-nah) nee-nyoh (nee-nyah) poo-eh-deh sehr eh-bah-loo-ah-doh(dah) pah-rah ehl proh-grah-mah deh eh-doo-kah-see-ohn ehs-peh-see-ahl seen ehl kohn-sehn-tee-mee-ehn-toh deh soos pah-drehs

Parents can accept or refuse the recommendations for placement of their child.

Los padres pueden aceptar o rechazar las recomendaciones para la colocación de su hijo (hija).

lohs pah-drehs poo-eh-dehn ah-sehp-tahr oh rreh-chah-sahr lahs rreh-koh-mehn-dah-see-oh-nehs pah-rah lah koh-loh-kah-see-ohn deh soo ee-hoh (ee-hah)

If you do not agree that your child needs special education or if services are denied, you are entitled to an impartial hearing.

Si no cree que su hijo (hija) necesita educación especial, o si se le niegan estos servicios, Ud. puede pedir una audiencia imparcial.

see noh kreh-eh keh soo ee-hoh (ee-hah) neh-seh-see-tah eh-doo-kah-see-ohn ehs-peh-see-ahl oh seh seh leh nee-eh-gahn ehs-tohs sehr-bee-see-ohs oo-stehd poo-eh-deh peh-deer oo-nah ah-oo-dee-ehn-see-ah eem-pahr-see-ahl

If you want to increase or decrease services, you must make a request in writing.
Si Ud. quiere aumentar o disminuir los servicios, debe pedirlo por escrito.
see oo-stehd kee-eh-reh ah-oo-mehn-tahr oh dees-mee-noo-eer lohs sehr-bee-see-ohs deh-beh peh-deer-loh pohr ehs-kree-toh

You have the right to get an independent evaluator.
Ud. tiene derecho a conseguir un(a) evaluador(a) independiente.
oo-stehd tee-eh-neh deh-reh-choh ah kohn-seh-geer oon (oo-nah) eh-bah-loo-ah-dohr (eh-bah-loo-ah-doh-rah) een-deh-pehn-dee-ehn-teh

This can be expensive.
Puede ser caro.
poo-eh-deh sehr kah-roh

There can be a long wait.
Es posible que la espera sea larga.
ehs poh-see-bleh keh lah ehs-peh-rah seh-ah lahr-gah

If the school can't help your child, he (she) may be entitled to free private school.
Si la escuela no puede ayudar a su hijo (hija), él (ella) puede tener derecho a asistir gratis a una escuela privada.
see lah ehs-koo-eh-lah noh poo-eh-deh ah-yoo-dahr ah soo ee-hoh (ee-hah) ehl (eh-yah) poo-eh-deh teh-nehr deh-reh-choh ah ah-sees-teer grah-tees ah oo-nah ehs-koo-eh-lah pree-bah-dah

A Child's Progress

Your child does (doesn't) _____.
Su hijo (hija) (no) _____.
soo ee-hoh (ee-hah) (noh) _____

behave well	se comporta bien	seh kohm-pohr-tah bee-ehn
complete	termina el	tehr-mee-nah ehl
his/her work	trabajo	trah-bah-hoh ah
on time	a tiempo	tee-ehm-poh
cooperate	coopera	koh-oh-peh-rah
follow (complex) instructions	sigue instrucciones (complejas)	see-geh een-strook-see-oh-nehs (kohm-pleh-hahs)

follow directions	**sigue instrucciones**	*see-geh een-strook-see-oh-nehs*
follow rules	**sigue las reglas**	*see-geh lahs rreh-glahs*
have a good vocabulary	**tiene un buen vocabulario**	*tee-eh-neh oon boo-ehn boh-kah-boo-lah-ree-oh*
imitate words with speed and accuracy	**imita palabras con rapidez y precisión**	*ee-mee-tah pah-lah-brahs kohn rrah-pee-dehs ee preh-see-see-ohn*
initiate activity	**inicia actividades**	*ee-nee-see-ah ahk-tee-bee-dah-dehs*
interact well with his peers	**se relaciona bien con sus compañeros**	*seh rreh-lah-see-oh-nah bee-ehn kohn soos kohm-pah-nyeh-rohs*
listen attentively	**escucha atentamente**	*ehs-koo-chah ah-tehn-tah-mehn-teh*
make a big effort	**hace un gran esfuerzo**	*ah-seh oon grahn ehs-foo-ehr-soh*
participate eagerly	**participa con entusiasmo**	*pahr-tee-see-pah kohn ehn-too-see-ahs-moh*
play well	**juega bien**	*hoo-eh-gah bee-ehn*
prefer music (art, computers, gym)	**prefiere la música (el arte, las computadoras, la educación física)**	*preh-fee-eh-reh lah moo-see-kah (ehl ahr-teh, lahs kohm-poo-tah-doh-rahs, lah eh-doo-kah-see-ohn fee-see-kah)*
respect others	**respeta a los demás**	*rrehs-peh-tah ah lohs deh-mahs*
respond verbally to visual prompts	**responde verbalmente a ayudas visuales**	*rrehs-pohn-deh behr-bahl-mehn-teh ah ah-yoo-dahs bee-soo-ah-lehs*
share	**comparte**	*kohm-pahr-teh*
show self-control	**demuestra autocontrol**	*deh-moo-ehs-trah ah-oo-toh-kohn-trohl*
speak well	**habla bien**	*ah-blah bee-ehn*
understand	**comprende**	*kohm-prehn-deh*
use his/her free time well	**usa bien su tiempo libre**	*oo-sah bee-ehn soo tee-ehm-poh lee-breh*

| work well with others | **trabaja bien con los demás** | *trah-bah-hah bee-ehn kohn lohs deh-mahs* |
| work independently | **trabaja independientemente** | *trah-bah-hah een-deh-pehn-dee-ehn-teh-mehn-teh* |

Your child's _____ is (are) improving.
_____ de su hijo (hija) está(n) mejorando.
_____ deh soo ee-hoh (ee-hah) ehs-tah(n) meh-hoh-rahn-doh

He (She) shows mastery in _____.
Demuestra dominio _____.
deh-moo-ehs-trah doh-mee-nee-oh _____

activities of daily-living skills	**de las actividades relacionadas con las destrezas del diario vivir**	*deh lahs ahk-tee-bee-dah-dehs rreh-lah-see-oh-nah-dahs kohn lahs dehs-treh-sahs dehl dee-ah-ree-oh bee-beer*
behavior	**del comportamiento**	*dehl kohm-pohr-tah-mee-ehn-toh*
communication skills	**de las destrezas de la comunicación**	*deh lahs dehs-treh-sahs deh lah koh-moo-nee-kah-see-ohn*
eating habits	**de los hábitos alimenticios**	*deh lohs ah-bee-tohs ah-lee-mehn-tee-see-ohs*
language skills	**de las destrezas del lenguaje**	*deh lahs dehs-treh-sahs dehl lehn-goo-ah-heh*
math skills	**de las destrezas matemáticas**	*deh lahs dehs-treh-sahs mah-teh-mah-tee-kahs*
penmanship	**de la caligrafía**	*deh lah kah-lee-grah-fee-ah*
reading skills	**de las destrezas de lectura**	*deh lahs dehs-treh-sahs deh lehk-too-rah*
social skills	**de las destrezas sociales**	*deh lahs dehs-treh-sahs soh-see-ah-lehs*
speech	**del habla**	*dehl ah-blah*
spelling	**de la ortografía**	*deh lah ohr-toh-grah-fee-ah*
verbal skills	**de las destrezas verbales**	*deh lahs dehs-treh-sahs behr-bah-lehs*

vocabulary	**del vocabulario**	*dehl boh-kah-boo-lah-ree-oh*
word-recognition skills	**de las destrezas de reconoci-miento de palabras**	*deh lahs dehs-treh-sahs de rreh-koh-noh-see-mee-ehn-toh deh pah-lah-brahs*
writing skills	**de las destrezas de escritura**	*deh lahs dehs-treh-sahs deh ehs-kree-too-rah*

Your child needs to see a speech therapist (doctor, school psychologist, nutritionist).

Su hijo (hija) necesita ver a un logopeda (médico, psicólogo escolar, nutricionista).

soo ee-ioh (ee-hah) neh-seh-see-tah behr ah oon loh-goh-peh-dah (meh-dee-koh, see-koh-loh-goh ehs-koh-lahr, noo-tree-see-oh-nees-tah)

You can try to modify your child's behavior by _____.

Ud. puede tratar de modificar el comportamiento de su hijo (hija) _____.

oo-stehd poo-eh-deh trah-tahr deh moh-dee-fee-kahr ehl kohm-pohr-tah-mee-ehn-toh deh soo ee-ioh (ee-hah) _____

giving him/her a time-out	**dándole un descanso**	*dahn-doh-leh oon dehs-kahn-soh*
giving him/her something else to do	**dándole otra cosa que hacer**	*dahn-doh-leh oh-trah koh-sah keh ah-sehr*
ignoring it	**ignorándolo(a)**	*eeg-noh-rahn-doh-loh(lah)*
taking something away that he/she likes	**quitándole algo que le gusta**	*kee-tahn-doh-leh ahl-goh keh leh goos-tah*

Your child has (You have [You have]) made a lot of progress in a short time.

Su hijo (hija) ha progresado mucho en poco tiempo.

soo ee-ioh (ee-hah) ah proh-greh-sah-doh moo-choh ehn poh-koh tee-ehm-poh

He/She can identify _____.

Puede identificar _____.

poo-eh-deh ee-dehn-tee-fee-kahr _____

colors	**colores**	*koh-loh-rehs*
days of the week	**días de la semana**	*dee-ahs deh lah-seh-mah-nah*
numbers	**números**	*noo-meh-rohs*
words	**palabras**	*pah-lah-brahs*

He/She has accomplished a lot.
Ha logrado mucho.
ah loh-grah-doh moo-choh

His/Her attention span is increasing.
Su capacidad de concentración está aumentando.
soo kah-pah-see-dahd deh kohn-sehn-trah-see-ohn ehs-tah ah-oo-mehn-tahn-doh

He/She likes a challenge.
Le gustan los desafíos.
leh goos-tahn lohs deh-sah-fee-ohs

He/She likes to help others.
Le gusta ayudar a los demás.
leh goos-tah ah-yoo-dahr ah lohs deh-mahs

He/She is acting more maturely.
Actúa más maduramente.
ahk-too-ah mahs mah-doo-rah-mehn-teh

He/She is more talkative.
Es más hablador(a).
ehs mahs ah-blah-dohr(doh-rah)

He/She has made significant changes since the beginning of the year.
Ha[s] cambiado notablemente desde el principio del año escolar.
ah[s] kahm-bee-ah-doh noh-tah-bleh-mehn-teh dehs-deh ehl preen-see-pee-oh dehl ah-nyoh ehs-koh-lahr

He/She should be mainstreamed.
Debería[s] ser normalizado(a).
deh-beh-ree-ah[s] sehr nohr-mah-lee-sah-do(a)

He/She made a smooth transition into his/her (your) new class.
Ha tenido una transición fácil en su clase nueva.
ah teh-nee-doh oo-nah trahn-see-see-ohn fah-seel ehn soo klah-seh noo-eh-bah

Please come in to discuss your child's goals (grades, deficiencies).
Por favor, venga a la escuela para discutir las metas (las notas, las deficiencias) de su hijo (hija).
pohr fah-bohr behn-gah ah lah ehs-koo-eh-lah pah-rah dees-koo-teer lahs meh-tahs (lahs noh-tahs, lahs deh-fee-see-ehn-see-ahs) deh soo ee-hoh (ee-hah)

Your child is reaching (has reached) (have reached) his/her (your) goals.
Su hijo (hija) está logrando (logró) sus metas.
soo ee-hoh (ee-hah) ehs-tah loh-grahn-doh (loh-groh) soos meh-tahs

Your child has disciplinary problems.
Su hijo (hija) tiene problemas disciplinarios.
soo ee-hoh (ee-hah) tee-eh-neh proh-bleh-mahs dee-see-plee-nah-ree-ohs

We need to have a conference.
Necesitamos tener una conferencia.
neh-seh-see-tah-mohs teh-nehr oo-nah kohn-feh-rehn-see-ah

14

Planning for the Future

Promotion and Graduation Requirements

Students are promoted based on their grades (test scores).
Los estudiantes son promovidos de grado según sus notas (los resultados de sus pruebas).
lohs ehs-too-dee-ahn-tehs sohn proh-moh-bee-dohs deh grah-doh seh-goon soos noh-tahs (lohs rreh-sool-tah-dohs deh soos proo-eh-bahs)

A student is held back in a grade if he/she doesn't succeed in class.
Un estudiante debe repetir un grado si no sale bien en su clase.
oon ehs-too-dee-ahn-teh deh-beh rreh-peh-teer oon grah-doh see noh sah-leh bee-ehn ehn soo klah-seh

Students must pass certain city (state) tests in _____.
Los estudiantes deben pasar ciertos exámenes de la ciudad (del estado) en _____.
lohs ehs-too-dee-ahn-tehs deh-behn pah-sahr see-ehr-tohs ehk-sah-meh-nehs deh lah see-oo-dahd (dehl ehs-tah-doh) ehn _____

Students have to maintain certain standards of academic performance.
Los estudiantes deben mantener ciertos estándares de rendimiento académico.
lohs ehs-too-dee-ahn-tehs deh-behn mahn-teh-nehr see-ehr-tohs ehs-tahn-dah-rehs deh rrehn-dee-mee-ehn-toh ah-kah-deh-mee-koh

Parents will receive notification if their child is in danger of repeating a year.
Los padres recibirán notificación si su hijo (hija) está a riesgo de repetir el año.
lohs pah-drehs rreh-see-bee-rahn noh-tee-fee-kah-see-ohn see soo ee-hoh (ee-hah) ehs-tah ah rree-ehs-goh deh rreh-peh-teer ehl ah-nyoh

They can appeal the decision to hold back their child by writing a letter to the principal.
Pueden apelar la decisión de reprobar a su hijo (hija) escribiendo una carta al director (a la directora).
poo-eh-dehn ah-peh-lahr lah deh-see-see-ohn deh rreh-proh-bahr ah soo ee-hoh (ee-hah) ehs-kree-bee-ehn-doh oo-nah kahr-tah ahl dee-rehk-tohr (ah lah dee-rehk-toh-rah)

Let's speak about graduation requirements.
Hablemos de los requisitos de graduación.
ah-bleh-mohs deh lohs rreh-kee-see-tohs deh grah-doo-ah-see-ohn

He (she) needs (You need [You need]) _____ credits to graduate.
Necesita[s] _____ créditos para graduarse[te].
neh-seh-see-tah[s] _____ kreh-dee-tohs pah-rah grah-doo-ahr-seh [grah-doo-ahr-teh]

The dropout rate in our school is low (high).
El índice de estudiantes que abandonan sus estudios es bajo (alto).
ehl een-dee-seh deh ehs-too-dee-ahn-tehs keh ah-bahn-doh-nahn soos ehs-too-dee-ohs ehs bah-hoh (ahl-toh)

He (She, You [You]) must pass a test (tests) in _____.
Tiene[s] que pasar un examen (exámenes) en _____.
tee-eh-neh[s] keh pah-sahr oon ehk-sah-mehn (ehk-sah-meh-nehs) ehn _____

He (She, You [You]) must pass all of your classes.
Tiene[s] que pasar todas sus [tus] clases.
tee-eh-neh[s] keh pah-sahr toh-dahs soos [toos] klah-sehs

He (She, You [You]) must perform _____ hours of community service.
Tiene[s] que trabajar _____ horas de servicio comunitario.
tee-eh-neh[s] keh trah-bah-hahr _____ oh-rahs deh sehr-bee-see-oh koh-moo-nee-tah-ree-oh

He (She, You [You]) must be in attendance at least _____ percent of the time.
Tiene[s] que asistir por lo menos _____ porciento del tiempo.
tee-eh-neh[s] keh ah-sees-teer pohr loh meh-nohs _____ pohr-see-ehn-toh dehl tee-ehm-poh

Your child (You [You]) may not attend graduation.
Su hijo (hija, Ud. [Tú]) no puede[s] asistir a la graduación.
soo ee-hoh (ee-hah, oo-stehd [too]) noh poo-eh-deh[s] ah-sees-teer ah lah grah-doo-ah-see-ohn

Applying for a Job

Our school offers _____.
Nuestra escuela ofrece _____.
noo-ehs-trah ehs-koo-eh-lah oh-freh-seh _____

| job placement services (counsel) | **servicios (consejería) de colocación de empleos** | *sehr-bee-see-ohs (kohn-seh-heh-ree-ah) deh koh-loh-kah-see-ohn deh ehm-pleh-ohs* |
| career planning | **planificación de carreras** | *plah-nee-fee-kah-see-ohn deh kah-rreh-rahs* |

What interests you [you]?
¿Qué le [te] interesa?
keh leh [teh] een-teh-reh-sah

Do you want to be a/an _____?
¿Quiere[s] ser _____?
kee-eh-reh[s] sehr _____

accountant	**contable**	*kohn-tah-bleh*
administrator	**administrador(a)**	*ahd-mee-nee-strah-dohr (doh-rah)*
architect	**arquitecto(a)**	*ahr-kee-tehk-toh(tah)*
baker	**panadero(a)**	*pah-nah-deh-roh(rah)*
banker	**banquero(a)**	*bahn-keh-roh(rah)*
bookkeeper	**tenedor(a) de libros**	*teh-neh-dohr(doh-rah) deh lee-brohs*
butcher	**carnicero(a)**	*kahr-nee-seh-roh(rah)*
carpenter	**carpintero(a)**	*kahr-peen-teh-roh(rah)*
cashier	**cajero(a)**	*kah-heh-roh(rah)*
civil service worker	**empleado(a) público(a)**	*ehm-pleh-ah-doh(dah) poo-blee-koh(kah)*
dentist	**dentista**	*dehn-tees-tah*
doctor	**médico(a)**	*meh-dee-koh(kah)*
driver	**conductor(a)**	*kohn-dook-tohr(toh-rah)*
editor	**redactor(a)**	*rreh-dahk-tohr(toh-rah)*
electrician	**electricista**	*eh-lehk-tree-sees-tah*
engineer	**ingeniero(a)**	*een-beh-nee-eh-roh(rah)*
firefighter	**bombero(a)**	*bohm-beh-roh(rah)*
flight attendant	**asistente de vuelo**	*ah-sees-tehn-teh deh boo-eh-loh*
hairstylist	**peluquero(a)**	*peh-loo-keh-roh(rah)*
jeweler	**joyero(a)**	*hoh-yeh-roh(rah)*
journalist	**periodista**	*peh-ree-oh-dees-tah*
laborer	**obrero(a)**	*oh-breh-roh(rah)*
lawyer	**abogado(a)**	*ah-boh-gah-doh(dah)*
librarian	**bibliotecario(a)**	*bee-blee-oh-teh-kah-ree-oh(ah)*
mail carrier	**cartero(a)**	*kahr-teh-roh(rah)*
manager	**gerente**	*heh-rehn-teh*
mechanic	**mecánico(a)**	*meh-kah-nee-koh(kah)*
merchant	**comerciante**	*koh-mehr-see-ahn-teh*
musician	**músico(a)**	*moo-see-koh(kah)*
nurse	**enfermero(a)**	*ehn-fehr-meh-roh(rah)*
optician	**óptico(a)**	*ohp-tee-koh(kah)*
painter	**pintor(a)**	*peen-tohr(toh-rah)*

pharmacist	**farmacéutico(a)**	*fahr-mah-seh-oo-tee-koh(kah)*
pilot	**piloto**	*pee-loh-toh*
plumber	**plomero(a)**	*ploh-meh-roh(rah)*
police officer	**policía**	*poh-lee-see-ah*
programmer	**programador(a)**	*proh-grah-mah-dohr(doh-rah)*
psychologist	**psicólogo(a)**	*see-koh-loh-goh(gah)*
researcher	**investigador(a)**	*een-behs-tee-gah-dohr (doh-rah)*
salesperson	**dependiente**	*deh-pehn-dee-ehn-teh*
sanitation worker	**basurero(a)**	*bah-soo-reh-roh(rah)*
secretary	**secretario(a)**	*seh-kreh-tah-ree-oh(ah)*
server	**mesero(a)**	*meh-seh-roh(rah)*
stewardess	**azafata**	*ah-sah-fah-tah*
surgeon	**cirujano(a)**	*see-roo-hah-noh(nah)*
tailor	**sastre (costurera)**	*sahs-treh (kohs-too-reh-rah)*
teacher	**profesor(a)**	*proh-feh-sohr(soh-rah)*

What are your qualifications (skills)?
¿Cuáles son sus [tus] títulos académicos (aptitudes)?
koo-ah-lehs sohn soos [toos] tee-too-lohs ah-kah-deh-mee-kohs (ahp-tee-too-dehs)

Have you ever worked before?
¿Ha[s] trabajado antes?
ah[s] trah-bah-hah-doh ahn-tehs

Do you have any experience?
¿Tiene[s] experiencia?
tee-eh-neh[s] ehk-speh-ree-ehn-see-ah

What did you do?
¿Qué hacía[s]?
keh ah-see-ah[s]

Do you like to work with people (alone)?
¿Le [Te] gusta trabajar con otras personas (solo(a))?
leh [teh] goos-tah trah-bah-hahr kohn oh-trahs pehr-soh-nahs (soh-loh(lah))

Do you like to work with your hands?
¿Le [Te] gusta trabajar con las manos?
leh [teh] goos-tah trah-bah-hahr kohn lahs mah-nohs

Are you creative?
¿Es [Eres] creativo(a)?
ehs [eh-rehs] kreh-ah-tee-boh(bah)

What is your average?
¿Cuál es su [tu] promedio?
koo-ahl ehs soo [too] proh-meh-dee-oh

You must have a Social Security card.
Tiene[s] que tener una tarjeta de seguro social.
tee-eh-neh[s] keh teh-nehr oo-nah tahr-heh-tah deh seh-goo-roh soh-see-ahl

This paper lists the job requirements.
Este papel enumera los requisitos del puesto.
ehs-teh pah-pehl eh-noo-meh-rah lohs rreh-kee-see-tohs dehl poo-ehs-toh

There are many job opportunities.
Hay muchas oportunidades de empleo.
ah-ee moo-chahs oh-pohr-too-nee-dah-dehs deh ehm-pleh-oh

How much would you like to earn?
¿Cuánto quisiera[s] ganar?
koo-ahn-toh kee-see-eh-rah[s] gah-nahr

Here is a list of available (suitable) jobs.
Aquí hay una lista de puestos disponibles (apropiados).
ah-kee ah-ee oo-nah lees-tah deh poo-ehs-tohs dees-poh-nee-blehs (ah-proh-pee-ah-dos)

What job would you like to apply for?
¿Para qué puesto quiere[s] solicitar?
pah-rah keh poo-ehs-toh kee-eh-reh[s] soh-lee-see-tahr

Applying to a College

Do you want to stay home or go away?
¿Quiere[s] estudiar en su [tu] área o afuera?
kee-eh-reh[s] ehs-too-dee-ahr ehm soo [too] ah-reh-ah oh ah-foo-eh-rah

Do you want to live on campus?
¿Quiere[s] vivir dentro del campus?
kee-eh-reh[s] bee-beer dehn-troh dehl kahm-poos

Do you want to go to a/an _____?
¿Quiere[s] ir a _____?
kee-eh-reh[s] eer ah _____

art school	**una escuela de bellas artes**	*oo-nah ehs-koo-eh-lah deh beh-yahs ahr-tehs*
business school	**una escuela de comercio**	*oo-nah ehs-koo-eh-lah deh koh-mehr-see-oh*
junior college	**un centro universitario de dos años**	*oon sehn-troh oo-nee-behr-see-tah-ree-oh deh dohs ah-nyohs*
military school	**una escuela militar**	*oo-nah ehs-koo-eh-lah mee-lee-tahr*
music school	**un conservatorio de música**	*oon kohn-sehr-bah-toh-ree-oh deh moo-see-kah*
nursing school	**una escuela de enfermería**	*oo-nah ehs-koo-eh-lah deh ehn-fehr-meh-ree-ah*
private college	**una universidad privada**	*oo-nah oo-nee-behr-see-dahd pree-bah-dah*
state college	**una universidad estatal**	*oo-nah oo-nee-behr-see-dahd ehs-tah-tahl*
technical college	**una universidad politécnica**	*oo-nah oo-nee-behr-see-dahd poh-lee-tehk-nee-kah*
training college	**un instituto profesional**	*oon een-stee-too-toh proh-feh-see-oh-nahl*
university	**una universidad**	*oo-nah oo-nee-behr-see-dahd*

Do you want a/an _____ degree?
¿Quiere[s] _____?
kee-eh-reh _____

associate's	**un grado asociado**	*oon grah-doh ah-soh-see-ah-doh*
bachelor's	**una licenciatura**	*oo-nah lee-sehn-see-ah-too-rah*
bachelor's in arts	**una licenciatura en letras**	*oo-nah lee-sehn-see-ah-too-rah ehn leh-trahs*
bachelor's in science	**una licenciatura en ciencias**	*oo-nah lee-sehn-see-ah-too-rah ehn see-ehn-see-ahs*
doctoral	**un doctorado**	*oon dohk-toh-rah-doh*
doctor of philosophy	**un doctorado en filosofía**	*oon dohk-toh-rah-doh ehn fee-loh-soh-fee-ah*
master's	**una maestría**	*oo-nah mah-ehs-tree-ah*

master's in arts	**una maestría en letras**	*oo-nah mah-ehs-tree-ah ehn leh-trahs*
master's in science	**una maestría en ciencias**	*oo-nah mah-ehs-tree-ah ehn see-ehn-see-ahs*
post-graduate	**un postgrado**	*oon pohst-grah-doh*

Where would you like to go?
¿Adónde quiere[s] ir?
adohn-deh kee-eh-reh[s] eer

What interests you?
¿Qué le [te] interesa?
keh leh [te] een-teh-reh-sah

What would you like to major in?
¿En qué quiere[s] especializarse [te]?
ehn keh kee-eh-reh[s] ehs-peh-see-ah-lee-sahr-seh [teh]

In order to apply you need _____.
Para solicitar admisión, necesita[s] _____.
pah-rah soh-lee-see-tahr ahd-mee-see-ohn neh-seh-see-tah[s] _____

to fill out an application	**llenar una solicitud**	*yeh-nahr oo-nah soh-lee-see-tood*
to write _____ essays	**escribir _____ ensayos**	*ehs-kree-beer _____ ehn-sah-yohs*
to get _____ letters of recommendation from your teachers	**obtener _____ cartas de recomendación de sus [tus] profesores**	*ohb-teh-nehr _____ kahr-tahs deh rreh-koh-mehn-dah-see-ohn deh soos [toos] proh-feh-soh-rehs*
to receive a grade point average (GPA) of _____	**recibir un promedio académico de _____**	*rreh-see-beer oon proh-meh-dee-oh ah-kah-deh-mee-koh deh _____*
to receive an SAT score of _____ in critical reading (math, writing)	**recibir un grado de _____ en el examen de ingreso a la universidad (SAT) en lectura crítica (matemáticas, redacción)**	*rreh-see-beer oon grah-doh deh _____ ehn ehl ehk-sah-mehn deh een-greh-soh ah lah oo-nee-behr-see-dahd (SAT) ehn lehk-too-rah kree-tee-kah (mah-teh-mah-tee-kahs, rreh-dahk-see-ohn)*

You must also take the SAT Reasoning Test.
Tiene[s] que tomar el Examen de Razonamiento del SAT.
tee-eh-neh[s] keh toh-mahr ehl ehk-sah-mehn deh rrah-soh-nah-mee-ehn-toh dehl SAT

The college requires _____ SAT subject tests.
La universidad exige _____ pruebas por asignaturas del SAT.
lah oo-nee-behr-see-dahd ehk-see-heh _____ proo-eh-bahs pohr ah-seeg-nah-too-rahs dehl SAT

These tests measure your command of language, math, science, history, and English.
Estas pruebas evalúan su [tu] dominio del lenguaje, matemáti-cas, ciencias, historia, e inglés.
ehs-tahs proo-eh-bahs eh-bah-loo-ahn soo [too] doh-mee-nee-oh dehl lehn-goo-ah-heh, mah-teh-mah-tee-kahs, see-ehn-see-ahs, ees-toh-ree-ah eh een-glehs

The dates of these tests are _____.
Las fechas de estas pruebas son _____.
lahs feh-chahs deh ehs-tahs proo-eh-bahs sohn _____

There are free reviews for students on the Internet.
Hay repasos gratuitos en el Internet para los estudiantes.
ah-ee rreh-pah-sohs grah-too-ee-tohs ehn ehl een-tehr-neht pah-rah lohs ehs-too-dee-ahn-tehs

Are you in the Advanced Placement program?
¿Está[s] en el programa de colocación avanzada?
ehs-tah[s] ehn ehl proh-grah-mah deh koh-loh-kah-see-ohn ah-bahn-sah-dah

What courses are you taking?
¿Qué cursos está[s] tomando?
keh koor-sohs ehs-tah[s] toh-mahn-doh

You should plan on taking the AP tests.
Debe[s] planificar tomar las pruebas AP.
deh-beh[s] plah-nee-fee-kahr toh-mahr lahs proo-eh-bahs AP

The college has entrance exams.
La universidad tiene exámenes de entrada.
lah oo-nee-behr-see-dahd tee-eh-neh ehk-sah-meh-nehs deh ehn-trah-dah

What are your extracurricular activities?
¿En qué actividades extracurriculares ha[s] participado?
ehn keh ahk-tee-bee-dah-dehs ehks-trah-koo-rree-koo-lah-rehs ah[s] pahr-tee-see-pah-doh

Colleges prefer well-rounded students.
Las universidades prefieren estudiantes balanceados académicamente.
lahs oo-nee-behr-see-dah-dehs preh-fee-eh-rehn ehs-too-dee-ahn-tehs bah-lahn-seh-ah-dos ah-kah-deh-mee-kah-mehn-teh

You may submit as many applications as you like.
Puede[s] mandar tantas solicitudes como quiera[s].
poo-eh-deh[s] mahn-dahr tahn-tahs soh-lee-see-too-dehs koh-moh kee-eh-rah[s]

You must also submit your transcripts.
Tiene[s] que presentar también una copia de sus [tus] expedientes académicos.
tee-eh-neh[s] keh preh-sehn-tahr tahm-bee-ehn oo-nah koh-pee-ah deh soos [toos] ehks-peh-dee-ehn-tehs ah-kah-deh-mee-kohs

How much can your family afford to spend for college?
¿Cuánto dinero puede pagar su [tu] familia para su [tu] educación universitaria?
koo-ahn-toh dee-neh-roh poo-eh-deh pah-gahr soo [too] fah-mee-lee-ah pah-rah soo [too] eh-doo-kah-see-ohn oo-nee-behr-see-tah-ree-ah

Do you need a loan (financial aid)?
¿Necesita[s] un préstamo (ayuda financiera)?
neh-seh-see-tah[s] oon prehs-tah-moh (ah-yoo-dah fee-nahn-see-eh-rah)

You must fill out this form.
Tiene[s] que llenar este formulario.
tee-eh-neh[s] keh yeh-nahr ehs-teh fohr-moo-lah-ree-oh

Your grades are excellent.
Sus [Tus] notas son excelentes.
soos [toos] noh-tahs sohn ehk-seh-lehn-tehs

You may receive a scholarship.
Puede[s] recibir una beca.
poo-eh-deh[s] rreh-see-beer oo-nah beh-kah